COME
HERE

STOP RUNNING
FROM THE LOVE
YOU WANT

GO
AWAY

COME HERE

STOP RUNNING FROM THE LOVE YOU WANT

GO AWAY

DR. RALPH EARLE
and Susan Meltsner

Kerri B. Blank, researcher

Produced by The Philip Lief Group, Inc.
and Cathy D. Hemming

POCKET BOOKS
New York   London   Toronto   Sydney   Tokyo   Singapore

POCKET BOOKS, a division of Simon & Schuster Inc.
1230 Avenue of the Americas, New York, NY 10020

Earle, Ralph (Ralph H.)
    Come here, go away : stop running from the love you want / Ralph
Earle with Susan Meltsner; Kerri B. Blank, researcher.
        p.   cm.
    Includes bibliographical references and indexes.
    ISBN 0-671-68435-3 : $19.95
    1. Love.   2. Intimacy (Psychology)   3. Interpersonal relations.
4. Mate selection—United States.   I. Meltsner, Susan.   II. Blank,
Kerri B.   III. Title.
HQ801.E17   1991
158'.2—dc20   90-44441
                                                                    CIP

First Pocket Books hardcover printing January 1991

10 9 8 7 6 5 4 3 2 1

To
Glenda,
Marcus,
and Michelle,
who best know the
"come here, go away"
side of Ralph.

THE TWELVE STEPS
OF ALCOHOLICS ANONYMOUS*

1. We admitted we were powerless over alcohol—that our lives had become unmanageable.

2. Came to believe that a power greater than ourselves could restore us to sanity.

3. Made a decision to turn our will and our lives over to the care of God, *as we understood Him*.

4. Made a searching and fearless inventory of ourselves.

5. Admitted to God, to ourselves and to another human being the exact nature of our wrongs.

6. Were entirely ready to have God remove all these defects of character.

7. Humbly asked Him to remove our shortcomings.

8. Made a list of all persons we had harmed, and became willing to make amends to them all.

9. Made direct amends to such people wherever possible, except when to do so would injure them or others.

10. Continued to take personal inventory and when we were wrong promptly admitted it.

11. Sought through prayer and meditation to improve our conscious contact with God *as we understood Him*, praying only for knowledge of His will for us and the power to carry that out.

12. Having had a spiritual awakening as the result of these steps, we tried to carry this message to alcoholics, and to practice these principles in all our affairs.

Acknowledgments

I would like to thank the following people for their generous help in making this book possible: Claire Zion, my ever-enthusiastic editor at Pocket Books, and her associate, Lisa Kazmier; Cathy Hemming, Nancy Kalish, and the late Jamie Rothstein for their encouragement and editorial guidance; Kerri Blank, whose preliminary research served as the foundation for this book; Emily Marlin, whose friendship and ideas have been invaluable; and most of all, the patients whose struggles with intimacy motivated this project. On a personal note, I am grateful to all members of Twelve Step fellowships, whose emotional support has been crucial in completing *Come Here/Go Away*. And I am forever indebted to my wise friend and gifted collaborator, Susan Meltsner.

RALPH EARLE

CONTENTS

INTRODUCTION

■ *REBECCA*

"Most of the time, I don't mind being single," Rebecca explained. "I sort of like the freedom to come and go as I please, to eat chocolate pudding for dinner, or not make the bed or do the dishes every day because nobody's going to see the mess but me. And I certainly don't buy into the idea that a woman isn't complete without a man. I have a full life. A good job. A nice apartment. Interests. So, I'm still single. Lots of people are single. It isn't a tragedy. It isn't that big a deal."

Yet there are also times when Rebecca, a striking woman with big blue eyes and dark wavy hair, does think being single is a big deal—when she feels particularly lonely or isolated, for instance. Or when she thinks about the high-school and college classmates who are married or living with someone, and wonders why she is not. "There are days when I feel like I'm wearing a neon sign saying, thirty-three, single, and desperate," Rebecca sighs. "It seems like the whole world is looking at me and asking, 'What's wrong with this woman? Why doesn't she have a boyfriend?'"

It is unlikely that anyone—much less everyone—pays much attention to Rebecca's single status or thinks less of her because she is not involved in an intimate relationship. However, like so many of the single patients I treat in my therapy practice, Rebecca thinks less of *herself* for being unattached and unable to connect with an attractive and compatible partner.

A self-proclaimed late bloomer, Rebecca dated occasionally during high school. She became sexually active her sophomore year in college. "I felt as if I'd jumped overboard into the ocean," she recalled, "only I didn't know how to swim."

Rebecca had sex with the first man who suggested it, believing he truly cared about her—which proved not to be the case. "I was incredibly naive," Rebecca explained. "I'd spent so many years fantasizing about it, that I actually thought I'd meet the man of my dreams, be swept off my feet, and live happily ever after. Boy did I have the wrong number. And for someone who calls herself intelligent, it took me a long time to figure that out. Each time I got involved with a guy I thought, 'He's the one. This time it's going to be different.' But it never was."

After a half-dozen "heavy doses of reality," Rebecca made a concerted effort to stay away from men she saw as potential heartbreakers. "Unfortunately, the guys who seemed safe were also boring or downright neurotic," Rebecca commented. "I went back and forth between being insecure and needy in exciting nonrelationships and being bored and suffocated in safe relationships. If there was a middle ground, I never found it." Periodically, she stopped looking, avoiding all social situations for months at a time. "But then I'd think, 'This is ridiculous. I can't spend my whole life curled up on the sofa reading trashy novels and eating Häagen-Dazs ice cream,'" she explained.

However, each time Rebecca ended her self-imposed ban on socializing, she found the prospect of getting to know a new man less appealing—so much so that on several occasions she had accepted blind dates or made plans to attend singles functions only to cancel them at the last minute, deciding that "it wasn't worth the aggravation."

"I want to get out of this vicious cycle before it's too late," she proclaimed during her first therapy session. "Before there's no hope of ever being in a real relationship."

Rebecca wanted that "real" relationship, but she did not want to risk failure, rejection, or pain. She looked for opportunities to be intimate, but when she found them she talked herself out of pursuing them. "Don't get your hopes up. You'll only be disappointed again," she thought and did not let down her guard or allow herself to be and share her real self with another person.

Over the course of my career as a family therapist, psychologist, and minister, men and women of all ages and from all walks of life have come to me for help with their intimacy and relationship problems. Some were married, some single. Each had their own unique life experiences and approach to relationships, but all shared Rebecca's dilemma. They were caught in the clutches of the *intimacy paradox*—the tentency to want, need, and strive for intimacy while at the very same time fearing and trying to protect themselves from it. Are you?

INTIMACY PARADOXES

A paradox is an idea that seems contradictary—even impossible—but is true nonetheless. Intimate relationships are full of them. There are, for instance, good relationships that occasionally feel bad, and unhealthy relationships which at times feel terrific. People who love us can and do hurt us, and we periodically become so furious at them that we want to wring their necks.

Intimacy itself is paradoxical. We want to be close but also need distance. We long to "be ourselves" with people but feel compelled to protect ourselves by concealing certain aspects of who we really are. We wish to be loved, cared for, even catered to but become wary and uncomfortable whenever it appears that our wish might be fulfilled.

We search high and low for people with whom we can have close, nourishing relationships. But what do we do when we find them? We begin to worry that they will prove to be untrustworthy, that once we let our guard down they will try to control us or ask too much of us, or worst of all, abandon us. Like Rebecca, some of us turn tail and run before we even make the connections that could lead to truly intimate relationships. Others among us connect, but create *pseudointimate* relationships—as Linda, a thirty-five-year-old attorney, and her husband, Robert, a thirty-seven-year-old financial planner, did.

When this attractive, achievement-oriented couple first met six years ago, both were already extremely successful in their respective fields and accustomed to working hard, putting in long hours, being tough competitors, and letting nothing—including their personal lives—interfere with the pursuit of their professional aspirations. Getting married would not change that, they agreed. Their careers would remain their top priority until they were ready to start a family. Then, like the rational business people they were, they would renegotiate.

Unfortunately, because both Linda and Robert were reluctant to take time and attention away from a "sure thing" (their professional lives) to invest it in something that might never "pay off" (intimacy), their relationship had all but died of neglect by the time they got around to the topic of having children. Indeed, by their fifth anniversary, Linda and Robert lived under the same roof but led completely separate lives, going for months without making love. Their marriage had no genuine intimacy in it. And although this bothered them, they still feared that they would not be able to remedy the problem without doing potentially irreparable damage to their careers.

Alisha, a forty-five-year-old schoolteacher, went to the opposite extreme. For twenty years her entire life revolved around her marriage. Believing that if she just tried hard enough, she could control her alcoholic husband's drinking problem, Alisha spent nearly every moment of every day worrying about Frank, trying to stay one step ahead of him and to make his life as carefree as possible, so that he would not need to get drunk. "I thought my love could cure him," Alisha said soon after she had joined one of the therapy groups I conduct. "I thought that if I could just make him see how much I loved him, he would stop destroying himself." But that was not what happened. What's more, Alisha was as "hooked" on changing and controlling Frank as he was on alcohol—and that sort of addictive attachment to another person is also pseudointimacy.

Although Rebecca's, Alisha's, Linda's, and Robert's intimacy or relationship problems may be more severe than your own, some of their attitudes and behaviors probably sound familiar to you. You may know all too well: When it comes to intimacy, *that which we want, we also fear,* and the resulting psychological tug-of-war can wreak havoc on our lives. This book explains *why* this happens. It describes the barriers to intimacy you construct when one part of yourself says, "Come here; I want to get close," while another part says, "Go away; I'm afraid you will hurt me." Then it tells you how to take down those barriers and build truly intimate, satisfying relationships.

WHY I WROTE THIS BOOK

I have been working with troubled individuals, couples, and families for thirty years, beginning in the 1960s, when I was a parish minister. I can vividly recall the couples and families who came to me for guidance back then and how they were being torn apart by polarizing social issues like racism and the Vietnam war. Marriages were literally being destroyed because one partner supported integration and the other did not. Husbands blaming their wives and wives blaming their husbands argued endlessly over children who were growing long hair, burning their draft cards, and participating in sit-ins.

By the early seventies I was a family therapist associated with an obstetrics and gynecology practice in Scottsdale, Arizona. The sexual revolution had arrived by then and, living up to the expectations it brought with it, was stirring up trouble in countless relationships. The vast majority of my patients had sexual problems that they believed were the sole cause of their marital strife.

For the past seven years a significant portion of my practice has been devoted to the treatment of addictions, compulsions, and codependency. One partner's drinking problem, compulsive gambling, sex addiction, or workaholism, and the other partner's obsessive effort to control the addicted partner's behavior are the barriers to intimacy I am most likely to hear about these days.

As I watched the divisive forces in our lives change from one decade to the next, I could not help but notice that the fundamental problem stayed the same. Intimate relationships do not get off the ground, or they crumble under the weight of conflicts in whatever form they may take, *because they are are built on a shaky foundation.*

Far too many of us are missing one or more of the essential ingredients for genuine intimacy. We do not like ourselves or trust other people and, as a result, cannot be or share our real selves with them. We have a low threshold for conflict and ambiguity. Expecting everything to go smoothly all of the time and suppressing our anger or frustration when it does not, fills the air between ourselves and others with tension. We retreat to our separate corners to hide behind the work we brought home from the office, a drug- or alcohol-induced haze, or some other self-protective shield. And of course, in one way or another, all of us have been hurt or disappointed during childhood or in our adult relationships. Our lives revolve around our determination not to be hurt again.

HOW THIS BOOK WILL HELP

The first section of *Come Here/Go Away* describes the many reasons why you may be *intimacy disabled.* Although your disability may be invisible to the naked eye, because of it you are at as much of a disadvantage in personal relationships as a dyslexic is in a schoolroom. And like the hearing-impaired individual who learns to read lips and sign, you find ways to compensate for your disability. Unfortunately, the methods you choose may become negative habits that do you more harm than good. The second section of this book describes four of the most common barriers to intimacy, or *intimacy substitutes,* and how relying upon them affects your life and relationships. In the third and final section, I share the practical advice and strategies that my patients have found most helpful for removing those barriers to intimacy from their lives. It will help you get out of your rut and break the negative habits that have compelled you to cling to people or to keep them at arm's length— to get stuck in a vicious cycle of looking high and low for intimacy one minute only to back away from it the next.

As a family therapist who is also a psychologist and a minister, I have long seen my role as helping people to achieve a balance in their lives and relationships by integrating body, mind, *and* spirit. Although I have taken a more psychological than inspirational approach in this book, I cannot stress strongly enough that developing a relationship with a higher power is an integral part of the process of forming intimate relationships with other people. So is *becoming intimate with yourself.* Indeed, a significant portion of this book is devoted to the idea of self-acceptance and self-healing, whether that involves working through unfinished business from your past, enhancing self-esteem, or recovering from addictions, compulsions, and codependency.

The people I write about in this book reflect the types of patients I treat in my therapy practice and as such may have had life experiences that were more traumatic than your own or seem to have more serious problems than you are encountering in your own life. Because I believe that they offer valuable insights for anyone and have confidence in your ability to discern those elements that do apply to your life, I have not attempted to dilute their stories. I have, however, changed names or other identifying information and, in some instances, created composite case studies based on more than one person's life. Finally, I have tried to avoid sex-role stereotyping and sexist language, but found the exclusive use of "he or she" and "himself or herself" at times a bit distracting. Therefore, unless I am referring to a specific individual, please keep in mind that the pronouns "he" or "she" can denote an individual of either gender.

A QUESTION OF BALANCE

Each year, in my ministerial role, I perform several weddings, and one part of the traditional wedding ceremony has always intrigued me. In my church—and I am sure many others—prior to the ceremony, three candles are set up beside the altar. The groom and bride light the third and center candle. In most religious ceremonies, they blow out the outside candles, signifying that "two have now become as one."

At this point in the ritual a part of me always wants to shout,

"Stop! Do not put out your separate flames." A truly intimate bond is not formed by merging identities and becoming one with another person, but rather by maintaining our separate selves and sharing them with each other. *That* is what makes intimacy a challenge to us all. And, after all is said and done, *that* is what this book is about.

COME HERE/GO AWAY:
The Intimacy Paradox

■ JOSH AND PAMELA

"Sometimes I wonder what I would do without Pamela," Josh said. A thirty-five-year-old sporting events promoter, he had lived with Pamela for almost a year and found it difficult to imagine unwinding after a stressful workday without her there to listen to him and make him laugh and massage his shoulders until the tension disappeared. When he awoke and saw her curled up on her side of the bed with only a few tufts of reddish brown hair visible above the covers, Josh felt reassured. He knew that he was not alone. Even her irritating habits were somehow comforting. Fussing at Pamela for leaving her shoes in the middle of the living room for him to trip over or for using his razor to shave her legs were some of the little rituals that defined their relationship. It was one of the better—and certainly the longest—of the intimate relationships Josh had ever had.

"But, I try not to think about that," he said. "I try not to think about how much I care about her and depend on her to be there for me. Because then I have to think about how rotten I'm going to feel when she leaves me." For Josh, it was always *when*, never *if*.

Short and stocky with a round face and curly blond hair, Josh resembled a teddy bear even in his designer-label suit. He was successful, articulate, and opinionated, sometimes to the point of seeming arrogant. Yet he also had a boyish sort of charm. The combination must have struck a chord with more than one woman, and it was not hard to believe Josh when he claimed that attracting members of the opposite sex had never

11

been a problem for him. "The problems begin *after* I attract them," he explained.

For Josh, intimacy was like a runaway train. "I buy a ticket for a nice leisurely ride, but end up barreling down a mountain at two hundred miles per hour." No matter how smoothly a relationship started, it inevitably "got completely out of control." No matter how independent and self-confident a woman seemed when Josh met her, as soon as he let his guard down, she "started having the screaming meemies or turned into a clinging vine, nagging, crying, and criticizing everything I said or did." He could spot the warning signs a mile away, he claimed, and was constantly on the lookout for them.

"Pamela wasn't like the other women I got involved with," Josh recalled. "Not as tough or aloof or ambitious. She was always cheerful and patient, but not a pushover either. I could tell she was strong and sure of herself on the inside where it really counted." As you might expect, Josh found these qualities enormously appealing. Yet, he never quite trusted them to last. He still "waited for the other shoe to drop" and periodically decided that it had.

In one instance, Pamela received complimentary tickets to the ballet and, knowing that Josh did not like the ballet and usually worked late on weeknights anyway, she offered the second ticket to her sister. She thought she was being considerate and undemanding. Josh thought, "Uh oh. That's just what my old girlfriend Brenda used to do when she was ticked off at me. Then she'd rub my nose in it for weeks, reminding me that she had to go everywhere by herself because I was never around to do things with her."

Although the danger existed only in his own mind, Josh was convinced that he would soon be riding that runaway train to disaster once again and felt compelled to pull on the brakes. "When Pamela got back from the ballet, I was watching TV," he recalled. "And she started to tell me all about the great time she had, but I just kept staring at the TV and ended up yelling at her, saying something stupid like, 'Can't you see I'm trying to watch this program.' Right away she clammed up—which I knew she would because she's not a fighter. She just backs away." According to Josh, Pamela immediately retreated to the bedroom and pretended to be asleep when he came to bed. "That was fine by me," he declared.

For the next few days, Josh buried himself in his work, so much so that he rarely saw Pamela and barely spoke to her when he did. "But I began to miss her," he continued. "I really wanted to be with her again." He rearranged his schedule, bought a dozen roses, and was waiting on the doorstep when Pamela got home from work. "Come here and give me a hug," he said. "I love you."

Based on what you have read so far, it will come as no surprise that ten minutes into her first therapy session, Pamela said, "Sometimes I wonder whether my relationship with Josh is worth the effort I put into it. One minute he's sending out signals that he wants to be close and the next he's shutting me out completely. First it's 'Come here, come here,' but when I do it's 'Go away, go away.' And just when I'm ready to walk away for good, he reels me back in again. I swear I've had a lump in my throat and knots in my stomach since the day I met him."

Pamela, a twenty-eight-year-old physical therapist with wholesome, "girl-next-door" looks and a sunny disposition, met Josh two and a half years ago. He had injured himself during a celebrity tennis tournament and wound up at the rehabilitation center where Pamela worked. "He was your basic pain in the neck," Pamela chuckled as she remembered how Josh "moaned and groaned and came up with truly ingenious reasons why he couldn't do what I asked him to do. He was really comical about it, though. After his sessions *I* was sore—from laughing so hard."

The laughter continued after Josh's treatment ended. "I'm not the type who gets swept off her feet," Pamela claimed. "But Josh managed to do that." According to Pamela, he made every date a romantic adventure. He also made sure to tell her about all of her predecessors and how disappointing and demanding they had been. "To tell you the truth, I got sick of hearing about them," she said. "And I thought it was pretty weird how the 'old girlfriend' stories always came out right after we'd spent an entire weekend together or been to a party where lots of people said how good I was for him and how he should hang onto me. It always felt like he was warning me not to be like them, not to suffocate him and hassle him the way they did."

If that was, in fact, Josh's intention, then his ploy worked. Thinking that "hell would freeze over before I gave him an excuse to put me in the same category with those other women," Pamela made sure to back off as soon as Josh gave the slightest indication that he felt crowded. This was not particularly difficult for Pamela to do. She had always prided herself on being cheerful, easygoing, and self-reliant. "He was never going to find a woman who was less demanding than I was," she asserted, adding that for as long as she could remember, she had made a point of "never asking anyone for anything."

No matter how insecure, angry, or neglected she felt, Pamela kept her feelings to herself. When Josh wanted space, she gave it to him. When he wanted to be close, she was there for him. And since he did not want to be close all that often, she cultivated friendships and pursued interests outside their relationship. "We're together when we're together and not when we're not," Pamela said, sounding resigned to the fact that she would never get more from this relationship.

"At first I wasn't even allowed to call our relationship a relationship," Pamela said and grimaced. "He'd say, 'Don't use the R word. We're only *seeing each other*,' and I'd wonder what that meant. That I only existed when I was in his line of vision? That he was seeing me until he saw someone better and dumped me? Sometimes I wanted to shake him and shout, 'Grow up already!'"

The relief Pamela felt when Josh finally acknowledged that they were a couple was short-lived. "After an argument, when everything seemed to be okay again, I could never really be sure it was," she explained. "I'd worry about what I said. I'd think that he was just pretending to be over the fight, but that once I left, he'd never call me again." Even after she began living with Josh, Pamela still "walked on eggshells," keeping tabs on Josh's moods and adapting herself to them.

By now the source of Josh and Pamela's relationship problems may seem obvious to you. You may have concluded that Josh withdrew and distanced himself from Pamela because he was afraid of intimacy, afraid that Pamela would demand more from him than he could comfortably give and that the relationship would grow "completely out of control" the way his other relationships had. To ward off his fears, Josh periodically pulled away from Pamela and slowed things down until he felt comfortable again.

If that was your diagnosis, you get a "B+" in armchair psychology. "A" grades are reserved for those of you who noticed that Pamela was more than an "innocent victim" of Josh's ambivalence about intimacy.

By remaining cheerful at all times, asking very little of Josh, and never letting him know how much she loved or needed him, Pamela was able to maintain the distance *she* required in order to feel safe and comfortable in the relationship. Playing the perfect, caring, undemanding mate, Pamela always responded to Josh's needs and tried to give him whatever he wanted but rarely divulged any information about her real self or her real feelings. This allowed her to maintain the control *she* needed. Believing that getting too close to or expecting too much from Josh would put her at his mercy, Pamela had difficulty being on the receiving end of the relationship. And so, although she claimed that Josh's emotional advances and retreats were driving her crazy (and I am sure that they were), deep inside herself Pamela felt relieved each time Josh decided to "go away." His ambivalence made it possible for her to ward off *her* fear of intimacy, so much so that when Josh finally let her know that he was certain he loved her and was committed to being with her, Pamela immediately began questioning her own commitment to the relationship. In fact, she called to set up her first therapy session two days *after* Josh proposed to her.

As you can see, even though Josh appeared to be causing the strife in their relationship, this couple's come here/go away dance was a pas de deux. Josh and Pamela were not always conscious of their moves and countermoves, but both were attempting to locate a comfortable space between closeness and distance and to stay within its boundaries. They were struggling to unlock the most basic and universal intimacy paradox—that which we need, we also fear. Chances are that you do this too. In one way or another you try to achieve the close, nourishing relationships you want without suffering the consequences you fear.

YOUR HEART'S DESIRE
What Do You Want?

Actually we do not merely *want* intimacy, we *need* it. Intimacy is not just icing on the cake of our lives. It is one of the basic ingredients. From earliest infancy—when our very survival is in another person's hands—through old age—when connecting with other people continues to be the only effective way to stave off loneliness—we are driven by our basic psychological need to con-nect and share our real selves with other people.

This need is stronger for some of us than for others. At certain times in our lives the desire to learn or achieve may take priority over our need for intimacy. But that need does indeed exist in all of us, and when it goes unmet, we definitely sense something vitally important missing from our lives. Although we may desperately want doctoral degrees or the words Chief Executive Officer etched on the door to our offices, we can live happy and healthy lives without these things. We can also live without romance or mar-riage or sex, but we die an emotional death if not a physical one without intimacy.

That is why, although I will be focusing primarily on intimate *couple* relationships, I want to acknowledge that throughout our lives we often turn to friends or family members in order to meet our need for intimacy. Anything you read about in this book can be used to make those relationships more intimate and fulfilling as well.

AN INTIMATE RELATIONSHIP IS . . .

. . . close, familiar, and usually affectionate or loving. In it, two people relate to each other as two individuals, each with his or her own identity. You are *with* each other rather than *part of* one another. Of course, there may have been a time when you felt so close to someone that your identities seemed to merge. You were falling in love.

The passionate, romantic love that brings couples together is intense and untarnished by anything so mundane as the details of daily living. Under the spell of new love, you idealize (and some-times idolize) the other person and the relationship. This is ex-tremely easy to do since both of you are on your best behavior. She does not yet know that he leaves soggy crumpled tissues on the nearest piece of furniture after blowing his nose, or will not eat chicken unless you remove the bones the way his mother did. He does not know that you can cook only what comes in a plastic wrapper with microwave instructions attached, or that you cry when you are happy or angry as well as when you are sad.

What's more, it would hardly matter if you did know these things. The "chemistry" between you is so intoxicating that the habits which will one day irritate you to no end are seen as "adorable" quirks and are outweighed by the countless endearing qualities that practically glow in the dark when you are together. Such skewed perceptions, as well as the sense that you and your lover see the world in exactly the same way and understand each other completely, are the stuff that romance is made of. They are, to a certain extent, inevitable—and necessary. It is quite possible that it takes precisely this sort of altered state of consciousness to propel us past our natural fear of getting close.

However, the dust stirred up by newness and passion must settle before true intimacy can develop. Although romantic relationships can be intimate and intimate relationships can be romantic, ro-mance and intimacy are not one and the same. For one thing, intimacy is a bit calmer and quieter than romance. For another, it cannot, by definition, be based on illusions.

The close connections and deep knowing bonds of intimacy develop between two "real" people, flawed as they may be. Or as Melody Beattie, author of *Codependent No More*, put it, in an intimate relationship, "I can be me, you can be you, and we can be us"—warts and all.

AN INTIMATE RELATIONSHIP INVOLVES...

. . . mutual caring. It involves sharing your innermost thoughts and feelings. The safety and acceptance you find in an intimate relationship make it possible to talk about your joys, your fears, old pain, new disappointments, your blissful discoveries, and your most embarrassing moments. In turn, these self-disclosures bring you closer to your partner, helping you feel even safer and more accepted. An intimate relationship also involves giving and receiving emotional support, as well as being on the same wavelength some of the time and feeling free to ask questions and disagree when you are not. Intimacy enables you to feel "at home with" another person even though he or she may not think or feel or be just like you.

INTIMACY ASKS YOU...

. . . to take down the barriers and step out of the roles you may play with others and be yourself. It asks you to trust; to believe that other people will not intentionally hurt you. It demands that you be trustworthy as well.

Intimacy asks you *not* to create the illusion that you are perfect or need no one. Nor will it permit you to maintain your illusions about your partner. As you will see, covering up other people's inappropriate or unacceptable behavior or pretending that it does not bother you creates dependency, not intimacy.

IN RETURN, INTIMACY GIVES YOU . . .

* mutual acceptance and the freedom to be who you really are
* the opportunity to combine your strengths and resources to weather any storm *together*
* happiness and emotional gratification
* a way to reduce the strain and uncertainty of daily living
* a tremendously reassuring sense that you fit somewhere and matter to someone—that you are not utterly alone in the world

These may sound like incredibly lofty promises, but those of you who have experienced intimacy—however briefly—know that they can be fulfilled. Having someone know, accept, and love who you really are is one of the most gratifying experiences you can have.

Yet, there are perils at every turn. To get close to another person, you must take substantial risks. You must act to fulfill your desire for intimacy even though you are afraid of the consequences that your actions may bring and though you have no guarantee that you will ever get what you want. For various reasons, many of us are unable or unwilling to do that.

THE SPECTER OF DOOM
What Are We Afraid Of?

Over the course of my career, I have endlessly encountered a seemingly innocuous three-letter word. I call it the telltale "but," and nearly every couple or individual who seeks my help utters it while describing their intimacy or relationship problems.

I heard it from Gary, a thirty-two-year-old electrical engineer, who found it virtually impossible to remain faithful to his wife, Ellen. "I love her," he assured me, "*but* sometimes when I'm with her or even when I'm just thinking about being with her, I feel like I'm suffocating, like I'm locked up in a vault with my air supply running out."

I heard it from Elizabeth. After thirteen years of marriage, she had divorced her hot-tempered, verbally abusive husband and wondered if she would ever be able to trust a man enough to remarry. "I don't want to be alone for the rest of my life," she said, "*but* I don't want to make the same mistakes I made the last time either."

Rebecca, the thirty-three-year-old computer software designer you met in the Introduction, used it too. "I know I'll never find a relationship unless I get out and meet men," she declared, "*but* I just can't take any more singles bars or blind dates. I always get my hopes up, always think that this time it'll be different and I'll meet someone I like who likes me too. *But* I end up being disappointed and feeling more inadequate then ever."

The telltale *but* marks the spot where your desire to be intimate collides with your fears about what might happen if you actually were. Chances are that you know about such collisions, especially if you want to establish an intimate relationship or want more intimacy in the relationship you have, *but* at the same time do not want to:

- get hurt again or risk hurting someone else
- have someone find out that you are not as together as you appear to be
- get so attached to someone that you will be devastated if he or she leaves you
- change your life-style
- lose control of your life
- give up your independence and the goals you want to accomplish

When your needs and fears collide, your vision of what you might derive from a truly intimate relationship is quickly replaced by thoughts of what you stand to lose. You try to assess the risks involved—weighing the chances of getting what your heart desires against the potential for failure or pain. You consider the price tag for intimacy, and sometimes you conclude that the price is more than you are willing to pay. Your fears override your desire for intimacy and, as it did for Josh and Pamela, your need to protect yourself short-circuits your efforts to get close.

Intimacy *is* a high-risk venture. There is no doubt about it. And unlike other risks you might take—skydiving, for example, or starting your own business—the actual odds of winning or losing at intimacy are impossible to calculate. You enter unknown territory, daring to reveal yourself to another human being with hardly a clue as to how he or she will respond.

Many of those who have written about intimacy before me concluded that fear of the unknown poses the most tenacious obstacle. However, I propose that it is not so much what we do not or cannot know that frightens us, but rather what we *have known and think could happen to us again.*

All of us at one time or another and in one way or another have bet on intimacy and lost. We have had intimate gestures rejected, self-disclosures greeted with icy silence, and confidences betrayed. Such common occurrences may not be particularly traumatic, but most of us try to avoid experiencing them again. Some of you have been devastated when your marriage ended in divorce or disappointed by any number of relationships that failed to be all that you hoped they would be. Or over the years your efforts to change your single status may have left you as pessimistic about connecting with people as Rebecca was.

From these and other disheartening experiences all of us accumulate plenty of tally marks in the intimacy "loss" column, and we may still feel the sting of rejection, the sense of inadequacy, or the pangs of loneliness that accompanied each one. We are not stupid. Indeed, when life's lessons cause pain, all of us are fast learners, and what we learn is to protect ourselves from experiencing that sort of pain again.

Some of your most persistent fears took root long before your adult relationships hurt or disappointed you. They date back to childhood and the relationships you had with your parents and other family members. For instance, if you are one of the twenty-two million Adult Children of Alcoholics (ACOA) in this country, you grew up in a home where an alcoholic parent's unpredictable behavior taught you that it was unwise and perhaps even dangerous to trust or depend on other people. You may have been neglected by parents who were workaholics, or who were absorbed in isolating pursuits such as compulsive eating, cleaning, gambling, or spending, and as a result were physically or emotionally unavailable to you. Some of you were abandoned. Others were physically abused or bombarded with brutal criticism and demands that you simply were not equipped to meet. Your youthful experiences left an indelible impression; since the people who were supposed to love and accept you unconditionally and to help you feel safe did not, you could not expect virtual strangers to do so either.

When you consider the combined effect of unsettling childhood experiences and disillusioning adult relationships, it is not surprising that your fear of suffering similar consequences has an enormous impact on your life and relationships today, or that you construct all sorts of barriers to protect yourself from:

- rejection
- disapppointment
- being burdened
- being a burden
- limiting your options
- being controlled
- being exploited or drained dry
- letting others down

- losing your identity
- abandonment
- disapproval
- feeling boxed in
- betrayal
- embarrassment
- losing your freedom

That is quite a list, and it is far from exhaustive. The horrors we imagine when we think about intimacy are especially powerful when we view intimacy as a threat to achieving other seemingly more important goals—which is precisely what Stacy did.

■ STACY

Stacy is a twenty-nine-year-old filmmaker who appears to be well on the way to achieving her lifelong goal of having her own film production company by the time she turns thirty-five. A five-foot-two dynamo, Stacy has a seemingly limitless energy supply and needs it to handle her hectic, demanding work schedule and jam-packed life-style. When she first came to me several years ago, Stacy was already riding the fast track to success. For as long as I have known her, she has claimed to have no time for emotional commitments that might interfere with her progress toward her goals. She does not date, and her business associates double as friends. "We're not really close," she admits, "but we always have plenty to talk about." Of course, there is only one topic to talk about—business.

Stacy was only sixteen when her father, whom she adored, died. He was an accountant by trade. However, in his youth, Stacy's father, an exceptionally talented pianist, once pursued a career as a jazz musician. She vividly recalls how his eyes would sparkle and his rarely seen smile would appear whenever he reminisced about the old days, the days when he toured with a well-known jazz band or drew large, appreciative crowds to the nightclub where he soloed on the piano.

"My father was an incredibly passionate man," Stacy explains, "but he was a hopeless romantic, and that was his downfall. He gave up his dreams when he fell madly in love with my mother. He asked her to marry him on their first date, and he kept asking her for months and months until she finally agreed." When Stacy's oldest sister was born, her father took a day job to supplement the money he made as a musician, and he eventually gave up his musical aspirations entirely in order to support his rapidly expanding family. By the time Stacy was old enough to comprehend family interactions, she quickly realized that "my dad was working himself to death and my mother was constantly putting him down for never amounting to anything. And then of course, he died."

Deeply affected by her father's death, Stacy, who was by then the only child still living at home, appointed herself the keeper of his memories, sorting through old photographs and newspaper clippings and putting together scrapbooks that chronicled his short-lived musical career. This only reinforced her conviction that he could have been a truly great musician if he had not abandoned his dreams to marry her mother.

"I guess that was when I got the impression that you could have love or you could have a life of your own, but you couldn't have both," Stacy says. However, that idea didn't sink in until, as she put it, "history almost repeated itself."

When she was nineteen Stacy fell head over heels in love with another film student at the university she attended. According to Stacy, Craig was brilliant and passionate and "an intense, emotional man who could describe things so vividly that you could almost see them appear before your eyes." Although he was not the first man she had an intimate relationship with, he was the last, and Stacy recalls that with each passing day she grew more attached to Craig, "more willing to give up another part of me so I could be closer to him." Six months into their relationship, Stacy discovered she was pregnant.

"He wanted us to get married and keep the baby," Stacy reports. "He had it all worked out right down to a house in the suburbs with a white picket fence. I just couldn't do it." She had an abortion and not long afterward her relationship with Craig ended. Although the loss was painful, Stacy comforted herself with the thought that her life was "back on track." Ten years later she still acts as if she can only stay on that track by making sure that love does not "complicate" her life.

Although you may think that Stacy has made a conscious, rational choice to focus all of her energy on her career right now, she is not just pursuing lofty career goals but also running away from a relentless pursuer—her need for intimacy, a need Stacy occasionally acknowledged.

"I travel a lot," she said with a sigh, "and on the way home it always hits me. I'm going to walk into my loft and it's going to be empty, exactly the way I left it except for the dusk that's settled while I was away. There will be no one there to greet me, no one who cares that I'm back or even knows that I am. No one to ask about what I did while I was gone. No one to bring me a glass of wine or listen to my latest scathingly brilliant idea. Just me and my briefcase and my permanent-press clothes."

These thoughts were fleeting, however, and Stacy never seriously considered giving in to the occasional twinges of loneliness she felt. "I snap out of it, of course," she continued. "I mean I've yet to meet a man who would do those things for me anyway. And if one did, he'd expect something in return—like my whole life and all my dreams, and that would just be for starters."

Stacy had sentenced herself to a life without a close, nourishing relationship in it because she sincerely believed that the only way to fulfill her desire for success was to suppress her desire for intimacy. She had encountered the intimacy paradox that may be the great-granddaddy of them all—that within ourselves exist two sets of what *appear to be* mutually exclusive needs. On one side are our needs for:

- *communion*—to unite with other human beings, surrender some of ourself and feel part of a larger whole
- *connection*—to discover the ways that we are like other people and come together around this common ground
- *intimacy*—being and sharing our real selves with others

On the other side are our needs for:

- *agency*—to assert ourself and grow as separate individuals, to master new skills and exert a certain amount of control over others and the world around us
- *autonomy*—to exist and function independently
- *selfhood*—to see ourself as unique and unlike any other human being, and to prove our worth through our own productivity and accomplishments

These seemingly contradictory needs *could* coexist harmoniously *if* we accepted that both were valid and made an effort to achieve a balance between them. It is through our connections and intimate interactions with people whom we allow to touch our lives that we actually become who we are anyway and are able to grow as individuals.

Regrettably, most of us do not seem to realize this. Some of us conclude, as Stacy did, that intimate relationships threaten our identities and retard our growth. Some of us, as you will see, go to the opposite extreme, sacrificing our individuality for the sake of our relationships, believing that our relationships actually define who we are. However, most of us—like Josh and Pamela—bounce around like Mexican jumping beans. As you will learn later in this book, we also build walls, burn bridges, create illusions of intimacy, and find substitutes which temporarily anesthetize the pangs of loneliness or fill the empty spaces inside ourselves. As a result, our efforts to preserve our autonomy and protect ourselves from the consequences we fear can trap us in a come here/go away holding pattern that not only prevents us from getting the intimacy we need but also limits or damages us and our lives in many ways.

The barriers to intimacy that you have built, what has happened to you because of them, and even your ability to dismantle them all ride on the *prerequisites* for intimacy that I will describe in the next chapter. Those prerequisites are like the ingredients in a soufflé recipe. If you want the recipe to work, you must have all of them in the right measure, but as you will see, many of us do not.

2

PREREQUISITES FOR INTIMACY

■ PAMELA

"Did you ever see the *Peanuts* cartoon where Lucy says she'll hold the football so Charlie Brown can kick it?" Pamela asked, shortly after coming to see me about her relationship with Josh. "Charlie Brown thinks that Lucy is going to pull the football away at the last minute because that's what she's always done before. She swears up and down that she won't do it this time, and he decides to believe her, but of course she does and 'good old' Charlie Brown goes flying through the air and ends up flat on his back—*again*. Well, that's me in my relationships. I've hit the ground so many times that it hardly even hurts anymore."

For Pamela, intimacy was what happened during the fleeting moments that preceded disappointment. She was convinced that, sooner or later, anyone she trusted enough to get close to would withdraw love and attention from her, pulling it away as Lucy did with Charlie Brown's football. Intimacy never lasted, she believed, and she had long ago stopped hoping that it would. She had learned to give affection and emotional support, but not to expect it to be given to her in return. Indeed, by the time she met Josh, Pamela was certain that she did not even need it.

"Some women are like ferns," Pamela explained, "they need constant care or they wither and die. I'm like a cactus. I can get by on almost nothing at all." Pamela said this proudly. Needing "almost nothing" and never asking anyone for anything topped her list of cherished personality

27

traits. It was not surprising then to discover as Pamela talked more about herself, that a cactus was just about the only living thing that could have withstood the climate in her childhood home.

Forced to adapt in an instant to her mother's unpredictable mood swings, Pamela became self-reliant and undemanding at an early age. "You just never made waves at my house," she explained. "You never knew what would push Mom over the edge." Actually, Pamela's mother, who suffered from manic-depression, went over the edge as a result of an internal chemical imbalance and not because of anything her children did. But Pamela did not know that at the time. She knew only that her mother would "act like Donna Reed" one day and be too distraught to get out of bed the next. "The worst was when we'd walk in the door after school and she'd start screaming at us. 'Take, take, take. That's all you ever do,' she'd say, and call us albatrosses hanging around her neck. Dad told us to just stay out of her way when she got like that." And that is what Pamela and her siblings did.

Not knowing what to expect from one day to the next, there was one thing Pamela was sure of—what she got in the way of love and acceptance had little to do with what *she* wanted. "You had to roll with the punches," she explained, "to take the good stuff when you got it and get by when it was taken all away." That was, as you may recall, precisely how Pamela handled Josh's emotional advances and retreats. Although far less dramatic or destructive than her mother's erratic behavior, Josh's changeability was familiar. His come here/go away dance confirmed what Pamela already believed about intimacy and enabled her to do the dance steps she herself knew best.

We all do the dance we know, the one that reflects what our unique life experiences have taught us about ourselves and how to relate to people who are important to us. Although our childhood experiences may not have been as extreme as Pamela's, we were all raised by the only kind of parents there are—imperfect ones. We also had imperfect friendships and imperfect adult lives that undoubtedly included encounters with people who hurt us. As a result, we may not have learned what we needed to know in order to have satisfying, truly intimate relationships. We may lack one or more of the prerequisites for intimacy—*the attitudes and abilities that make it possible for us to form close, lasting connections with other human beings.*

In this chapter you will read about eight of these prerequisites, why we need them, and what happens when they are sources of conflict and confusion for us. Each prerequisite is followed by a brief self-test—the first of many questions and exercises you will find throughout this book. You may wish to obtain a notebook in which to record all your answers.

TRUST

Trust—the firm belief in another person's honesty and reliability—is the foundation on which intimacy is built. It is the faith in other people that counteracts your fear of being hurt by them. When you trust others, you know in your heart that they will not willfully lie to or abuse you. If they make promises, they will keep them. If you share a confidence with them they will not reveal it to others or use it against you in the future. Trust convinces you that people are who they appear to be, that they have no ulterior motives. Trust is felt, not willed. You cannot talk yourself into trusting someone.

Intimacy requires consummate trust. With it you feel free to be yourself, to reveal your innermost thoughts, including those that expose what you believe are your weaknesses. Without it you feel compelled to play a role or maintain a facade, making it impossible for anyone to get really close to you. When you do trust, you can allow other people to be themselves as well. Since you can predict with reasonable accuracy how others will act in certain situations, you can relax and enjoy your relationship. When you do not trust, you anxiously monitor their behavior and your own, worrying about what will happen next. Or you may be so sure that others will hurt you that at the first hint of trouble you strike first, creating unnecessary conflicts.

Of course, if an intimate relationship is to work, the other person involved must be able to trust you too. And you must be able to trust your own feelings and decisions as well. Otherwise you'll never risk intimacy, for fear of making choices that will end up hurting you.

This may sound like a tall order, and you may be wondering how anyone can fill it. The truth is that you may not be able to at all times.

For starters, it isn't always easy to know who you *can* trust, especially when it comes to those who have repeatedly hurt or betrayed you. People with addictions of any kind are notoriously untrustworthy. And you are taking a foolhardy risk if you spill your guts to someone you barely know.

If you have trusted the wrong people in the past, you will naturally be suspicious of the people you encounter today. This was certainly the case for Kelly, a twenty-four-year-old graduate student, who was the victim of date rape several years ago.

"I don't know if I can ever trust anyone again," Kelly sighed, tears welling up in her eyes. "I mean, I trusted that guy. It never occurred to me that he would do what he did. He seemed so normal, so nice. Now when I meet someone who seems normal and nice, I automatically assume he isn't. Everyone seems like a wolf in sheep's clothing to me."

With or without a traumatic experience in your past, you may feel this way too. "I have no reason not to trust this person," you may say, "but I just can't." Although you may be responding to a gut instinct that is entirely accurate, more often your skepticism stems from a shortage of *basic trust*—the sense that the world is a safe place, that people are generally kind, and that life includes at least some situations with consistent, predictable outcomes.

The development of basic trust began for us during infancy after discovering—much to our dismay—that we were separate from our mothers, with needs that were not necessarily the same as, or even compatible with, hers. We got our first taste of anxiety when it dawned on us that we were still too helpless to meet our own needs and must rely on others to take care of us. If our parents picked up our signals, interpreted them accurately, and responded promptly and appropriately, we learned basic trust. If they did not, our most basic feeling was terror.

Your basic trust continued to develop (or deteriorate) throughout childhood and adolescence. Your physical survival may no longer have been at stake, but you continued to turn to parents and other adults for approval, acceptance, and supervision. The *consistency* of the treatment you received had the most dramatic impact on your ability to trust.

"Well, there's no one I'd trust with my life if that's what you mean," was Pamela's reply when I asked how trusting she thought she was. "I'm on my own in that department. People just aren't that reliable." This attitude, of course, was consistent with the extremely inconsistent environment in which she was raised and which taught her that the only person she could truly trust was herself.

As children we faced additional barriers to trust when we were told that our feelings or perceptions were wrong or inappropriate to express. We saw and heard arguments between our parents and were informed that no argument had taken place. We pronounced ourselves unhappy only to be lectured on why we had no right to be. People hurt us and claimed that what they'd done was for our own good. To this day we may wonder how much of what we think or feel is valid.

"Trust!" Bill, a divorced electrical engineer, hooted when the topic came up in a men's support group. "The last person I trusted was my ex-wife, and the last time I trusted was right before I found her in bed with my best friend. That was it for me as far as trusting people was concerned."

Trust is as fragile as porcelain and can be shattered at any time by anyone. You may have built a strong foundation for trusting others during your childhood only to have it shaken later in life. When this happens, the pain of betrayal can linger for years. Refusing to be hurt like that again, you may wear mistrust like an armored suit. Unfortunately, your suit of armor protects you from intimacy as well.

You can find out how a problem with trust may be influencing your intimate relationships by answering the following questions.
Use this rating scale:

> 5 = almost always
> 4 = frequently
> 3 = sometimes
> 2 = occasionally
> 1 = rarely if ever

_____ When someone appears interested in you or tries to engage you in a conversation about yourself, do you wonder what he or she really wants from you?

_____ When things are going well in your life or relationships, do you find yourself thinking, "This won't last"?

_____ When someone tells you there's nothing to worry about, do you automatically doubt his or her word?

_____ Do you feel the need to check up on people—making sure they haven't lied about what they've been doing or where they've been going?

_____ Do you often censor yourself, choosing your words carefully to prevent saying anything that could be used against you later on?

A total score of 15 or above tells you that you have work to do in this area; 20 or above means that this prerequisite may be preventing you from having the intimate relationships you want.

SELF-WORTH

■ REBECCA

Tall, poised, and stylishly dressed, it is difficult to imagine Rebecca, the single computer software developer, as an overweight teenager with braces on her teeth and horn-rimmed glasses that always seemed to be sliding down her nose. "I was big, clumsy, and self-conscious around everyone except other losers," she recalled. "During high school the only thing anyone wanted from me was help with their algebra homework.

"I used to tell myself that it didn't really bother me," Rebecca continues, "that God may not have given me great looks or a great personality or much to say, but he did give me brains and that was okay with me. But it really wasn't. I can't tell you how many nights I'd lie in bed crying because I truly believed that I would never be pretty or sexy or witty enough to have a boyfriend. I thought there was something so wrong with me that I was going to be alone my entire life."

Rebecca never completely let go of the image of herself as a lonely, unattractive teenager and as a result, lacked the second prerequisite for intimacy—a positive sense of self-worth. She doubted that she had what it took to be in an intimate relationship, and her actual experiences with men did not increase her self-confidence.

"I always felt like I was at a disadvantage," she continues. "Everyone said just be yourself. But the guys I went out with didn't want a girlfriend who was smart or assertive or opinionated or ambitious, and I was all of those things. I always felt like I was laughing too loud, saying too much, not saying enough . . . Even when I tried to play the game and be the way I thought they wanted me to be, I'd inevitably slip up and lose them somewhere along the line."

Rebecca had come to believe that her real self was not good enough, that it was not of much value at all—which is a sure sign that someone's sense of self-worth is too shaky to withstand the demands of an intimate relationship.

Self-worth is the belief that you are inherently lovable, capable, and entitled to a reasonable amount of happiness. This does not mean that you think you are perfect. Indeed, people who feel worthwhile are as aware of their limitations as they are of their strengths. They do not consider any weakness to be a fatal flaw, however. They do not bombard themselves with self-criticism; the mistakes they make are just mistakes and not more proof that they cannot do anything right. And although they have bouts of self-doubt now and then, they generally assume that other people think they are okay too.

Self-worth enables you to appreciate what you have to offer others and be convinced that you deserve the closeness you are hoping to find. Without this vision and the image of yourself as worthy of obtaining it, you may be repeatedly drawn to anyone who shows the least bit of interest in you, or you may go to the opposite extreme, rejecting anyone who seems willing and able to accept you as you are. Such people are bores or wimps or losers, you think.

(They have to be to want someone like you.) Or you may choose partners who give you what you need, but make you pay for this service by mistreating or negating you—reinforcing your belief that such treatment is all you really deserve.

A strong sense of your own worth makes you better able to open up and share yourself with others, while a shaky self-image prompts you to erect all sorts of barriers so no one discovers your deficiencies and rejects you because of them. Without self-worth you may cling to a mediocre relationship for dear life, fearing that without it, you would lose your entire identity. Or like Rebecca, you may be so convinced that no one could love you that you isolate yourself or run from opportunities to be intimate.

Of all the prerequisites for intimacy, self-worth is the most difficult to hang onto. There are just so many ways to damage or destroy it, and some of us started out with very little of it in the first place.

Like trust, your basic sense of self-worth developed during childhood when you discovered how to feel about yourself by observing your parents' reactions to you. Your parents were your mirror, and you became what you saw reflected in their eyes. Parents who encouraged and praised you built up your sense of control and accomplishment. Unconditionally loved and accepted, you learned to respect and accept yourself.

Unfortunately, many of us looked into cracked mirrors. We were raised by parents who, because of their own insecurities and experiences, were unable to be as sensitive and encouraging as we need them to be. They may have subscribed to the "spare the rod, spoil the child" school of child rearing and believed they were building our character by being strict and doling out far more criticism than praise. At worst, they ignored us or led us to believe we were to blame for their unhappiness.

"I remember being very young, maybe three or four," said Beverly, a twice-divorced secretary. "I was riding in the car with my mother and one of her friends, and Mom was talking about how rotten her life was, how she had given up all of her dreams, married too young, gotten pregnant too soon, you name it. She kept saying, 'What about me? When will it be my turn?' Which was something I was going to hear a million times before I left home to get married. But that was the first time I felt like my mother would have been happy if only I hadn't been born."

Despite the times her mother showed she did care for her, Beverly grew up feeling like a burden and never quite shook the sense that her mere presence could make other people miserable. Indeed she had two ex-husbands and two unruly teenage sons to prove that she still was the horrible, "good for nothing" person she had always believed herself to be.

Less drastic and more common than the near total rejection Beverly experienced, were our encounters with conditional love—receiving attention and affection only when we behaved in a certain way. Conditional love teaches us that our actions and our identities are one and the same, that we are what we do. If we "did good" (based on others' definitions of what was good), we were good people. If we misbehaved, we were bad people. To this day you may only like yourself when you are doing and saying what you think will please other people, even when it means denying your own needs.

Throughout our lives our self-worth continues to be influenced by both the things other people tell us ("You're such a klutz, troublemaker, brat") and our actual success or failure at various

---

Is self-worth a problem area for you? Answer the following questions to discover if you are having trouble believing that you are worthy of intimate relationships.

Rating scale:

5 = almost always
4 = frequently
3 = sometimes
2 = occasionally
1 = rarely if ever

_2_ Do you make decisions based on what you think other people expect?

_3_ Do you feel helpless to get what you want, thinking, "This is just how it is; there is nothing I can do about it"?

_3_ When you are interested in getting closer to someone, do you feel anxious and then tell yourself, "He or she would never be interested in me"?

_2_ Are you surprised when people you do not know very well remember your name or something you said?

_3_ Do you criticize yourself for not being smart, pretty, creative, or ambitious enough to somehow do the right thing in any situation?

_4_ Do you feel your value as a person is defined only by your job, your relationship, or other external sources of self-esteem?

A total score of 18 or above tells you that you have work to do in this area; 24 or above means that this prerequisite may be preventing you from having the intimate relationships you want.

endeavors. As a result we may have developed a long list of things we believe we cannot do and an even longer list of things we try to avoid because we cannot hope to succeed at them. Intimate relationships may have topped the list.

POSITIVE REGARD FOR OTHERS

The flip side of self-worth is a positive regard for others, which involves a willingness to view *other people* as lovable and capable. It is the ability to recognize them as separate and unique individuals and to respect their thoughts and feelings even though they may be different than our own. It requires a certain amount of sensitivity to other people's needs—which does not mean that you must be able to read their minds, but rather that you be willing to consider how your behavior may affect them.

Intimacy grows from your willingness to do things with another person, to spend time together and to make personal sacrifices for each other and the good of the relationship. Without positive regard for others, there would be no reason for you to want to get close. However, you are bound to meet people from time to time who are unable to view other people in a positive light at all.

■ JEFFREY

Jeffrey, a thirty-five-year-old professional baseball player with an eye on a sportscasting career (or at the very least, a lucrative commercial contract), had been a robust baby born after several miscarriages, and throughout his childhood, was the center of his parents' universe. Because nothing was too good for their miracle child his parents tried their best to give him whatever he wanted. On the rare occasions they realized his behavior was getting out of hand, they got angry and yelled at their son, but felt immediate remorse, imploring him to tell them how they could make up for their outburst. Naturally, Jeffrey had a few suggestions.

As luck would have it, Jeffrey was bright, attractive, and charming enough to garner similar treatment from people outside his home. The admiration of his teachers and friends, his athletic trophies, scholastic honors, and sexual escapades all served to reinforce his perception of himself as special and superior to others. He came to expect preferential treatment and to have the spotlight trained on him at all times.

He had never married, however, because he was still "looking for the right woman." She would have to have the right image, he told me. Although he did not say it in so many words, it was apparent that "the right image" was one that would enhance his own and increase his feeling of superiority. She could not be demanding, of course, and should be willing to focus on his career and his success—much like his parents had.

Jeffrey was beginning to think that a woman meeting his requirements did not exist. And he was right. Women who projected the image he wanted were too smart and self-confident to cater to him. And the ones who catered to him were not ambitious or successful enough for his tastes. "I'm thinking about calling up Disney studios and having them make me a perfect mate," he joked. He wasn't really joking, of course, but wishing he could really do so. Jeffrey saw women only in terms of what they could do for him. He really had no positive regard for them at all. And as a result, he was truly incapable of having an intimate relationship.

Though you may not think of others in quite so limited a way, you may still have difficulty with this prerequisite for intimacy. If your parents were only half as indulgent as Jeffrey's, you may unwittingly ride roughshod over others because you sincerely believe that if they really cared about you they would want to make you happy by meeting your demands.

More typically, you may not think highly of others because you do not think highly of yourself. Their most irritating behaviors may be the ones you cannot tolerate in yourself, or were severely criticized for in the past. What appears to be their insensitivity to your feelings may be your guilt over having those feelings in the first place. Or you may unconsciously project the unacceptable aspects of yourself onto others and become disgusted with them as an alternative to being disgusted with yourself. The people on whom you hang your projections may very well have some of the characteristics you attribute to them. However, if your sense of self-worth were stronger, those traits would merely annoy you rather than offend you so.

In addition, if you have received unfair or abusive treatment from some person in the past, you may conclude that all people of that gender, minority, or profession are untrustworthy, abusive, and so on. Naturally, this perception limits your ability to relate to them.

Men more than women—but very achievement-oriented people of both genders—have less positive regard for others than is needed for intimacy because they are used to interacting with others based on what they do rather than who they are. Like Stacy, the career-focused film producer described in the previous chapter, you may network instead of getting close, having a friend for every purpose and a purpose for every friend. Putting people into categories such as "drinking buddy," "prospective client," or "racquetball partner," means you find people useful, but not necessarily lovable, and therefore little intimacy may exist in your life.

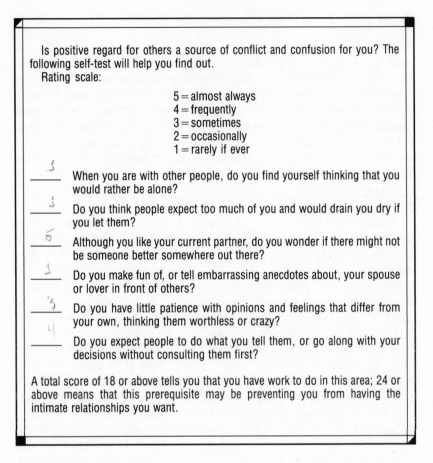

Is positive regard for others a source of conflict and confusion for you? The following self-test will help you find out.

Rating scale:

5 = almost always
4 = frequently
3 = sometimes
2 = occasionally
1 = rarely if ever

_3_ When you are with other people, do you find yourself thinking that you would rather be alone?

_4_ Do you think people expect too much of you and would drain you dry if you let them?

_5_ Although you like your current partner, do you wonder if there might not be someone better somewhere out there?

_1_ Do you make fun of, or tell embarrassing anecdotes about, your spouse or lover in front of others?

_3_ Do you have little patience with opinions and feelings that differ from your own, thinking them worthless or crazy?

_4_ Do you expect people to do what you tell them, or go along with your decisions without consulting them first?

A total score of 18 or above tells you that you have work to do in this area; 24 or above means that this prerequisite may be preventing you from having the intimate relationships you want.

INTERDEPENDENCE

Interdependence is one word for the give-and-take that makes intimate relationships work for *both* people involved in them. It is the delicate balance that enables you sometimes to act independently and sometimes to operate as a team—to take care of your partner when he or she needs it and to allow him or her to take care of you when that is what you need. It is perhaps the greatest challenge in any intimate relationship and one that is difficult to face for those of us who, for one reason or another, never learned what healthy dependency on others means.

■ ALISHA

A forty-five-year-old schoolteacher who recently separated from her alcoholic husband after more than twenty years of marriage, Alisha never
knew her father. He abandoned the family before she was born. "For a
long time I was sure he left because of me," she said. "He'd stuck around
when there were four kids, but number five was more than he could
handle. I was the straw that broke the camel's back, the one that drove
Daddy away. Then there was the whole stigma of not having a father
when all my friends did, and how that made me feel. But most of all I was
convinced that no man would ever care about me enough to stick around."

During adolescence and early adulthood, Alisha seemed determined to
prove her point. She got involved with men who were so obviously
undependable that they may as well have had "I'll get going when the
going gets tough" tattooed on their foreheads. She devoted herself to
making them love her and getting them to stay with her forever, waiting
on them hand and foot, supporting them financially and boosting their
egos in every way she possibly could. When playing willing slave lost its
effectiveness, she reversed roles, in an effort to convince them that she
could not live without them—even going so far as to threaten suicide.
Naturally, this only sent them packing.

At twenty-four she met and married Frank, who already had a serious
drinking problem which Alisha was in fact aware of. "I guess part of me
knew no one else would put up with him and that he knew it too," she
sighed. "He was already such a mess that he couldn't possibly get along
without me. He wasn't going to leave me and that was that. Or at least, it
was until recently." Dragged to an Al-Anon meeting by a friend, Alisha
realized that she had her "priorities all screwed up. I was so terrified that
he would abandon me, that I didn't even realize he wasn't really there for
me at all." As you will read more about in Chapter 7, Alisha had a
codependent relationship with Frank, not an *interdependent* one.

The most basic human fear is the fear of being separated from
other human beings, and if this did indeed happen to you at an
early age—whether you were abandoned by a parent as Alisha was,
or experienced separation because of death, illness, or divorce—
dependency is liable to be a source of conflict and confusion long
afterward. But even if you've never experienced a traumatic separation, depending on others and having them depend on you may be
a source of anxiety. To a certain extent it is for all of us.

Our dependency needs cause us to question our own strength and
self-reliance. We may see depending on others as a trap, a way for
them to wield power over us and prevent us from acting on our own.
We are prone to this point of view if our parents or other important

people in our lives made us pay for depending on them, inducing guilt by reminding us of every sacrifice they ever made on our behalf. In those old relationships, as well as our new ones, we may be reluctant to express our needs for closeness and nurturance. The price of dependency is just too high.

Because of a parent's alcoholism, illness, or demanding job, some of us took on adult responsibilities at an early age. Others had our needs addressed inconsistently at best. Still others were praised only for being independent and self-reliant. If any of these descriptions fit you, chances are that somewhere in the back of your mind resides the idea that depending on others is not as good or as safe as depending on yourself. You may even believe, as Pamela did with Josh, that you do not have needs or that you are flawed for having

---

Is interdependence an issue for you? Here is another self-test to let you know where you stand.

Rating scale:

5 = almost always
4 = frequently
3 = sometimes
2 = occasionally
1 = rarely if ever

_3_ Do you latch onto people, turning to them for reassurance and advice whenever you feel uncertain or upset?

_3_ Do you feel responsible for other people's happiness, bending over backward to take care of them?

_1_ Do you feel you must obtain the approval of others before making decisions that affect your life?

_4_ Do you feel anxious when you are away from your partner and feel more comfortable or self-confident in his or her presence?

_3_ Do you refuse offers of assistance, wondering if such offers stem from the belief that you are weak or incompetent?

_4_ When you realize that other people are counting on you, do you get nervous or worry about letting them down?

_5_ When you are in an intimate relationship for any length of time, do you feel suffocated, itchy, trapped?

A 4 or 5 rating in one or more of these areas is a pretty good indication that you have not yet achieved interdependence and may have difficulty doing so in the future.

them. Your determination to take care of everything on your own diminishes your capacity for intimacy. You may even unintentionally hurt people who want to get close to you by showing you they care.

Problems with interdependency are varied and complicated. They include:

- compulsively catering to our loved ones
- having an almost insatiable need to be reassured and coddled
- running at the first sign that someone is becoming dependent on us
- worrying about somehow failing to meet others' needs, hurting them, and then being unable to live with ourselves

These problems are definitely worth untangling since interdependence creates the bond that keeps two people together through the tough times, as well as the easy ones.

TOLERANCE FOR CONFLICT, AMBIGUITY, AND IMPERFECTION

There is no such thing as an intimate relationship that proceeds according to a preprogrammed game plan. Only in our fantasies do we meet a person with whom we are perfectly compatible, have a perfect romantic courtship, wed, rear children, and grow old together in perfect harmony.

Real-life relationships are full of surprises. They can be a source of great joy but also a source of emotions that range from upsetting to seemingly overwhelming. In real life the people you love will think or act differently than you expect them to. Now and then they will say or do hurtful and even repulsive things. They will change while you are not looking. They will butt heads with you and try to meet their needs at your expense.

These occurrences come with the territory of any intimate relationship. If you are tolerant and flexible enough to compromise, you can resolve conflicts in a manner that allows both of you to get some of what you need. If you are tolerant and accepting enough to allow others to be themselves even if the way they are is not exactly the way you wish they would be, you will let the "small stuff" roll off your back and stay in the relationship long enough to get a shot at experiencing true intimacy. Such tolerance is sometimes hard to come by, however, especially for people who expect perfection and for people who are "allergic" to anger or dissension of any kind.

Perfection is our ultimate illusion. The assumption that we can actually attain it is often an outgrowth of the demands for perfection that were placed upon us during childhood, the very same ones that may have turned us into maniacally driven high achievers in other areas of our lives. At work, in school, during athletic competitions, we succeeded by setting goals and forging ahead to achieve them, simply trying harder whenever they seemed to be slipping from our grasp. Once we reached our goals, we set new ones and started the entire process all over again. To this day we are never satisfied with where we are, never really comfortable unless we are striving for something better.

Nowhere is this approach more self-defeating than in personal relationships, where intimacy unfolds ever so slowly, and closeness is obtained in a spiral path rather than a straight line. Consequently, if you are a perfectionist and goal-oriented, you quickly grow impatient with a process that simply does not make sense to you. You want instant intimacy and find close relatonships too frustrating and unpredictable to enjoy. All too often you give up and go back to something that seems more manageable—your work or one-night stands.

The second grand illusion—one that leads to an intolerance for conflict—is the assumption that a good relationship is peaceful and harmonious at all times, that people who care about each other rarely argue and that anger is a "bad" emotion best kept under wraps.

■ ELIZABETH

"I don't do anger," said Elizabeth, sounding as if she believed anger was an activity like washing windows instead of an emotion that is part of all human beings. But then Elizabeth was never aware of feeling anger. She had stopped feeling it soon after marrying Howard, who had seemed to be such a mild-mannered man, right up until the first time he got really angry and threw the porch furniture through the picture window. His destructive temper tantrums became routine, and although he never laid a hand on Elizabeth or their children, she was always afraid that he would—that he would lose control completely and end up killing them all. What's more, sometimes *her* rage at him became so overwhelming that she wanted to strangle Howard with her bare hands. The magnitude of her fury frightened her, so she shut it off like a faucet. "I just pushed it down deep inside," she explained, "buried it because I thought that if I didn't I really would kill him."

Elizabeth eventually left Howard, but by then all of her feelings were frozen. In an effort to eliminate one emotion. Elizabeth deadened them all—which is a common occurrence whenever we try to anesthetize our feelings instead of dealing with them. We end up with an almost zombielike existence that does not make us much fun to be around and pretty much squelches any hope of attaining intimacy.

Like Elizabeth, you may be afraid of what might happen if you unleashed your anger. Perhaps you would cause the sort of damage you witnessed firsthand by angry and abusive people with whom you were involved in the past. You may remember the unpleasant response you received from your parents when you expressed anger or frustration during childhood and now, to avoid present-day rejection or disapproval, would rather do almost anything but fight. If you grew up in a home where people argued constantly and there was always tension in the air, you may have promised yourself that your adult relationships would never be like that. Now, the slightest expression of negative emotions by your spouse or lover sends you into a tailspin. You are sure that unless you give in immediately and makes amends, your relationship will become as out of control as your family once was.

Regardless of the reason behind it—if you cannot tolerate conflict, ambiguity, and imperfection, if they create more discomfort than you can bear—then you will run from a relationship long before it provides the intimacy you were hoping to find. You may quite literally flee, ending relationships as soon as they hit troubled waters. You may make yourself comfortably numb, using alcohol, drugs, food, or compulsive behaviors to avoid feeling or facing what is happening. Or you may try with all your might to force other people to measure up to your expectations. No matter which path you choose, you lose.

SELF-DISCLOSURE

Self-disclosure is the process of sharing your inner self with others and talking about your real thoughts or feelings even if they are not pretty. For many of us the mere thought of doing this leaves us quaking in our boots.

The most nerve-racking question we face in dealing with others concerns what is, and is not, appropriate to disclose to whom at what point in any relationship. Our search for an answer sends us back to square one and the issue of trust. Certainly it would be foolish to reveal tidbits of who we are to people who would use that information against us. But how can we know in advance if this will happen?

Is tolerance for conflict, ambiguity, and imperfection a problem area for you? Answer the following questions to find out.

Rating scale:

> 5 = almost always
> 4 = frequently
> 3 = sometimes
> 2 = occasionally
> 1 = rarely if ever

_____ When things do not go according to plan or people do not act the way you expect them to in a relationship, does it raise serious doubts about your continuing to put energy into that relationship?

_____ When someone makes what you consider to be a mistake or disagrees with you, do you take it personally, thinking, "I *deserve* better than this" or, "He *owes* me an apology" or, "I am *entitled* to an explanation"?

_____ Do you have relationships that seem terrific at first, but end quickly because the other person involved turned out not to be who you thought he or she was?

_____ Do you go out of your way to avoid arguments?

_____ When you feel angry, are you more likely to flee the scene, otherwise bury your emotions in food, drink, or work, than to explain the reason for your anger?

_____ If someone you love does something that hurts or irritates you, does the offense linger in your mind long after the incident is over?

_____ Do you silently keep track of the insensitive things people do, until you cannot take it anymore, then regurgitate all of their transgressions during one monster argument?

_____ Do you find yourself walking on eggshells in order to avoid upsetting the people who matter to you—especially those who have been known to become angry or argumentative?

A total score of 24 or above tells you that you have work to do in this area; 32 or above means that this prerequisite may be preventing you from having the intimate relationships you want.

The second question involves knowing who we really are to begin with, and whether we feel comfortable being ourselves or rather have gotten into the habit of disowning our own ideas and values in order to please others. Many of us have. We have created a false self to conceal our real, but presumably unlovable and inadequate self. And some of us have been "in character" for so long that we feel as if our false self is the person we are supposed to be.

■ SYLVIE

A pediatrician and recovering addict, Sylvie—who you will get to know later in this book—has been clean and sober for three years. She was the oldest of four children in a family where both parents worked long hours, leaving her in charge of her siblings. "I was the strong one and the smart one," she recalled. "I got so used to hearing my parents and everyone else say, 'Sylvie can handle it,' that I really believed I could handle anything. And whenever I got tired or upset and especially if I'd cry, I would hear, 'Pull yourself together, Sylvie. You're too smart to feel that way.' I believed that too. Even now in my twelve-step meetings, where I know I can be completely honest, I still catch myself using humor to make what I'm saying easier to take or being real intellectual about something I'm feeling. It's like this ancient voice inside my head is saying, 'You're Sylvie and Sylvie does not admit when she's hurting.'"

Most likely to have trouble with this prerequisite for intimacy are those of us with chaotic backgrounds that taught us we could retain some semblance of control by sealing off parts of our identity and refusing to reveal our doubts and fears. Those of us who were severely criticized or ridiculed learned to create a facade that concealed our vulnerabilities. Others among us grew up in families burdened with secrets of a member's alcoholism or inappropriate sexual behavior and were forbidden from discussing what was happening and how we felt about it. It was only a small step from there to concluding that telling anyone anything personal about ourselves was dangerous and should be avoided.

But perhaps the greatest obstacle to self-disclosure is that many of us never learned *how* to disclose. We don't recognize the signs that others are open to intimate conversation—smiling and making eye contact, for instance. When people approach us we automatically train our gaze on our toes and during conversations, especially those of a personal nature, we seem utterly fascinated with our fingernails. We hide behind newspapers, wait until we are walking out the door before saying what is really on our minds, and even seduce our spouses or lovers to prevent them from probing our thoughts and feelings. We cannot help it. Our experience with self-disclosure is limited at best, and the few effective communication skills we have do not get the job done. Indeed, they can create more distance instead of bridging the intimacy gap.

Blaming, coercing, begging, bribing, yelling, not saying what we mean or meaning what we say, are not conducive to intimacy and limit or eliminate self-disclosure completely. Yet they are some of the most common ways we attempt to communicate our points of view.

Is self-disclosure a source of conflict or confusion for you? Take the following self-test.
Rating scale:

> 5 = almost always
> 4 = frequently
> 3 = sometimes
> 2 = occasionally
> 1 = rarely if ever

_____ Do you try to create and maintain an image that helps you appear more like the people you assume are more competent and confident than you are?

_____ Do you think that people who talk about themselves are considered bothersome by others?

_____ Do you think talking about your concerns or problems is like "washing your dirty laundry in public," or that it makes you seem weak?

_____ After disclosing information about yourself, do you replay those conversations in your mind and end up regretting what you said?

_____ If you do start to reveal personal information, do you find yourself making light of serious matters?

_____ Do you become uncomfortable when other people talk about personal matters or express emotions like sorrow, self-doubt, or fear?

_____ Do you want to express your innermost thoughts and feelings, but find yourself at a loss for words or fear that if you start you won't be able to stop?

_____ Do you use some or many of the poor communication tactics I described in this section?

A total score of 24 or above tells you that you have work to do in this area; 32 or above means that this prerequisite may be preventing you from having the intimate relationships you want.

Few of us are itching to share our innermost thoughts with people who do not talk, do not listen, have no sense of humor, refuse to admit they are wrong, or routinely criticize others. How can we expect to find intimacy if we are one of those people?

Although women can and do develop communication habits that discourage self-disclosure, men are far more likely to. They have had less practice and have received less encouragement for participating in conversations that have no other purpose than to bring two people closer together and enable them to feel good about each other. Verbalizing their feelings is not something that comes naturally to men who have for years been conditioned not to. They are much more likely to hide their feelings or to believe their actions speak for them. In fact, the average man's idea of an intimate exchange is the average woman's idea of a casual conversation—which may be why so many relationship conflicts seem to begin with a woman saying to the man in her life, "You never tell me how you feel."

COURAGE

In our quest for intimacy we can never know in advance if our efforts to form close lasting connections with others will fulfill our heart's desire or bring to life our worst nightmares—and that is why courage is a prerequisite. We need it to take the risks that are necessary in any intimate relationship, to reach out for intimacy's probable gains in spite of the possible losses.

Many of the people you have read about so far could not take those risks. Pamela could not. She believed that if she let herself depend on Josh or asked for anything from him, he would disappoint her. Rebecca could not. She thought there was no point in trying to attract and get close to men because she would only fail. Alisha could not. She wanted an ironclad, money-back guarantee that people would not abandon her.

Whenever you are reluctant to take risks, the negative outcomes you fear are blown up to catastrophic proportions, overshadowing the more positive possibilities. Indeed, you may completely blind yourself to the plus side, believing that should you try to have an intimate relationship, you could *only* lose. With those kinds of odds, is it any wonder that so many of us stand at the threshold of intimacy only to turn tail and run at the last minute?

If you look at a risk as doing something you may never have done before but which you will not know you *can* do successfully until after you have tried it, then it becomes clear that you have already taken an infinite number of risks. What's more, the vast majority of them—from walking for the first time to passing your driver's test—have had positive outcomes. Yet, when you face a new challenge, you invariably forget the successful risks you have taken and remember only the ones that have backfired. Your failures are clear in your mind whether they happened yesterday or thirty years ago when you asked Peggy Sue to the prom and she turned you down, or

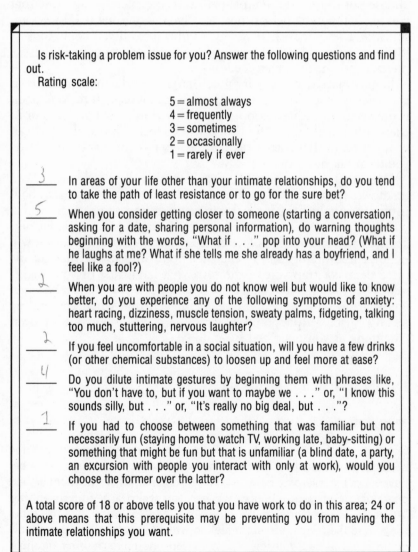

Is risk-taking a problem issue for you? Answer the following questions and find out.

Rating scale:

5 = almost always
4 = frequently
3 = sometimes
2 = occasionally
1 = rarely if ever

_3_ In areas of your life other than your intimate relationships, do you tend to take the path of least resistance or to go for the sure bet?

_5_ When you consider getting closer to someone (starting a conversation, asking for a date, sharing personal information), do warning thoughts beginning with the words, "What if . . ." pop into your head? (What if he laughs at me? What if she tells me she already has a boyfriend, and I feel like a fool?)

_2_ When you are with people you do not know well but would like to know better, do you experience any of the following symptoms of anxiety: heart racing, dizziness, muscle tension, sweaty palms, fidgeting, talking too much, stuttering, nervous laughter?

_2_ If you feel uncomfortable in a social situation, will you have a few drinks (or other chemical substances) to loosen up and feel more at ease?

_4_ Do you dilute intimate gestures by beginning them with phrases like, "You don't have to, but if you want to maybe we . . ." or, "I know this sounds silly, but . . ." or, "It's really no big deal, but . . ."?

_1_ If you had to choose between something that was familiar but not necessarily fun (staying home to watch TV, working late, baby-sitting) or something that might be fun but that is unfamiliar (a blind date, a party, an excursion with people you interact with only at work), would you choose the former over the latter?

A total score of 18 or above tells you that you have work to do in this area; 24 or above means that this prerequisite may be preventing you from having the intimate relationships you want.

twenty years ago when you gave a party and no one came, or ten years ago when you got to the podium to give your speech and forgot what to say.

The most influential memories of risking and failing are those directly related to intimacy. But *anything* you ever tried which did not turn out as you hoped it would or caused you pain is still stored in a file stamped, "You blew it." You haul out that file each time you consider taking another risk. Not wanting to blow it again, you choose not to try for the probable gains, completely forgetting that you are a different person now and have more maturity, wisdom, skills, and resources than you ever did before. If you could look at intimacy risks objectively, you would see that you actually have a pretty good chance of succeeding.

Unfortunately, objectivity goes out the window when fear is in the driver's seat. And fear is indeed what drives you to look upon intimacy as an if/then proposition and to think, "If I do X, Y, or Z, then only horrible, painful things will happen." Ironically, you can only get rid of that fear by taking the very risk the fear is preventing you from taking.

Does this mean that you should rush full speed ahead into unknown territory? Of course not. Confronting your fears about intimacy involves *gradually* letting go, testing the waters, and if your intimate gestures are well received, wading in a little farther. Yes, you will feel vulnerable every step of the way, and yes, that will be unpleasant. But most of the time you will discover that getting close does *not* trap you in the terrifying landscape of your nightmares but rather gives you a taste of how satisfying life can be when you share it with someone else. And even that when you end up feeling hurt or disappointed, it will not be as horrible or overwhelming as you imagined it would be.

INTIMACY ROLE MODELS

■ GARY

Gary, the thirty-two-year-old electrical engineer who came to see me because he feared he had developed a sexual addiction, honestly believed that the interplay between himself and women with whom he had one-night stands was intimacy. "We were sort of close," he said sheepishly. "At least we were for a couple of hours. We talked some. Not much but some, and there was this warm feeling when I knew they were probably g to go to bed with me. I'd connected—no more than an alcoholic ects with a bartender or a drug addict connects with his dealer, but still it was a connection. The best I could do, 'cause when it came to real connections I didn't have a clue."

Why didn't he? Because the interactions he had observed between the two most influential people in his life—his parents—left him with more misconceptions about intimacy than realistic behavior patterns to emulate. This may also be true for you.

In addition to adopting attitudes and behaviors based on how you were treated by others during childhood or other times in the past, you also learned about intimacy from what you saw going on around you, by *observing* the influential people in your life, most notably your parents, but also others. You did not sit around staring and taking notes, of course, and may not have realized you were learning at all. You absorbed information and formed impressions unconsciously, almost by osmosis. And like your experiences, your observations may not have been as positive or useful as you needed them to be in order to build a sturdy foundation for your future relationships. In fact, you may have started out at a disadvantage when it came to intimacy because you had few, if any, *positive intimacy role models*—people you admired or respected whose relationships with people besides yourself were healthy, mature, caring, honest and non-manipulative.

For instance, Gary was an adult child of alcoholic parents. Both his mother and his father had drinking problems, and as a result they modeled many things, but intimacy was not one of them. When Gary talked about the relationship between his parents, he mentioned screaming matches at three in the morning, icy silences at the breakfast table when one or both had hangovers, and sitting in the local bar watching them flirt with strangers to make each other jealous. He recalled no expressions of affection, no signs of concern for each other's welfare, and no common interests other than drinking (and even that seemed to be a competition over who could hold the most liquor). "The only times I saw them sit down and really talk to each other was when they were making a pact to quit drinking," he said. "But even those discussions were a joke, because sooner or later one of them would slip up and they'd be right back to where they started."

Of course, our families are not the only intimacy role models available to us. In fact, by lacking role models inside his home, Gary learned most of what he knew about getting close from outside sources, most notably the media. He sought the unbridled passion and instant intimacy he saw portrayed in movies and on television. And he sought it over and over again because he had only a hazy notion of what a warm, close, long-term relationship could be like.

Although emulating the idealized version of intimacy presented

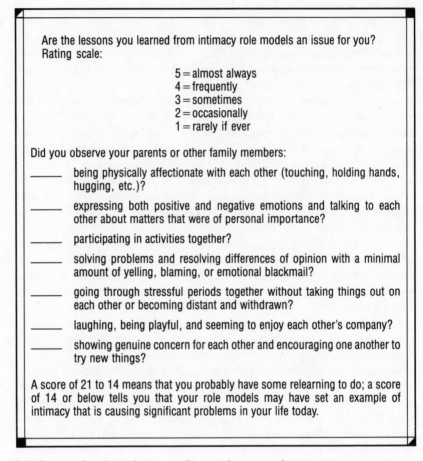

Are the lessons you learned from intimacy role models an issue for you? Rating scale:

5 = almost always
4 = frequently
3 = sometimes
2 = occasionally
1 = rarely if ever

Did you observe your parents or other family members:

_____ being physically affectionate with each other (touching, holding hands, hugging, etc.)?

_____ expressing both positive and negative emotions and talking to each other about matters that were of personal importance?

_____ participating in activities together?

_____ solving problems and resolving differences of opinion with a minimal amount of yelling, blaming, or emotional blackmail?

_____ going through stressful periods together without taking things out on each other or becoming distant and withdrawn?

_____ laughing, being playful, and seeming to enjoy each other's company?

_____ showing genuine concern for each other and encouraging one another to try new things?

A score of 21 to 14 means that you probably have some relearning to do; a score of 14 or below tells you that your role models may have set an example of intimacy that is causing significant problems in your life today.

by the media can do more harm than good, positive impressions formed by observing friends, lovers, or spouses can help you relearn the meaning of intimacy, repairing at least some of the damage that was done earlier in your life.

Now that you are familiar with the eight prerequisites for intimacy and have completed eight self-tests to determine which ones may be sources of conflict and confusion, you may have discovered that you have some difficulty with almost all of them. But don't despair. Any prerequisite you now lack *can* be replenished, and I will show you how to do that throughout this book.

But before you can move forward to change your approach to intimacy or even fully understand what you may now be doing to compensate for the prerequisites you lack, you must take another look back at your past experiences. You see, your present-day relationships are influenced not only by what you did *not* get in the past but also by what you did get—disappointment, rejection, indifference, disapproval, and other forms of psychological pain.

The next chapter describes how, in our efforts to cope with unsettling past experiences, we unwittingly adopt an approach to life and relationships that reinforces the lessons we have already learned, intensifies our fear of intimacy, and prevents us from effectively meeting our need for it.

3

I WON'T GET HURT AGAIN:
Intimacy and Unfinished Business
from the Past

■ STACY

"It's like Stacy isn't even part of this family anymore," her sister commented. "She started shutting the rest of us out when Dad died."

"Stacy is one of those people who walks through life with her dukes up," her oldest brother added. "No matter what kind of financial trouble she got herself into trying to build her film company, she refused to take a dime from any of us. She actually got mad at us for offering to help. To tell you the truth, she always seems angry to me—something about the way she moves, says, 'Don't cross me.'"

Stacy firmly believed that she had to be tough to survive in her business. But she did not reserve her intimidating facade for business settings only.

"A friend of mine dated her once," her brother continued, "but he didn't stand a chance. He knew that if he made just one mistake, she'd cut him to shreds . . . apparently she did."

Why did Stacy walk through life with her dukes up, acting as if she needed no closeness at all? Why did she intimidate people into keeping their distance and end potentially intimate relationships before they had a chance to get off the ground? Because she was acting out a script based on seemingly unalterable beliefs about herself, other people, and relationships. Those beliefs were backed up by past experiences that not only diminished her supply of intimacy prerequisites but also caused her pain that she preferred not to experience again.

55

As a sixteen-year-old mourning the death of her father, Stacy coped with her pain by trying to explain and learn something from the tragedy. If she could make sense out of the situation, if she could find some message in her father's life and death, then she could accept it, she thought. As you may recall from Chapter One, poring through old scrapbooks and photo albums, Stacy concluded that her dad had died young and full of regrets because love and marriage had forced him to give up his dream of becoming a renowned jazz musician. It does not really matter that Stacy's perception might not have been accurate. She believed it. "He could have been happy," she explained thirteen years later, "but he just got by. He did work he hated. He let my mother push him around. He compromised himself to death."

The message Stacy gleaned from her loss was not to do that. She never would, Stacy decided. Never. But several years after her father's death, she almost did when she fell in love with Craig, got pregnant, and almost married him at his urging. "My father's life passed before my eyes," Stacy told me, "and it made me realize that I was about to sacrifice *my* life for love. I couldn't do it. I got away in the nick of time." And she has been staying away from "distracting" personal attachments ever since.

"I'll never forget the agony of having to choose between a life with Craig and my dream of making it as a filmmaker," Stacy said. "I knew I was hurting him. I was hurting myself. It was a horrible position to be in. I should never have let things go so far." Now she does not. Her intimidating behavior keeps her out of that "horrible position." Although she is not fully aware of what she is doing or why she is doing it, her every move ensures that no personal relationship will force her once again to make a painful choice between intimacy and her dreams.

MAKING SURE NOT TO GET HURT AGAIN

Imagine for a moment that you have slipped on an icy sidewalk or tripped over a child's toy and injured your knee. Your knee throbs. It swells. Your physician assures you that no serious damage has been done and advises you to stay off your feet as much as possible for a few days. You try to follow his advice, but you have a job to go to, children to watch, errands to run. Because putting your full weight on your injured leg causes excruciating pain, you have to find a way to move around as painlessly as possible. You must compensate for your injury in order to get on with your life—and you do. You learn to keep your bad leg slightly bent and your foot pointed downward so that when you walk, only your toes and the ball of your foot touch the ground before you quickly shift your weight to your good leg.

You hobble around like this for weeks. Slowly and carefully, you try to resume walking normally. You test out your leg and if you feel the slightest twinge of pain, you conclude that you are not ready, that your knee has not yet healed. You hobble for another day or another week, and your knee stiffens. So does your ankle and your foot. Your back aches, and the hip joint of your good leg throbs. Because of the injury to your knee and the way you adapted to it, your entire body is out of alignment. Consequently, when you do resume walking "normally," you may continue to favor one leg or lean forward slightly to compensate for your back pain. In addition, you are acutely aware of conditions that might cause you to reinjure your knee. You avoid icy sidewalks and scream at your kids when they leave toys lying around. You may give up jogging or overflow with righteous indignation when you notice spilled liquids on the grocery store floor. Your knee has healed, but your life is not the same as it was before you sustained the injury. There is a new concern—*making sure that you do not get hurt again.*

Each of us goes through a similar process in response to any *emotional* injury we sustain. Whether you suffered painful losses as Stacy did or were neglected by your parents, ridiculed by your peers, rejected by a lover, or hurt in any other way, you found the strength to go on with your life in spite of the pain. You compensated for your losses and established elaborate defense systems both to minimize the immediate impact of a painful situation and to avoid being hurt like that again. You did what you had to do, and you did it in the best way you possibly could at that time under those circumstances.

Yet, just as coping with a knee injury throws other parts of your body out of alignment and changes the way that you move, your adaptation to psychological pain alters your entire outlook and continues to influence your attitudes and actions long after the original wounds seem to have healed. Because the methods you use to cope with unsettling past experiences are woven into the fabric of your personality and firmly fixed in your subconscious mind, you may develop a limited view of the world and a rigid set of beliefs and behaviors that predispose you to approach life and relationships in a certain way. Everything you think, feel, and do may be colored in some way by your old pain, your unfinished business from the past, and the *stance* you adopted because of it. This was certainly the case for Stacy, who adopted one of the four approaches that I come across most often in my psychotherapy practice—the intimidator stance.

THE INTIMIDATOR STANCE

Perhaps you know someone like Stacy who rejects intimacy or avoids it by wearing an intimidator mask at all times. You may take this stance yourself, making it perfectly clear to all onlookers that you need no one. Oblivious to the wounds you inflict in the process, you reject everyone who attempts to get close to you, keeping them at a distance with your icy demeanor or scaring them away with angry outbursts.

If you approach life and relationships from the intimidator stance, you are emotionally guarded and suspicious. Constantly on the lookout for signs that other people are going to trick you into depending on them only to turn around and abandon you, you make sure to land the first blow—one which the recipient rarely sees coming and may not deserve. You are unforgiving. Like Stacy, the people in your life get one strike and then they are out. Once you have shut the door and pulled up the drawbridge, there is no way back into your emotional fortress.

Convinced that you can count on no one but yourself, it is of the utmost importance to see yourself as strong and independent. Since, in your mind's eye, asking for support of any kind is a sign of weakness, you will not do so, nor will you accept any assistance offered to you. In addition, you may believe that anything you receive from other people comes with strings attached and you are determined to remain unencumbered. As Stacy put it, "The only person I want to answer to is myself. I won't blame my failures on anyone else, and I don't want anyone else to take credit for my success."

When you feel an urge to be comforted or cuddled, you squelch it. Indeed, the needier you feel, the tougher you act, appearing hostile, selfish, or downright irrational to those around you.

You are using intimidation to ward off your fear of intimacy. However, you would never acknowledge this fear and in fact, may not be aware of it. *You believe that you do not need or want intimate relationships, and that you are happier without them.*

■ *ELIZABETH*

Elizabeth, who you'll recall stopped feeling and expressing anger because she was afraid of the damage she might do to her violent tantrum-throwing husband, felt like a new woman when she finally divorced him three years ago. Unlike Stacy or other intimidators, Elizabeth definitely wanted an intimate relationship. However, she *believed that she would never find one.*

"It's hopeless," Elizabeth informed her therapy group, as she described her latest effort to find a man to love her. In spite of a seemingly endless litany of excuses why she could not take the group's advice and place a personal ad, Elizabeth had finally gone ahead and done it. "You'll see, I'll be the only person in the world who gets no response," she had sighed. But the responses came pouring in. She had immediately begun to worry that the men who sounded good on paper would turn out to be "ax murderers or child molesters." Making sure to mention that she was not getting her hopes up, Elizabeth eventually called one of the men who had written to her.

"It was a problem just trying to work out where and when we would meet," Elizabeth told the group. "With our work schedules and my unreliable car, finding a baby-sitter and not wanting to go to a cocktail lounge, well it's a wonder we ever got the details ironed out." Even then, Elizabeth had almost canceled. "What is the point?" she'd asked herself. "I know I'll only be disappointed again." This pessimism came through loud and clear during her date.

"We talked a lot about how hard it was to meet people," Elizabeth continued. "He agreed that there were plenty of wolves in sheep's clothing running around and that some men find it difficult to get involved with a woman who has children. I told him how much I loved my kids and that they took up most of my time and attention. I let him know that any guy who went out with me would have to accept that fact and how other guys hadn't been able to. He said he understood that and the other things I told him too—about my marriage and my divorce and how depressed I got about my life sometimes."

Did they discuss anything *positive*, asked one of the group members (who claimed to be getting depressed herself).

"Oh, we talked about his job," Elizabeth replied. "He's an accountant or an auditor or something like that."

No one in the therapy group was surprised to learn that Elizabeth never heard from this man again. They could not imagine anyone coming back for another dose of her negative outlook on life and relationships. Elizabeth interpreted the situation differently, however. "Nothing good ever happens to me," she sighed. "I should just accept the fact that I'll never be happy. I should just get used to being alone. Nobody wants me. No one ever has."

THE VICTIM STANCE

Do you approach life and relationships the way Elizabeth did, expecting the worst, believing that the fates have conspired to ruin your life, and feeling powerless to change things? Then you have adopted the victim stance and may be unwittingly fulfilling your own prophecies of gloom and doom.

Just as Elizabeth was victimized by her ex-husband's unpredictable and terrifying rages, at some time in the recent or distant past, you may have been the victim of abuse, neglect, abandonment, or discrimination. You were rendered powerless by people or events and could not stop them from hurting you. The victim stance often begins with such experiences, but it goes beyond the reality of what happened to you at that time. It is an attitude that invades all areas of your life, a perception of yourself as first, foremost, and in all situations a helpless victim of circumstance.

Since, in your mind, external events and other people are the cause of your misery, they must also be the cure—or so you think. As a result, what you look for in an intimate relationship is someone who will take care of you and make you feel better about yourself. At the same time, however, you are completely convinced that no one could accomplish this feat.

If you operate from the victim stance, you cannot imagine why anyone would be interested in someone as helpless and hopeless as you perceive yourself to be, and so discount anyone who seems willing to get close to and accept you. Only someone who is not good enough to attract anyone better would choose you, you think, and the relationship never gets off the ground.

Whenever you do receive the attention you crave, it makes you uncomfortable. You have never been known to accept a compliment gracefully, and your efforts to deflect positive attention often make you appear to be fishing for more compliments and more reassurance. If, by chance, you find yourself in a relationship that fulfills your need for intimacy, you mistrust it. Poised for rejection, you are easily hurt and offended, and your partner can make amends until the cows come home without ever satisfying you. He or she is not sincerely sorry, you think, but merely trying to placate you.

Trying the patience of everyone around you, your hypersensitivity, whining, complaining, and pessimism drive people away. The intimate relationships you really do want cannot survive in the climate your misery creates, and you end up with precisely what you predicted—more disappointment, more loneliness, more despair, and more proof that your situation is hopeless.

■ GARY

Gary was neither an intimidator nor a victim. He was friendlier than Stacy and did not share Elizabeth's negative outlook at all. In fact, he was an entertaining fellow, charming, amusing, and enormously appealing. Overflowing with charisma, Gary had a passion for living on the edge but an aversion to commitments.

"Before I met my wife, Ellen, I never had a relationship that lasted more than a couple of months," Gary admitted. "I was always falling madly, passionately in love. I'd see a woman and feel that magic, that chemistry between us, and I just couldn't get enough of her. But it never seemed to last." Gary, as you may recall, was raised by alcoholic parents and was a whiz at the romantic phase of relationships, but lacked staying power. Prone to making impressions rather than being himself, Gary gave women just enough to pique their interest but nothing substantial to hang onto. In fact, any relationship began to unravel as soon as the woman in his life tried to add some substance to it.

"I'd start feeling like I was being swallowed alive," Gary said. "And like I was naked all of the time. I've never been real comfortable with what women call 'getting to know me better.'" Indeed, believing that his lover was going to see through his carefully constructed facade, Gary would begin feeling nervous. "Like I was on the witness stand waiting to see if I'd be convicted by a jury of my peers," Gary continued, chuckling at his own analogy which hit disturbingly close to home.

Believing that any examination of his real self would turn up glaring inadequacies, Gary immediately took the heat off by criticizing and picking fights with his lover. Then he "stirred up more trouble" by disappearing or "forgetting" to call for days at a time. Becoming fed up with him, Gary's lover would end the relationship, and since she rejected him rather than the other way around, Gary got to move on to his next relationship guilt-free. Gary was an *escape artist*.

THE ESCAPE ARTIST STANCE

Footloose and fancy free, the escape artist is determined to remain that way. If you are one, you may consciously desire an intimate relationship but unconsciously fear being swallowed up or suffocated should you find and stick with one. You may be an *impression manager* who hides what you believe are fatal flaws behind a mask of some kind. Genuine intimacy threatens to expose the real you, and you cannot let that happen so you "dance away" before it does. Or you may worry about committing yourself to the wrong person. What if I am making a mistake, you ask yourself; what if there is someone better out there somewhere? The possibility haunts you, and you feel compelled to keep your options open, to keep moving and searching for your perfect soul mate.

You may be the sort of escape artist who wants only what you cannot have—your best friend's lover, your married boss, someone who makes no demands whatsoever, or a fantasy lover you hope to find in the real world someday. The people with whom you *can* have relationships pale in comparison, and you just cannot seem to settle for "second best."

Or you may actually make poor choices and be forced to extract yourself from relationships you should never have embarked upon. Hooked on excitement and passion, you may be drawn toward people possessing "animal magnetism" or a moody, almost dangerous emotional intensity. But once the "high" of the romantic phase wears off, and you can look at your lover more objectively, you realize that you have nothing in common, no foundation on which to build a lasting relationship.

Regardless of your underlying motives, if you are an escape artist, you love the thrill of the chase and begin missing it as soon as it ends. You feel antsy, anxious, like an animal who belongs in the wild but has been captured and caged. The longer you remain in a relationship, the more powerful your urge to get out of it becomes, and you ultimately give in to that urge. You may do this by engineering your own rejection the way Gary did or you may simply leave—with or without explaining your departure. "On Saturday he loved me and wanted me to move in with him," said one of my patients as she described the demise of her relationship with an escape artist. "Wednesday he needed space and canceled our weekend plans. Monday he informed me that I was great but something he referred to as 'it' was missing. By Friday he had found someone new."

Fleeing from the intimacy you had been so intent upon finding only weeks or months before, you immediately begin another chase. You see, you do not fully comprehend that you are running from relationships because of the intimacy prerequisites *you* lack. You are convinced that the relationship did not work out because it was not the right relationship. The partner you had was the wrong partner. Each had some flaw that you will make sure your next lover does not have—and then you will stop running and searching. You will know that you have found "it" and will finally settle down and commit yourself to the relationship.

But this does not happen. It cannot happen because you do not actually know what you want. However, you *believe that whatever you have is not good enough to be "it."*

■ *ELLEN*

"I had to marry Ellen," Gary told me. "I couldn't get her to leave me." Although he laughed at his own comment, Gary was not really joking. By the time he met Ellen, he had repeated his escape pattern countless times and, in fact, treated Ellen in precisely the same way he had treated all his other lovers. But unlike her predecessors, Ellen put up with Gary's shenanigans. Indeed, hanging onto her relationship with Gary was so vitally important to Ellen that she was willing to put up with almost anything.

When Ellen met Gary she was twenty-eight years old and had already survived a four-year marriage to a cocaine addict, a three-year affair with a married man, and a two-year relationship with a chronically depressed hypochondriac. Gary was easily the healthiest man she had ever attracted, and Ellen recognized this immediately. "I thought, 'My God, he's so normal, so sure of himself, so fun to be with,' " Ellen recalled. "It seemed like such a miracle. I kept telling myself, 'Ellen, this is your big chance, maybe your last chance, so don't blow it.' "

Although Gary had, as usual, been infatuated with Ellen from the moment he laid eyes on her, Ellen felt that she had made Gary love her by behaving in ways that she defined as "lovable"—concealing her desperation with nonchalance, hanging on Gary's every word, flattering him constantly, and repeatedly bending her own will to fulfill his wishes. These were the ritualized ways that Ellen earned her keep socially, and she returned to them time and time again as her relationship with Gary progressed. "I wanted to make him happy," Ellen said. "I was willing to do almost anything to please him. No sacrifice was too great. I loved him that much." She was also terrified of losing him.

"I didn't think I could survive another divorce," Ellen sighed. "I couldn't stand the pain or the loneliness or feeling like such a failure. When I agreed to marry Gary, I promised myself that I would make our marriage work—no matter what it took." Unfortunately, for Ellen to make her marriage work it was going to take patience and a capacity to forgive that a saint would be hard pressed to find. Exchanging wedding vows did not affect Gary's escapist approach one iota. He spent the night before his wedding with a woman he had been "seeing on the side" for months and, by his own estimation, has had close to one hundred one-night stands or short-lived affairs since marrying Ellen. Ellen knew about many of these indiscretions and responded in much the same way to all of them—by renewing her commitment to make Gary happy, so happy with her and their life together that he would have no reason to be unfaithful. Over the next few years, Ellen withstood enormous heartache and made sacrifices far above and beyond the call of duty because she was absolutely convinced that if she just hung in there long enough and tried hard enough, Gary would become the person she desperately wanted him to be, and their relationship would be what she desperately needed it to be.

THE DESPERATELY SEEKING STANCE

I will not be happy until I find someone to love and make him or her love me is the fundamental belief behind the desperately seeking approach to life and relationships. If you are not in a relationship, and have adopted that stance, you may be obsessively looking for the love that you are convinced will heal you and make you feel whole. Everyone you meet could be the one, the person who will make your life complete. Plagued by the sort of "last chance" energy that Ellen experienced, merely feeling attracted to this potentially perfect partner creates internal chaos. You must be perfect too, you think. You must make this person love you by molding yourself into whomever he or she wants you to be. Unlike the escape artist, the chase and the early stages of a relationship do not thrill you. They scare you to death! You are a bundle of raw nerve endings as you anxiously review every detail of every interaction. One wrong move could land you right back where you started—alone, lonely, and desperately seeking love.

Like Ellen, you will make countless sacrifices and suffer endless heartache in order to hold onto what you have. Convinced that you would not survive without your partner and wanting to avoid the pain of rejection, the loneliness and sense of failure you know you will experience if you do not make your relationship work, you try harder and harder to be and do whatever it takes to ward off this unthinkable disaster. You literally lose yourself in the process, which naturally makes the relationship seem even more vital. You would be nothing without it, you believe.

Some of you who desperately seek intimacy are perpetual people pleasers and round-the-clock caretakers. You do all the giving in your relationship. Or you may operate from the opposite extreme. You have such deep longings for intimacy that you expect your partner to meet your every need, to fill every nook and cranny of emptiness inside you. You drain people dry and try so hard to pull them in closer that you end up pushing them away. Still others among you may be so anxious about intimacy that you throw everything but the kitchen sink at your partner—clinging one day, distancing the next, giving your spouse the silent treatment in the morning only to be overflowing with sweetness that night.

PERSONAL HISTORY 101

The *intimidator, victim, escape artist,* and *desperately seeking* stances are not the only ones available to us, simply the most common. Of course, even if you are lacking numerous intimacy prerequisites and have suffered serious traumas in the past, you are *not* predestined to adopt a stance or adhere to it rigidly. However, if you are prone to a certain point of view about intimacy and knowingly or not find ways to confirm it time and time again, then you have indeed adopted one. Like missing intimacy prerequisites, its source can be traced to the past lessons you learned about yourself, other people, and relationships.

GROWING UP IN A DYSFUNCTIONAL FAMILY

If you grew up in a *dysfunctional family,* you cannot help but approach life and relationships with a skewed perspective. In such a family you received insufficient nurturing, and your home life was unpredictable because:

- a parent's addiction, compulsive behavior, mental illness, or some other dysfunction was the central focus in your household
- your parents were either too overwhelmed by their own problems to meet your needs *or* instead focused all of their attention on you—invading your privacy, inappropriately confiding in you, and giving you the impression that you existed only to meet their needs
- family members routinely broke promises and kept secrets from one another, lying and covering up for the dysfunctional member
- there were rigid, unspoken rules that may have made little sense to you but which you knew all too well were never to be broken
- the open expression of feelings and direct discussion of personal or family problems was prohibited

If your family fits any of these descriptions, then at least one family member's unpredictable and at times downright dangerous behavior forced you to find a way to survive in the midst of chaos and hopefully to restore some order to your life. Though you may have pretended that upsetting circumstances in your home neither existed nor adversely affected you, they of course did. Because of them you stopped trusting people or became dishonest. You suppressed your fears and anger, and indeed numbed all unsettling emotions. You stifled your real self and developed habits that you would carry with you into your adult life.

With your formative years constricted by rigid rules reminding you that you were not to trust, talk, or feel, you missed out on the opportunity to test yourself and discover your unique strengths or establish an independent identity. Indeed, as a member of a dysfunctional family you survived by playing a role and rarely, if ever, deviating from it.

For instance, Ellen, the oldest child in a family turned upside down because her mother had a chronic heart condition and her father was a workaholic, took on the role of *hero*. She assumed responsibility for taking care of all of the problems in her family. Repeatedly hospitalized and regularly confined to bed for weeks at a time, Ellen's mother relied on Ellen to run her household and raise her children. "I don't know how we would survive without you," she told her daughter, reinforcing Ellen's sense of responsibility and intensifying her fear that she would somehow fail to take care of things adequately. "I had to make sure things ran smoothly," Ellen recalled. "If I didn't, my mother might get upset and have to go into the hospital or some other terrible thing might happen. I didn't necessarily know what I dreaded, but I was always worried." The most difficult person for Ellen to satisfy was her father, who seemed to be in a sour mood whenever he did spend time at home. "If I cooked a really special dinner or massaged his shoulders the way he liked, then I might be able to coax a smile out of him," Ellen said. "Maybe I thought he'd stay home more or take care of some of the things that I got stuck with; I don't know. But it seemed terribly important to please him, like it was my mission in life to make him happy." By getting involved with men who were dysfunctional in one way or another, Ellen continued to carry out her mission in every intimate relationship she ever had.

Gary, on the other hand, played the *mascot* in his dysfunctional family. The youngest child, he reduced the tension in his household by distracting and entertaining his parents and his older siblings. Being cute and amusing was his full-time job then, and it is still the approach to people that he is most comfortable with now. In chameleonlike fashion, he changed with the prevailing winds in his household, learning to manipulate the family hero—his eldest sister—in order to get his own way. As an adult, most of the women he set his sights on had hero tendencies and assumed the lion's share of responsibility for maintaining the relationship and—in everyone's case but Ellen's—ending it.

Other family roles include the *scapegoat*, who causes trouble to take the heat off the truly troubled family member, and the *lost child*, who fades into the woodwork, believing that the best thing he can do for his family is to stay out of the way.

If you grew up in a dysfunctional family, you learned to define yourself by your role and not by your real thoughts, feelings, hopes, and fears, which you lost sight of at a young age (if you were ever in touch with them at all). Since it was all you ever knew yourself to be, like Ellen and Gary, you may still be playing that role today, and it may be preventing you from having truly intimate relationships. If you are interested in learning more about each role and its impact on your present-day beliefs and behavior, a good source of additional information is *Following the Yellow Brick Road* by Joy Miller and Marianne Rippes and Melody Beattie's *Codependent No More*.

OTHER PERSONAL HISTORY LESSONS

■ *ELIZABETH*

"My stepfather worked second shift," Elizabeth said, "and by the time he got home, my mother, who had to be up for work by six, was asleep. So was everyone else. But not me. I was wide awake with my heart pounding, listening for his footsteps and praying that he wouldn't come into my bedroom that night. If he walked by, I knew I was safe. But once I heard the footsteps stop and the doorknob turn, it was all over. There was nothing I could do to keep him from molesting me and no one I could tell about what he was doing. He said it would be my word against his. Since my mother and everyone else seemed to think he was the best thing that ever happened to our family, I knew that I wasn't the one they would believe."

After her stepfather abruptly departed for points unknown, Elizabeth managed to erase the memories of his sexual abuse from her mind. In fact, until she entered therapy nearly two decades later, she recalled very little about the four-year period when her stepfather was molesting her. Her entire adolescence was a blur and what she did remember "seemed like it happened to someone else." Yet, she lived in the *emotional atmosphere* of the past. Her adult life was permeated by perceptions that dated back to her youth—overwhelming feelings of powerlessness; a sense that unhappiness was her lot in life; and a belief that her rage, if unleashed, would be uncontrollable. Those perceptions were the reasons Elizabeth stayed married for thirteen years in spite of her husband's explosiveness. They were the reason she predicted gloom, doom, and disaster for herself. They, along with a diminished capacity to trust, low self-esteem, and sexual anxieties, are sources of conflict and confusion for any sexual abuse victim and they can be stirred up into an absolute frenzy by the mere possibility of establishing an intimate relationship.

If an adult *physically* used you for his or her own sexual gratification, the sexual abuse was overt and once old memories and feelings emerge, the connections between past and present quickly become apparent. However, you may have been covertly sexually abused. Even though there was no actual sexual contact, your childhood interactions with parents or other adults may have been sexually charged.

For instance, your father might have used you as a confidante, talking about his sexual exploits or frustrations. You may have been elevated to the status of man of the house or surrogate wife by parents who expected you to provide the emotional gratification their actual spouse did not. The normal boundaries that defined who the parent was and who the child was were violated, and that is frequently as terrifying as actually being molested by a trusted adult—but far more difficult to identify at a later date.

Abandonment or prolonged separations from a parent, especially during the first three years of your life, also leave emotional scars that can last a lifetime. Being a child of divorced parents may mean that you are extremely vulnerable to rejection. Before a relationship is even off the ground, you may anticipate its dissolution and prepare yourself for it by keeping your guard up and sharing your real self as little as possible.

Even your mother's and father's parenting style can have an impact on your present-day approach to life and relationships. According to W. Hugh Missildine, M.D., author of *Your Inner Child of the Past*, the child you once were lives on inside you and in almost any situation, but especially in intimate relationships, that *inner child* can prompt you to think, feel, and behave as you did during your actual childhood. Consequently, ask yourself:

- if your parents were *oversubmissive* and gave into your every whim during childhood, then you may have little impulse control or respect for the rights of others in your adult relationships.
- if your parents were *overindulgent* and showered you with unsolicited gifts, you may drift through your adult life neither initiating nor following through with any project or relationship.

- if your parents were *overcoercive* and anxiously controlled your every move, you may continue to rely on others to make decisions for you and provide you with a direction for your life.
- if your parents were *punitive* and believed they were disciplining you when they were actually venting their own anger, you may be self-punishing and vengeful.
- If your parents were *neglectful*—too busy or preoccupied to pay attention to you, you may be willing to go to any lengths to obtain and hang onto the closeness and warmth you did not get during childhood.
- If your parents *rejected* you, psychologically abusing you by belittling or ignoring you completely, then you may have an extremely difficult time believing that anyone could accept you the way you are.

Your parents also remained a part of you. Their old messages inside of you can quickly douse your burning desire for intimacy or ignite your fears: "Men are only interested in one thing—sex, so don't trust them" or "Women will do anything to get that ball and chain around your ankle" or "You're making a fool of yourself wearing your heart on your sleeve like that."

Where did the beliefs and behavior patterns that make up your present-day approach to life and relationships come from? The following personal history quiz, which you may want to answer on a separate sheet of paper, can help you find out.

1. Which of the following words or phrases describe the family in which you grew up? Feel free to think of descriptive words of your own.

- Warm
- Relaxed
- Accepting
- Tolerant
- Cold
- Violent
- Flexible
- One for all and all for one

- Close-knit
- Closemouthed
- Chaotic
- Fun-loving
- Argumentative
- Critical
- Rigid
- Safe
- Supportive

- Expressive
- Emotional
- Tense
- Stable
- Deceptive
- Every man for himself

2. How did you get your parents' attention or approval? Were you "rewarded" for:

- listening to their problems
- being cute and charming
- being neat and organized
- having problems (health, discipline, etc.)

- staying out of the way
- being smart or "good"
- excelling at sports
- assuming adult responsibilities like taking care of younger siblings, etc.

---

3. Which of the following sayings could pass for rules that your family lived by?

- Children should be seen and not heard.
- Don't wash your dirty linen in public.
- If at first you don't succeed, try, try again.
- Promises are made to be broken.
- If you don't have anything pleasant to say, don't say anything at all.
- Do as I say, not as I do.
- If you want something done right, do it yourself.
- Do unto others as you would have them do unto you.
- Do unto others *before* they do unto you
- You should be grateful because other children don't have it this good.

---

4. Take a few more moments to think about the experiences you had while growing up in your family and then complete the following sentences. (You can complete each more than once.)

- I wish my parents had . . .
- I wish my parents had not . . .
- I wish my family had been more . . .
- I wish my family had been less . . .
- While I was growing up, I promised myself that as an adult I would or would not . . .

---

5. Now go back over your answers to the first four questions and place an asterisk (*) beside any that are *still influencing or operating in* your family life today (i.e., words that described your family

which *also* describe your adult relationships; ways that you still use to get attention and approval; rules you still live by and things you are still trying to make turn out right).

REPEATING THE PAST

■ GARY AND ELLEN

From their first meeting, Gary and Ellen seemed prematched. Both recalled feeling as if they had known each other all of their lives and in a way, they had. Ellen, like all the women Gary instantly fell in love with, subtly expressed attitudes and displayed attributes that reminded him of his oldest sister—the family hero who took care of him and allowed him to "get away with murder" as long as he promised to reform. And Gary was the fourth man who had subconsciously reminded Ellen of the workaholic father she could never seem to please or get to assume his parental responsibilities. Their "lock-and-key" relationships *re-created the circumstances they had encountered in their childhood homes,* confirming their beliefs, utilizing their habitual behaviors, and most of all providing an opportunity to complete *unfinished business of the past.* It was as if they had been given a second chance (or a third or a fourth) finally to succeed at something they previously failed to do.

The fact that Ellen and Gary were repeating their pasts and using their present-day relationship to complete unfinished business was far more obvious to an outsider observer than it was to them. Indeed, they were not really aware of it at all. Ellen realized that she was in yet another relationship that she couldn't make work no matter how hard she tried. But she did not know why. Gary loved Ellen and knew his infidelities hurt her, but he could not resist the urge to escape by charming and having sex with other women. Although they both remembered their past experiences, they did not recognize their connection to the present, and so they blindly continued down the same old path.

Having old habits and unfinished business does not mean that you cannot have satisfying relationships or that you will never fulfill your need for genuine intimacy. However, *being unaware* of your unresolved issues and missing intimacy prerequisites usually means that you will do only what you have always done and get more of what you have always gotten.

The course you unwittingly pursue is comparable to having a travel agent present you with a dozen marvelous vacation alternatives, but you decide to go back to the same spot you went to last year and the year before that, and indeed every year since you first started taking vacations. You know how to get there. You know what to expect once you arrive. You know that you will not be required to do anything you haven't already learned how to handle. Because you have never really enjoyed yourself during these vacations, each year you promise yourself that next year you will vacation someplace else. But, somehow when the time comes you cannot bring yourself to do it. You stick with what you know.

Please remember that traveling the same route to the same destination in one relationship after another does not mean that you are stupid or masochistic. You are simply trying to obtain the love and acceptance you need by relating to people in the way that is most comfortable and familiar to you. The relationship feels right, but somehow it turns out wrong. Unfortunately, each time this happens, your original beliefs and especially your old fears about intimacy are reinforced. And if this happens often enough, you may stop trying to "get it right" and start trying to get something else instead. You may:

1. put your need for intimacy on the back burner, embarking upon a single-minded quest for something more tangible than love, such as success in your career.
2. create "intimacy illusions," establishing relationships that boost your ego and allow you to conceal your vulnerability, but that lack real warmth or closeness.
3. get hooked on intimacy substitutes—addictive substances and compulsive behaviors that temporarily anesthetize the pangs of loneliness and fill the emptiness inside of you.
4. develop one-sided relationships, in which you do all the giving, and in the worst-case scenario, become so dependent on your partner that you truly believe you will cease to exist without him or her.

In the next four chapters of this book I will describe each of these four barriers to genuine intimacy, and I will use one individual or one couple's history as an example of each. These people may have problems or backgrounds that are more traumatic than your own, but I believe that their insights and experiences will, nevertheless, be of value to you—so will each chapter's summary of the specific intimacy prerequisites that you are apt to be lacking if you have erected that particular barrier. It sets the stage for the final section of this book, which contains practical strategies for replenishing those prerequisites so that you can finally unlock the intimacy paradoxes in your life and have the intimate relationships you desire.

MOVING UP—AND AWAY— FROM INTIMACY:
Giving Up Relationships While You're on a Quest for Success

■ LINDA AND ROBERT

A striking twosome, Linda and Robert's photograph graced the cover of a regional magazine. It showed a slender blond woman in a designer gown and diamonds, her head tilted upward to look at a man with dark wavy hair and chiseled features. He cut a dashing figure in his tuxedo and directed his gaze at her. They certainly looked like two people in love, and according to the cover story titled, "Dynamic Duos: Couples Who Have It All," they had found the secret to success in both business and marriage.

At thirty-five, Linda was an attorney and a full partner in a prestigious law firm. An expert on occupational health and safety issues, she traveled extensively, crisscrossing the country to testify at legislative hearings, organize class action suits and litigate individual negligence cases. Her husband, Robert, thirty-seven, was a financial planner whose monthly newsletter and recently published book on tax shelters had earned him a national reputation and a schedule of speaking engagements that kept him out of town at least three days each week.

When Linda and Robert were at home, their careers remained their top priority. They worked late into the night in separate studies—the two most lived-in rooms of their custom-designed home. Linda ran five miles every morning. Robert worked out at a local health club in the evening. Linda donated her services as an advocate for the homeless. Robert, an accomplished clarinetist, spent his weekends "puttering around" in his home recording studio. They never argued.

"We used to," Linda explained to me. "I hated attending parties with Robert's money-mad associates. And Robert was bored to death accompanying me to charity events. We'd snipe at each other beforehand and have a full-blown fight on the way home. But we worked all that out years ago." They resolved the conflict by agreeing to go to those social functions alone.

"We're the happiest couple we know," the magaine article quoted them as saying. Yet, one year after those words appeared in print, Linda and Robert found themselves in a marital therapist's office. As admirable as their professional achievements were, and as enviable as their seemingly conflict-free marriage appeared to be be, Linda and Robert had begun to realize that they did *not* have it all.

One thing they definitely did not have was time for each other. Their hectic schedules and separate interests made sure of that. In fact, the hour it took them to drive to the airport on days when they had both booked outgoing flights was probably the longest stretch of uninterrupted time they spent together—and it was not time spent on personal conversations. "My mind was usually on whatever I was flying out to take care of, and Robert is busy cursing the traffic and screaming at lousy drivers," Linda explained.

"We have sex once in a blue moon," Robert complained, "and even then I don't think either one of us is really into it. Our bodies participate, but our minds are always someplace else."

They had tried scheduling time to be together, but invariably one of them ended up canceling their "date." Something always came up, something that took priority over togetherness. "We were halfway through our fifth year of marriage," Linda said. "That was the year we had planned to start a family, but I was busier than ever, and Robert had been holed up in his office for months working on a new book. He didn't even come to bed most nights, just crashed on the sofa in the study."

"The nights I did make it to the bedroom," Robert continued, "she would be asleep with the lights on and her briefcase open on her lap. We were more like roommates than husband and wife."

Determined to revitalize their relationship, the couple went on a second honeymoon, returning to the luxurious Hawaiian resort where they had spent the first. Their high hopes for a romantic getaway were quickly dashed. "All we did was fight," Linda reported. "I was exhausted and wanted to sleep late. But Robert got me up at eight so we would have enough time to get through the sight-seeing itinerary he had planned."

"We agreed not to work," Robert commented, "but she brought a stack of legal briefs with her to the beach. And then she got mad because I struck up a conversation with a retired couple who wanted some financial planning advice."

"Struck up a conversation?" she retorted. "You opened up a branch office by the pool. You were constantly surrounded by at least a half dozen guys discussing tax shelters and annuities."

But the biggest blow came on the third evening of their vacation. They had gone down to dinner at the hotel's terrace restaurant. Seated at a candlelit table for two, they had a breathtaking view of the ocean sparkling in the moonlight and couples walking arm in arm along the water's edge. They were surrounded by more couples—newlyweds holding hands and talking softly about their dreams for the future; middle-aged couples reminiscing about moments they had already shared; longtime lovers laughing over the private jokes they had accumulated over the years. Linda and Robert were the only pair who seemed to have nothing to say.

"Our silence was deafening," Linda sighed. "I was actually relieved when Robert told me that he had to go back up to the room to make a phone call to Tokyo." And neither one of them seemed to mind when a crisis developed at Linda's law firm and they had to cut their vacation short. They resumed the life-style and relationship to which they were accustomed, one in which they were alone even when they were together.

"But it wasn't enough anymore," Linda explained. "Before that trip to Hawaii, working hard and seeing the results of all that hard work seemed like enough. Our lives felt full, maybe even overflowing. But now it's impossible not to notice that something's missing." That something was intimacy.

Because they had wanted to pursue their separate careers and interests without the demands of a close relationship to distract or deter them, there had never been much intimacy in Linda and Robert's marriage, and the emotional connections they did have had fallen by the wayside over the years. What's more, they were so used to getting by without intimacy that any additional closeness made them nervous and irritable. As their ill-fated second honeymoon so clearly demonstrated, without work or other "productive" activities to occupy them, Linda and Robert did not know what to do with their time or each other.

They had encountered the most common barrier to intimacy—squelching or shelving our need for closeness while we fulfill our needs to achieve, be productive, and succeed.

HAVE YOU PUT INTIMACY ON HOLD?

Are you currently involved in a relationship, but:

- find that your own and your partner's jam-packed work schedules prevent you from spending much time together?
- are too tense and preoccupied with work-related issues to truly enjoy the time you do spend together?
- feel so pressured and exhausted that you wish you did not *have* to spend time with your partner?

If you are not in a relationship, do you tell yourself that you really are not ready for one, that you:

- see your career as your top priority right now?
- are too busy to date or are too tired after work to socialize?
- value your independence too much to give it up yet?
- probably could not find anyone who would tolerate the amount of time and energy you devote to your career?

Whether you are in a relationship or not, do you:

- feel ill at ease with people unless you are discussing business?
- find it virtually impossible to sit still and do nothing, feeling compelled to fill up your downtime with some sort of activity?
- feel anxious, impatient, and irritable in social situations because you think that you have "better things" to do with your time?

If your answer to one or more of these questions was yes, then your quest for success may be diminishing your capacity for closeness and causing you to neglect or avoid intimate relationships. Although it was not your intention, your determination to get ahead may have carried you farther and farther away from genuine intimacy.

LOVE AND WORK

There is nothing wrong with having a career that interests and challenges you. There is nothing wrong with deriving satisfaction from your accomplishments or setting goals and devoting time to achieving them. Tangible success in the work world is proof of your competence, a source of pride and pleasure that contributes to a positive self-image and a well-balanced life. However, success is not all you need to be happy and healthy. As Linda and Robert discovered, a *single-minded* quest for success fills certain spaces in our lives while virtually guaranteeing that others remain empty.

I stress the word *single-minded* because it is this tunnel vision, this all-or-nothing approach to life and *not* your desire to succeed that poses an obstacle to intimacy. When you devote all of your energy to achieving success, you become what I call a "production unit," and you leave no room in your life for relationships. You develop *all* of the attitudes and skills that enable you to get ahead in the work world (being competitive, keeping your emotions under wraps, never trusting anyone completely, and making choices based on "what's in it for me") and *none* that genuine intimacy requires. As a result, you feel completely out of your element when it comes to sharing your true feelings, trusting, and considering another person's needs and interests as well as your own. You even come to believe that *all* of the satisfaction and self-confidence you feel comes from your achievements, while relationships seem to offer *nothing* but frustration and confusion.

Going to these extremes is the end result of turning the intimacy paradoxes in your life into either/or propositions. You believe that you can either be intimate and share yourself with others *or* be autonomous. You can look for common ground and seek the pleasure of another person's company *or* develop your unique abilities and seek the pleasure of competing with other people and winning the tangible rewards individual achievement offers you. You can have love *or* work, you think, not both. Indeed, you may be convinced that you *must* give up one in order to get the other—at least temporarily.

Instead of looking for a middle ground that enables you to meet your needs for both accomplishments *and* relationships, you choose between the two and find that there is plenty of support for selecting the former rather than the latter. After all, our society promotes the work ethic, presenting work as an absolute necessity, not a matter of choice. Intimacy, on the other hand, has long been regarded as a frill, one of those extra bonuses that some of us are lucky enough to receive, but most of us can get by without.

Belabored as the term may be, the yuppie culture that has shaped our values over the past decade has placed enormous emphasis on having something to show for oneself. Chances are the first signs of success your peers look for are not the warm, nourishing relationships in your life. Bank statements, status cars, luxury condominiums, job titles, exotic vacations, and the like are used to measure a person's worth, and intimacy simply does not supply these things.

Your personal beliefs—based on your own past experiences—can also make a quest for success seem far more appealing than would a quest for intimacy. If you already harbor doubts and fears about forming close relationships—and most of us do—you have a perfect out. Work is a permissible, indeed sanctioned, way to avoid intimacy. Some of us even have employers who *expect* us to sacrifice all else for our jobs.

In addition, work is, on the whole, more reinforcing than relationships. If you work hard, you reap numerous rewards—tangible, predictable results for your efforts. Money and all that it can buy, praise, prestige, promotions, power, finalized sales, done deals, and much more come your way when you set career goals and dedicate yourself to achieving them. If you want more "goodies," you simply work harder. Relationships, on the other hand, seem to defy the laws of cause and effect. There is no way to predict their outcomes or control them, no guarantee that you will get out of them what you put into them. What you do get are vague, nebulous feelings that you cannot see or touch and therefore are never quite sure are real. You have absolutely no idea if there will be more of these intangible rewards forthcoming. Trying harder to push a relationship to produce whatever you want from it is, more often than not, a prescription for disaster and frustration.

With the deck stacked to favor a quest for success, we may unwittingly sacrifice our personal life and relationships in order to meet our need to achieve. Or we may consciously decide to forgo intimacy *for the time being*. Believing that we must strike while the iron is hot where our career goals are concerned, we put our need for intimacy on hold, fully intending to get back to it as soon as we have accomplished what we set out to accomplish. This makes perfect sense to us. It might even work if the intervening years and our single-minded devotion to achieving our goals did not change us. But they do.

WORK NOW, LOVE LATER

■ LINDA

"I was definitely a daddy's girl," Linda said. A federal court judge and political activist who was always rational and in control of his emotions, Linda's father was unquestionably the most important influence in her life. "We'd play trivia games around the dinner table," Linda recalled. "I always won and I loved it. My dad would say, 'That's my girl' and I'd be in seventh heaven.

"My mother was okay," Linda continued, "but my dad was brilliant and always doing something exciting. I mean, who else had a father who took them to marches on Washington and brought civil rights leaders home for dinner? As far back as I can remember, I wanted to grow up to be just like him and to make him proud of me." The admiration was mutual. Linda's father adored her and never failed to tell her how brilliant, coolheaded, and exceptional he thought she was. The only conflicts they ever had were over Linda's dates.

"Every time I went out with someone," Linda said, "my dad would launch into these lectures about keeping my priorities straight. I never understood why he got so worked up. I wasn't exactly a prolific dater in the first place. I'd rather prepare for a debate or cover a peace rally for the school newspaper than go on dates."

Linda's father rewarded her for being smart, curious, active, and motivated to achieve, while discouraging her from dating or wasting her time on "frivolous" activities such as going to parties or spending Saturday afternoons at the mall. Since Linda adored and respected the man, his message carried a great deal of weight, and the traits he cherished she valued as well. She never doubted that she had what it took to accomplish any goal she set for herself.

"I always knew exactly where I was going, careerwise," Linda said. Indeed, by the time she entered college, she had the next ten years of her life planned and a number of ideas for the following decade as well. "I knew what courses I would take, what organizations I would join, which law school I would attend, the kind of law I would practice. I had it all mapped out down to the smallest detail." Her plans called for her to fall in love during her senior year of college and get married right after she graduated from law school. "But of course you can't really plan those things," she said thirteen years later.

Linda fell in love ahead of schedule, during the summer between her freshman and sophomore years. "Eddie worked for our gardener," Linda explained. "His family was poor, but he had taken out loans to go to the local community college and had just received a scholarship to the state university. He wanted to be a teacher or a social worker, and I thought he was probably the most sensitive guy on earth. I fell head over heels in love with him. The whole summer rushed by in a blur, and I thought I was going to die when I had to leave to go back to school."

In the beginning Linda and Eddie wrote letters every day. She got a part-time job so that she could fly home or he could fly in without her parents knowing about it. "It was the first big secret I ever kept from them," she said. Her schoolwork suffered. Her plans did not seem as important as they once had. But when Eddie asked her to transfer to the state university so that they could be together all of the time, Linda balked. "I thought about what my dad would say," she recalled. "I thought about what my life might be like in the long run. Would I still be able to get into law school? Would Eddie even want me to be a lawyer if he was only going to be a teacher? And in the end I couldn't do it. I told him I wanted things to stay the way they were." Eddie seemed to take the news well, but by spring break he had found another girlfriend. "Someone who could be there for him, he said. I was a basket case and when I finally leveled out, I remember praying never to have to go through anything like that again."

Devastated by the untimely demise of her relationship with Eddie, Linda began to wonder whether she was really "cut out for relationships" at all. Although doubting that she was lovable was painful for Linda, she did know that she was capable and decided to "stick with my strong-points." She went back to her game plan with a vengeance. "First things first," she told herself. "Get what you want out of life, then you can worry about sharing that life with somebody else."

SETTING PRIORITIES AND STICKING TO THEM

Linda's upbringing, her identification with her rational, intellectual, successful father, and her real-life experiences with intimacy all influenced the order in which she set her priorities.

The combined effect of similar factors had an impact on your perception of what was important and what was not as well. Whether you reached a specific turning point or instinctively chose one path over another throughout your life, you may have drawn the same conclusion as Linda—that you would be more satisfied overall if you concentrated on what was most important (achieving success) and stuck with your strongpoints. "For now," you thought, "I'll do what I'm good at and get ahead. Later, when I've achieved these truly important goals, I'll be ready to tackle a real relationship." Intimacy could wait, you believed, never realizing that, seduced by success, you would end up postponing it over and over again.

Opting to work now and love later certainly paid off for Linda in the work department. By devoting *all* of her energy to her lofty goals, she achieved them in record time. By her twenty-six birthday she had finished college, graduated with honors from law school, put in two years at the state attorney general's office, and was about to move one thousand miles away from her hometown to work for a law firm that specialized in the types of cases that most interested her. She had made her father proud. She was proud of herself. Yet whenever she slowed down long enough to feel anything, she felt empty. Her need for intimacy, which had been simmering on the back burner for years, was trying to attract her attention.

"I can't say I never thought about taking another stab at a real relationship during those years," said Linda. In fact, she had had about four short-lived relationships since her painful breakup with Eddie. They had been, for the most part, convenient liaisons with men who were as focused on their careers as she was on hers. "I still wasn't sure I was ready for anything serious," she continued. "There seemed to be so many other, more important things to do."

Linda quickly put her need for intimacy back on hold as soon as she walked through the doors of her new office. She had her sights set on being the first woman to be offered a full partnership in the history of the firm, knowing she'd have to prove that she would not "wimp out like other female lawyers I've known in the past. They had all come on like gangbusters in the beginning," she explained, "but then they fell in love with one of the partners and left the firm or had babies and decided to work part time." It seemed that intimate relationships had proved to be their downfall. Linda was not going to let them be hers.

"I felt like I couldn't just be as good as the guys," she added. "I had to be better." And that took an enormous amount of time and effort.

Linda got what she wanted at the expense of her personal life, but that didn't bother her. "I loved my work. It was exciting, challenging, completely fulfilling. I wouldn't have traded it for anything."

Linda's words reflect another reason that our short-range decision to postpone intimacy often becomes a long-range life plan. We develop such a strong attachment to work that intimacy pales in comparison. We know what we are getting from our quest for success and grow more and more reluctant to risk losing this "sure thing" by pursuing something that might not net us anything of value at all.

In the meantime, we may attempt to obtain feelings of closeness through our relationships with people at work. These relationships are far from intimate, however, because we do not want to jeopardize our chances to move up the professional ladder and therefore can never be completely open or trusting. If co-workers get to know us too well, they will have ammunition to use against us, we think. Mentors provide some emotional support and encouragement, but we are not their equals, and their superior status and power ensures that a certain amount of distance is maintained. Likewise, when we befriend underlings, our position keeps them at arm's length. What's more, as close as we may feel to our business associates, those feelings last only as long as the situation does. If we or they leave the company, the friendship usually ends.

NOW I WANT IT, BUT I DON'T KNOW
HOW TO GET IT

No matter how dedicated you are to your career, from time to time your need for intimacy will rise to the surface and demand your attention. When it does, you can try to ignore it. But more often than not you will respond to it, deciding to start looking for a relationship. However, if your quest for success has been your top priority for any length of time, and there are still a number of mountains left to climb, rather than changing your life-style in any way, you will try to fit a relationship into it. With a limited amount of time or energy to spare, you are apt to look for the most efficient way to meet people and may in fact search for a suitable mate in the same manner that you would conduct a job search—placing or answering classified ads, getting "leads" from your network of relatives, friends, and colleagues, or signing on with a dating service. In spite of the multimillion-dollar industry that has been created by the need to find a quick, logical way to meet potential partners, the process can still be disheartening to say the least.

"I developed this binge/purge mentality about relationships," Linda explained. "There would be stretches of time when I was very aware of the fact that there was no man in my life. I'd start going out a lot, to bars and singles functions and on blind dates. Then I'd decide I'd rather be alone than deal with that crap and go for months without noticing the emptiness. Or I'd get involved with a guy, sometimes for six or eight months, but I'd always reach a point where I said, 'Oh, my God, what have I gotten myself into? This isn't what I really want.' So I'd end the relationship and throw myself into my work again. I just couldn't get it right."

Linda found herself in a come here/go away cycle, trying to "get it right" but repeatedly missing the mark. And you may be too.

Part of the problem is that you tend to be a harsh judge of the people you do meet. If you are achievement-oriented in general, it is not at all uncommon to look upon relationships as yet another potential accomplishment. If the relationship is to fit into your game plan, the person you want for a partner must create the right impression—look attractive, be from a good family, have a career or a level of success that you would be proud to reveal to your colleagues, and so on. Men or women with children may be completely out of the question because you are "not ready for that kind of responsibility." You want someone who is ambitious but does not try to compete with you; someone whose schedule is flexible enough to accommodate yours but who does not expect you to change your plans to accommodate him or her; someone who is an attentive sexual partner but never complains when you are too tired or preoccupied to be one yourself. If you manage to find someone who meets all of your criteria, there is yet another hurdle to be jumped. The "right" partner is one who will support your quest for success, you believe. And so you look for someone who makes few (and preferably no) demands on you and agrees that the relationship will never be allowed to interfere with your career. There are very few people who can fill this slot.

"I got involved with guys who had high-powered careers and guys who did construction work; college professors and bartenders," Linda said. "I had bicoastal romances and an affair with the guy next door. But no one could handle my life-style, and all of them ended up wanting more from me than I was willing to give." This is the most common complaint of people who put professional achievement above all else, and it is right on the money. Everyone you meet *does* demand more than you are willing to give.

But perhaps the most tenacious barrier to achieving intimacy once you decide you want it is that you have forgotten or never learned how to be yourself with someone. You may not have taken your relationship skills off the shelf for so long that they do not seem to "fit" you at all anymore. As a result, you may find yourself at a distinct disadvantage in forming and maintaining personal relationships. Having developed an achievement-oriented behavioral style that is not conducive to intimacy but, which nonetheless becomes the only behavioral style that seems to suit you and that you feel comfortable with, you do what you are good at—only to discover that what worked for you during your quest for success works against you during your quest for intimacy.

For instance, working from what you believe are your strengths, you try to impress people with your accomplishments and other tangible evidence of your self-worth. The concept of sharing who you are instead of what you do or what you have is foreign to you. Or you present yourself as someone who is completely self-sufficient and independent—an image that was absolutely essential to maintain in order to get ahead in your career but that undermines relationships.

"I saw myself as secure and self-confident," Linda recalled, "but a lot of men I met saw me as intimidating. We'd get through one date, and I'd think that we had really hit it off well, but they'd never call again. Finally, I just asked one of them what had happened and he said, 'You already have it all. What do you need me for?' I thought not needing anyone was an admirable trait, but apparently he didn't. He wasn't that secure himself, I guess." Most people are not. The sense that they have nothing to offer that you could not as easily obtain on your own diminishes their self-worth and creates enough self-doubt to scare them away.

Linda also encountered men who told her how refreshing it was to meet someone who was not clingy or dependent. "I learned that that was a sure sign they weren't the least bit interested in a real relationship," Linda explained. "I may not be a needy person. But I do need some affection and emotional support once in a while. If I let them know that for even an instant, those guys were out the door."

Your behavioral style may also include habits that make it difficult for you to *give* emotional support and be there for your partner. Problem solving may be the only way you know how to show your concern. Consequently, as soon as someone you care about expresses sadness, anger, frustration, or jealousy, you will rush in to make those feelings go away and make everything "all better." The other person, at best, experiences this as an attempt to discount his or her feelings and more often than not perceives your unsolicited advice as an attempt to control him or her.

What does all this add up to? The combined effect of your lack of relationship skills and your tendency to be your professional self even in personal interactions practically guarantees that your quest for intimacy will net you nothing but self-doubt and disappointment. You will *fail* to get what you are looking for, and failure is something that you, as an overachiever, definitely cannot tolerate. Your response to it will invariably be to *go back to what you are good at*—being productive and accomplishing things. As Linda did, you "throw yourself into" your work, immersing yourself once again in undertakings at which you excel.

Each time you come close to intimacy but, for one reason or another, end up backing away from it, your confidence and comfort in the world of relationships takes a nosedive, and your attachment to the measurable performance standards and tangible rewards of the work world grows stronger. You may even convince yourself that professional achievements are the *only* reliable source of personal fulfillment and pursue them even more relentlessly. The tide has now turned. Your quest for success is not just more important than intimacy. It has become a way to avoid intimacy, to ward off feelings of anxiety, inadequacy, failure, and other feared consequences of trying to get close. But then, that is what it has been for some of you all along.

SUPERACHIEVERS

■ ROBERT

Robert was a superachiever, and his quest for success made Linda's look like a stroll through the park. Having what has come in recent years to be known as a "Type A" personality, Robert was driven not only to achieve more and more, but to do so in less and less time, barreling past or running over anyone or anything standing between him and his goals. Anyone in his immediate vicinity could not help but notice the extreme sense of urgency and impatience with which he conducted his business and indeed all aspects of his life. He always had to have the last word and was always on the move. He ate fast, talked rapidly, never did just one thing at a time, and found it impossible to sit still and relax without feeling guilty. With little tolerance for delays, disruptions, or incompetence, he was pushy and controlling, constantly urging others to hurry also and becoming irritated, even irate, if they did not move fast enough for him. His abrasive take-charge personality was intimidating and anxiety provoking. People kept their distance, which was just fine as far as Robert was concerned.

"I wasn't trying to win any popularity contests," he said. "I didn't care if people went along for the ride, but if they didn't plan to, they were going to have to get out of my way."

With this attitude, it should come as no surprise that Robert did not place personal relationships high on his list of priorities. In fact, for most of his adult life intimacy did not make it onto his list at all. He had not witnessed it in his childhood home and had never experienced firsthand the pleasures of being in a warm, nourishing relationship.

The middle child of seven, Robert was raised in a home where nurturing was seen as coddling, and emotional outbursts of any kind were discouraged. "If you got excited, you were told to calm down and 'get a grip' on yourself," Robert recalled. "And you never cried. Never." Members of his family did not do that, Robert was told time and again.

"We *looked* like a Norman Rockwell painting," Robert said of his large family, "but we didn't act like one. None of us were abused or anything like that. We were pushed, though. There was this overwhelming sense that you had to justify your existence, that you had to do something great with your life or it wasn't worth living."

Robert's father, a career military officer, treated his children like little soldiers who were supposed to, above all else, be obedient. "Self-discipline is the key to greatness" was a phrase Robert heard at every turn. "My mother was second in command," Robert explained. "My dad actually referred to her that way and I suppose with seven kids underfoot I shouldn't fault her for running the household like a boot camp. It kept things from getting out of control, that's for sure." It also meant that there was little warmth or closeness in Robert's family. He could not recall ever seeing his parents show affection toward each other, and when he or his siblings were upset, they invariably received a pep talk rather than emotional support or validation of their feelings. "If I heard it once, I heard it a thousand times—adversity builds character," Robert said. "Whenever anything went wrong, there was one and only one way to deal with it: 'Next time try harder.' "

To be loved, you must produce, was the message that came through loud and clear during Robert's childhood. The worst thing anyone in Robert's family could be labeled was "good-for-nothing." According to Robert, "You knew you had really blown it if Mom or Dad called you that. You had shirked your responsibility to the family. You had failed them, not necessarily because you had done something wrong, but because you had not done enough. Our job was to make our parents proud, and I think we all took it very seriously."

Robert and his siblings were encouraged to find something at which they excelled and to pursue it. Robert found music and became an accomplished clarinetist, winning early admission and a full scholarship to a prestigious school of the arts. "It wasn't hard to be the best in the suburbs near whatever military base my dad was assigned to," he said. "But the competition was intense once I got to college." At first, Robert thrived on it. His experience with self-discipline and his drive to always try harder equipped him to handle it. But these traits could not compensate for the fact that he had neither the raw talent many of his fellow students had nor the emotional attachment to music that made going on even in the face of defeat worthwhile. Music was something they loved. It was something Robert did, and when he realized that he might never do it well enough to make a living or a name for himself, he switched his focus to business.

"It was a tough call," Robert explained. "I knew that getting out of music and into something else was a reasonable, logical thing to do. But I spent a lot of time feeling like a loser, like I had failed as a musician and was settling for second best. No one else in my family had done that. No one had ever quit anything—at least not up until that point." Robert resolved his dilemma by promising himself to do everything in his power to be a "monumental success" as a businessman. Nothing would get in his way or slow him down, he vowed—and nothing did. At age thirty he had more money, professional accomplishments, and public recognition than most of us will have in a lifetime, but he had never been in love.

"I was completely out of my element in relationships," Robert admitted. "They frustrated the hell out of me. I liked sex and had no problem finding bed partners. And anyone I saw on a regular basis, I treated like a queen. I sent roses, gave expensive gifts, took her to the best places, made sure that she had anything money could buy. But women always seemed to want what I *didn't* have to give—time, my undivided attention, long pointless talks about my feelings and their feelings and where our relationship was going. It was going wherever I was going, I told them, but that obviously wasn't what they wanted to hear. I constantly felt confused and inadequate." And he coped with those feelings—as superachievers do—by avoiding the intimate relationships that created them.

SUPERACHIEVERS IN RELATIONSHIPS

Being a superachiever does not make you a bad person or prevent you from ever having intimacy in your life. It does put you at a distinct disadvantage, however. Apprenticed to discipline, you give so little credence to your desires that you may not recognize the aching feeling in the pit of your stomach as an urge to get closer to people. Indeed, you are apt to attribute any and all unsettling emotions to work-related problems, concluding that you feel uncomfortable because you are behind schedule or wasting time.

Even though superachievers may be oblivious to their need for intimacy, they still want to be involved in relationships. They want sex or offspring. They believe settling down with someone is expected of them or view marriage as a logical part of their overall game plan. They tire of hearing people ask why someone as bright and attractive as they are is still single. Or they do want some closeness, companionship, and sharing—just not too much.

If you are a superachiever, you may find yourself in a *serial monogamous* relationship pattern. Unwilling or unable to make commitments, you stay in a relationship for a while, at some point decide that it is not the "right" one for you, and then move on to another relationship that eventually "just isn't right" either. You use your quest for success to justify ending each relationship. But the real culprit is your limited capacity for closeness. You have a low threshold for intimacy and once your partner crosses it, you start looking for the exit—and another relationship.

Superachieving men may find what they are looking for in traditional marriages, ones in which they can be the primary breadwinner and take care of the practical end of things while their wives assume responsibility for the "emotional stuff." Although wives in these marriages may work outside the home, the marriage is still traditional in the sense that the husband's career takes precedence and he is not expected to be an equal participant on the home front. Some achievement-oriented husbands in traditional marriages are "nice" guys who work hard but believe bringing home a paycheck is all the giving they have to do. In response to their wives' complaints that there is not enough intimacy in their marriage, they reply, "I'm here, aren't I?" Then there are the SOBs, men who bring their work habits home with them, expect to rule the roost, and are constantly surprised when their wives or children seem reluctant to give them their own way. They dictate rather than relate, and their spouses long for the warmth they believe an intimate marriage should have, often nagging or manipulating in order to get it.

Both types of men, as well as many other success-oriented men and women, become involved in relationships in which both partners are *highly committed to their careers.* Because these dual-career couples marry later and delay having children, their marriages can be quite stable. Recent research studies have revealed other advantages as well. Sometimes women with careers are considered to be more stimulating marital partners, for instance, and men in dual-career couples tend to be more involved in parenting and better parents than their more traditional counterparts. Even so, when both partners are superachievers, these relationships rarely live up to the ideal of mutual support and total equality that frequently women in particular hoped to find. They may have a high level of intimacy at the outset, but closeness invariably diminishes as you and your partner struggle with:

- *identity dilemmas*—conflict and confusion that result from behaving in ways that are not traditionally male or female. With no models of truly egalitarian relationships to emulate, you unwittingly fall back on your old gender programming.
- *role overload*—for women who, falling back on their gender programming, automatically assume more responsibility for household management and childrearing. You wear so many hats—businesswoman, wife, mother, household manager, nurse, chauffeur, social planner, and so on—that you feel pressured and exhausted all of the time and frequently end up neglecting yourself, your spouse, and your relationship.
- *competition*—whether this is carried over from the work world or the result of insecurity on your part or your partner's, the issue of who is more successful and whose career is more important may be your downfall.
- *spillover*—of work-related problems and stress as well as difficulty switching gears at the end of the workday, which can leave one or both of you too tense and preoccupied to be emotionally available

to each other. You are physically present, but your mind and spirit are elsewhere.

Unable to resolve effectively these and other issues, you and your partner may start out with strong emotional connections but stretch them to the breaking point. And if one or both of you are superachievers whose attachment to accomplishments is stronger than your attachment to relationships, you—like your single counterparts—will escape from marital stress by pouring more energy into what you are good at—achieving in the work world. You do not take care of your relationship, and it dies of neglect.

Finally, if you sincerely believe that intimacy is a frill that you can live without, or a serious threat to your independence and dreams for the future, you may not mind not spending time with your partner. You may be one of a growing number of superachievers who make a relationship commitment based on practicality instead of passion. Linda and Robert did this. Five years after their wedding had taken place, they still had not quite decided to be married.

"Good timing," Robert replied when asked what brought him and Linda together. A mutual friend set them up on a blind date soon after both had decided that it was time to "get serious" about someone. They fulfilled each other's criteria for suitable mates. "Linda had her own life," Robert said. "Unlike the other women I'd dated, she didn't expect me to provide one for her."

"Robert was easy," Linda explained. "He wasn't looking for someone to cook and clean and drop everything to meet his needs."

IS IT REALLY A PROBLEM?

If the prospect of actually starting the family that both Linda and Robert wanted hadn't caused Linda to begin reevaluating her priorities, would this couple have lived happily ever after in their "alone together" marriage? If they had not taken that second honeymoon and noticed that something was missing, would they have avoided the conflicts that eventually led them to a marriage counselor's office? Probably not.

At some point in our lives our unmet intimacy needs catch up with us and, in one way or another, we pay for having sacrificed them in order to pursue our single-minded quest for success. We are plagued by unshakable feelings of loneliness, isolation, and distress. Never allowing anyone to get close enough to provide the emotional support we need to reduce stress and replenish our energy supply, we buckle under the burden of our own self-sufficiency. We live a one-dimensional existence for decades, only to "wake up" at middle age or upon retirement or on our death beds and regret the experiences we missed out on and the people we neglected over those years. Or we realize that we are estranged from our children who have followed in our footsteps and are too busy climbing mountains of their own to be close to us in our old age.

GETTING BACK ON TRACK

A way of seeing is also a way of *not* seeing, and what you do not see when you turn intimacy paradoxes into either/or propositions is the middle ground and the fact that you can *actively pursue accomplishments and relationships simultaneously.* Intimacy and autonomy, sharing yourself and being independent, being a tough competitor and being a cooperative partner are not mutually exclusive. You can have both love and work.

As a superachiever you may have less tolerance for genuine intimacy than people who are less goal-oriented, but that does not mean you cannot have more intimacy in your life than you have now. You can even use *some* of your business know-how to get it. Most notably, you can identify what you want and what you need to do more of in order to be intimate. You can define the realities of your current circumstances and the compromises that *can* be made to take you from a one-dimensional existence to a well-balanced life. You cannot, however, go out and look for intimacy the way you would conduct a job search, or apply to your personal relationships the "try harder" principle that has worked so well for you in business. You can't compel your partner to talk about his or her true thoughts and feelings, schedule time for togetherness and expect to be close during those times. As Linda and Robert as well as countless couples like them discovered, this approach can result in frustration, disappointment, and conflict, not intimacy.

You find intimacy by simply being open to the possibility of it. And you become open to it by replenishing the intimacy prerequisites you lost during your single-minded quest for success, or may have been lacking in the first place. The four predominant sources of conflict and confusion for superachievers are:

1. Self-Disclosure. As Linda and Robert discovered, simply finding time to spend with another person does not lead to intimacy. You must fill that time with what I call "emotional intercourse"—an honest exchange of your innermost thoughts and

feelings which is, of course, discouraged in the business world. As a result of your quest for success, you may have become so accustomed to maintaining your composure, saying what you think other people want to hear, concealing your vulnerabilities and wearing the mask of the cool, calm, completely self-sufficient professional, that you have lost touch with what is going on inside you. You may be at a loss to express what you do know. You may negotiate over feelings instead of sharing them ("If you promise you won't be sad or angry I will do . . .") or you may be so intent on winning that the slightest disagreement becomes a full-fledged conflict, a fight to have it your way in a battle of the wills. Whether you have gotten out of the habit of self-disclosure or it has never been your strong suit, you must do more of it if you want a genuinely intimate relationship.

2. Self-Worth. As a superachiever you are extremely self-confident and secure in professional settings, but frequently overwhelmed with self-doubt and feelings of inadequacy during personal interactions. You may see yourself as capable but not lovable, as Linda did, or think that producing and achieving are the only things that make you worthwhile, as Robert did. You may measure your self-worth by the outward signs of success you have accumulated. Or you may have fallen into a comparison trap, defining who you are and how good you feel about yourself by how your life stacks up against other people's. This is particularly damaging to intimacy when you idealize other people's relationships, concluding that you are somehow deficient because your relationship does not feel as good as theirs looks. Or you may judge other people's relationships harshly, holding them up as proof that intimacy is unattainable and foolhardy to pursue. Until you come to view yourself as a multifaceted person and restore your faith in yourself as a potentially loving and lovable human being, your path to fulfilling personal relationships will be blocked.

3. Tolerance. One of the reasons that you were able to find your niche in the business world was that it allowed you to indulge your need to control people and events. Indeed, you were rewarded for doing that. Unfortunately, personal relationships defy your efforts to control them. They do not run on schedule. You can never be sure that when you do "A," your partner will do "B." He or she may do "C," "D," or "E" instead. You are apt to find this unpredictability, which comes with the territory of any relationship, inconvenient at best. To add intimacy to your life, you must become more flexible and willing to accept situations that do not conform to your expectations.

4. Interdependence. Over the years you have developed a fundamental belief that has a deadly effect on intimate relationships. You have come to believe that you can, and indeed that you are supposed to, manage every aspect of your life without assistance from other people. You see your own dependency as a defect and try to eliminate it. In addition, you see other people's dependency as a trap. If you acknowledge their needs, they will expect you to meet them, taking time and energy away from the really important things you want to accomplish. Blind to your own needs and trying not to see your partner's, you go your way and he goes his. But two people each doing their own thing equals coexistence, not interdependence. To form and maintain an intimate relationship, you must stop worrying so much about giving in to your own dependency needs or giving up your autonomy in order to meet your partner's needs. Giving to and getting from, pooling your emotional resources, developing a team spirit that carries you through the bad times and makes the good times even better is what intimacy is all about.

ALL DRESSED UP
WITH NOWHERE TO GO:
Impression Managers
and Intimacy Illusions

■ REBECCA

"I'm not really sure why I'm here," Rebecca said only moments after entering my office. "I want a relationship, but I don't think there's any way to find one that I haven't already tried."

As you may recall from earlier chapters, Rebecca, the computer software developer, sometimes did not mind being single, sometimes minded a lot, and always saw herself as a "big, fat failure in the intimacy department." She had indeed tried in dozens of ways to improve herself and her relationship track record. "I watch my weight and work out four nights a week," she explained. "I learned how to apply makeup from a makeup artist and how to move by an expert on body language. I've gotten advice on how to dress and what colors to wear. I even took voice lessons." Determined to make herself perfect on the outside, Rebecca also had her breasts augmented and her teeth straightened and is saving money for a nose job. "If I could find a way to be five-six instead of five-eight, I would do it," she said half-seriously. "Men find tall women intimidating."

They don't like them to be too smart or too ambitious or too talkative either, Rebecca assured me. She knew this because she had read almost every word ever written about what men want. It seemed that she had

memorized the advice she found in countless self-help books on relationships as well. "I know fifty great opening lines," Rebecca claimed. "I
know how to listen, and I always make sure to let men talk about
themselves. If that doesn't work, I try sports or the stock market or
whatever else they seem to be interested in. I find out what that is right off
the bat and then if they ask me out, I go to the library and read up on it, so
they'll think we have common interests." She rarely talks about herself or
her actual interests. "Guys hate that," she insisted.

As Rebecca continued describing how she behaved in the presence of
men whom she found attractive, it became apparent that everything she
said or did was influenced by her preconceived notion of what she thought
a particular man wanted. If he liked home-cooked meals, she cooked for
him. If he liked to sail, she took a Dramamine and sailed with him. In fact,
with the exception of camping or hiking in areas where she might
encounter snakes, Rebecca was willing to do almost anything to convince
a man that she liked what he liked and was whatever he hoped she
would be.

But in spite of her efforts, the relationships she had were short-lived.
Each time they ended, Rebecca would retreat to ponder what went wrong.
Then, when the loneliness of avoiding social contact would catch up with
her, she'd institute a new self-improvement plan and put herself back in
circulation, more determined than ever to conduct herself in precisely the
way she believed she must if she were to ever find the love and acceptance she so desperately wanted. The only approach she did not try was the
one that stood the best chance of working and the one that truly intimate
relationships required—being and sharing her real self.

Rebecca was stymied by the second barrier to genuine intimacy—
attempting to manipulate and control external circumstances in hopes of
getting the closeness you need *without* taking the risks you fear.

HAVING YOUR CAKE AND EATING IT TOO

No matter how Rebecca altered her appearance or behavior, she
could not alter her *fundamental belief that she was not good enough the
way she was.* Perceiving her real self as too flawed and inadequate to
attract the right man or hang onto a real relationship, she turned
the basic intimacy paradox into an if/then equation that added up
to certain disaster. *If* she tried to fulfill her *need* for genuine
intimacy (which required her to be and share her real self), *then* she
would get what she *feared*—rejection, failure, and pain. Believing
that these unwelcome consequences were virtually guaranteed,
Rebecca was understandably reluctant to take the risks that forming
and maintaining truly intimate relationships require—and you may
be also.

Imagine that you have just been given two tickets to a concert and are trying to decide whom to invite to that concert with you. The first person who comes to mind is someone you do not know well but would like to know better. You are attracted to this person and although you think that he or she may be attracted to you, you have no way of knowing for sure. Which of the following if/then equations most closely resembles the thoughts that would be going through your mind?

If I ask this person to go to the concert with me, *then* he or she will:

_____ say yes and we'll have a great time

_____ say no and I will feel foolish for asking

_____ make up a transparent excuse for not going and I will feel like a *real* loser because this person not only knows that I am attracted to him or her but feels so sorry for me that he or she is trying to let me down easy

_____ say no and explain that he or she wants to be "just friends," dashing my hopes for a romance and making me feel embarrassed for wearing my heart on my sleeve

_____ say yes, go to the concert, and *then* give me the "just friends" rap (making me feel even *more* disappointed since he or she raised my hopes by accepting my invitation)

_____ say yes and come on too strong after the concert

Now, imagine that you and someone you've been involved with for only a short period of time have made plans for a fun evening out on the town. Unfortunately, you are in a rotten mood because you had a miserable day at work or received some news that upset you. By the time dinner is half-over, your date, who has noticed that you seem depressed or anxious, asks what is wrong. Which of the following if/then equations most closely resemble the thoughts that would run through your mind while you were deciding how to respond to your date's question?

If I tell this person what is really bothering me, *then* he/she will:

_____ understand and be supportive, and I will feel better for having shared these feelings with someone

_____ laugh at me or think less of me for feeling the way I do

_____ realize that I am not as strong and together as I should be and wonder if I am really someone he or she wants to be involved with

_____ think that because I cannot handle this problem, I am weak and needy—someone who will become dependent and suffocating (which should put a quick end to this relationship!)

_____ say something insensitive which will not only make me think less of him or her but also ruin the entire evening and maybe any chance we had for a lasting relationship

If you chose the first option in both of these examples, you are optimistic and self-confident enough to take the risks that come with the territory of intimate relationships. If you checked any other option, you may not be. Indeed, your desire to get close to people may pale in comparison to what you fear would happen if you really did. To ward off your fears, you _could_ suppress your need for intimacy and devote yourself to fulfilling some other need the way individuals on a single-minded quest for success do. However, if the second obstacle to intimacy is operating in your life, you will try to have your cake and eat it too, to meet your needs and ward off your fears in one fell swoop.

- _You will say what you think other people want to hear,_ censoring yourself as you go along because you are afraid that revealing your true thoughts and feelings will prompt other people to reject or think less of you.
- _You will choose your words in advance and conceal your true motives_ because you believe that improves your chances of getting what you want or avoiding what you fear.
- _You will try to make other people feel special and important_ by paying rapt attention to every word they say and acting as if you are enthralled—even when you are barely interested.
- _You will see to it that your composure never cracks and your vulnerabilities are never revealed,_ presenting yourself as understanding, smart, or witty at all times.
- _Or you will create an image, a fictional self,_ that conceals your flaws and makes you look and sound like someone who is "good enough" to be loved—as Rebecca did.

What she called and sincerely believed to be self-improvement was actually self-protection. What I call the "fraud syndrome." If she came up with the right combination of desirable physical attributes and personality traits, she could have the relationship she wanted without putting her real self on the line to be rejected. If she missed the mark, only her facade was rejected, and she could improve it in some way before putting herself back in circulation.

Each of these maneuvers is part of an overall effort to reduce risks and keep anxiety at bay by manipulating and controlling an external circumstance—the impression you make on other people. This is by far the most common way we try simultaneously to meet our needs and ward off our fears; to have our cake and eat it too. Unfortunately, while using it, we can end up strangling ourselves with our own double binds.

IMPRESSION MANAGEMENT

If you are an impression manager, you have re-created yourself to match a composite picture that you pieced together by observing other people—both those you encountered throughout your life and those the media presents as role models. You looked around, saw people who seemed to have their act together, and drew certain conclusions about how someone of your gender, age, profession, and social status was supposed to think, feel, act, and look. Then you molded yourself to fit that image and tried to live up to those standards at all times. What you did seemed desirable, and there is certainly nothing wrong with trying to improve yourself. However, when your self-improvement effort involves teaching yourself to make the right impression, you change only what *other people* see and not your opinion of yourself.

In fact, you feel like a fraud and are more convinced than ever that if people saw the real you, they would reject you. You create your fictional self to ward off your anxiety, your distaste for uncertainty, your fear of losing control. But trying to juggle the reality of who you know yourself to be and the false image you want people to accept actually creates more fear and uncertainty.

"Going out to a nightclub or on a blind date is sheer torture," Rebecca claimed. "I agonize over what to wear and try on half my wardrobe before I finally settle on something. I starve myself all day so I won't look fat, and if I'm going out on a weeknight I leave work early to give myself time to get ready." Fully dressed an hour early, Rebecca stands in front of a mirror to rehearse clever comebacks and practice seductive gestures. A world-class impression manager, Rebecca does not want to leave anything to chance.

"Dinner dates are the worst," Rebecca continued. "Just deciding what to order is a nightmare. You can't order anything too expensive or you'll look like a gold digger, and you don't want to order the cheapest thing on the menu because your date might think that you think he doesn't make a decent living. Anything with ingredients like garlic or onions is out. And then you have to worry about actually eating what you order. It's really nerve-racking to chew in front of someone you hardly know."

Yes, Rebecca's concern with making the right impression had crossed the border to obsession, but even if you do not go to such extremes, the need to maintain your facade, and your fears about what might happen if you fail to do so can be paralyzing.

Since impression managers are convinced that *one wrong move could ruin everything,* spontaneity is out of the question. Thinking about what to do next keeps you much too busy to be in the moment or to feel comfortable socializing. The pressure to be something you are not increases the anxiety that you are already trying to compensate for and conceal. Since you instinctively respond to unsettling feelings by covering them up, naturally you will act as if you are not feeling anxious and this will—yes, you guessed it—make you even more anxious. Round and round you go in a self-defeating cycle of keeping up appearances, feeling like a fraud, and trying harder to keep up appearances so that no one finds out you are a fraud.

Of course, trying to make a good impression is useful at times— in job interviews, at business meetings, even during your initial encounters with people to whom you are attracted. Maintaining a certain image is actually called for in certain settings, most notably professional ones. In fact, you would be courting disaster to let down your guard at all times, in all places, and with all people. But choosing to wear a mask *after* assessing the real risks involved is not what impression managers do. They are reluctant to let their guard down with anyone—and that invariably keeps the intimacy they both want and need just beyond their reach.

As you will see, there are a number of different masks people can wear. Although they generally will settle on the one that works best for them, sometimes people use masks in combination, depending on the situation and risks involved.

THE PERFECT PERSON MASK

■ REBECCA

Designed to convince people that you have no flaws at all, the *perfect-person* mask is the one Rebecca wore and, in fact, had been wearing since childhood. She was raised by a master fault-finder.

"Once I baked my father a birthday cake and tried to write 'Happy Birthday, Dad' on it," Rebecca recalled. "I was only seven and he should have been impressed, but he wasn't." Rebecca had run out of writing room on the cake so that the letters in the word "Dad" ran together. "That was the only thing he commented on," Rebecca sighed. " 'It wouldn't have happened if you planned ahead,' he said. He was like that about every-thing. No matter what I did, he pointed out how I could do it better. He always found some little mistake and yelled at me for not being careful. As far as he was concerned, I couldn't do anything right."

Each time her father criticized her, Rebecca took that criticism to heart and tried harder to perform to her father's standards. But somehow she always managed to fall short of his expectations. If she brought home a report card with straight A's and one B, her father would ask why she got the B. Accidentally spilling a glass of milk at the dinner table could prompt a ten-minute lecture on how clumsy and careless she was. And if one of his periodic "neatness inspections," found Rebecca's room in disarray, she was grounded until it was spotless.

Although her father's expectations were clearly too rigid and too high for a young child to meet, Rebecca did not know that at the time. All she knew was that being careful, planning ahead, and never making mistakes was what she had to do if she wanted to be loved and accepted by her father. "But no matter how hard I tried, I failed," Rebecca said sadly.

Proof of just how miserably she had failed came when she was nine years old and her parents were divorced. "I was absolutely convinced that I had driven my father away with my carelessness. If I had only tried a little harder, done something a little better, not made so many mistakes, maybe he would have stayed."

She no longer feels responsible for the dissolution of her parents' marriage, but it is clear from Rebecca's present-day behavior that she still believes being "perfect" is a prerequisite for being loved.

If you wear a perfect-person mask, you believe this too. Like Rebecca, indeed like most youngsters, you tried to please your parents. Unfortunately, your parents may have held their love and acceptance just beyond your reach. Like a carrot dangled several feet in front of a donkey to get him to keep moving forward, your parents (possibly in a well-meaning attempt to help you live up to your potential) may have led you to believe that their approval and affection would be delivered *as soon as you showed them that you could be a little bit better than you already were.* Then when you did, they found something else to criticize or demanded still more effort. You had to be perfect—and you are still trying to be.

If you wear a perfect-person mask, you can never run fast enough, perform well enough, or go far enough to live up to what used to be your parents' and are now your own exceptionally high standards. You can excel at many endeavors, especially in business or athletics or any other area where excellence can be measured by the competitors you leave behind or the tangible rewards you obtain. Yet, excellence is not enough. Nothing seems to silence the little voice inside your head that constantly whispers, "You could have done better. You should be trying harder."

With this old, familiar refrain ringing in your ear, you anxiously search for and try to fill any chinks in your armor. Since the not-quite-perfect parts of you are generally the first and often the only aspects of yourself that you see, "mask maintenance" becomes a full-time job. Like Rebecca, you may even create a different version of your perfect-person mask to suit whomever you are trying to impress at a given moment. And you do indeed impress that person. In fact, you are dazzling the first time the two of you meet, and he or she may remain in awe of you forever after, but will almost always have a hard time loving you.

You see, the perfect-person mask comes with its own paradox: "If I can fool people into believing that I am perfect, they will like me. However, if they like me, they were too dumb or inept to figure out that I was fooling them, and I'm not sure I should settle for someone so dumb or inept." Although you may not be consciously aware of the impact of this convoluted idea, it, along with the "you could have done better" message that prevents you from being satisfied with what you have, almost immediately shows itself in your actions. At best, you doubt your partner's ability to do things the right way, giving instructions or reminders of things he or she is quite capable of remembering without your assistance. You may be hypercritical, demanding, or intent upon monitoring and constantly discussing the state of your relationship. He or she feels pressured, discounted, rejected, and the relationship crumbles under the strain of your nit-picking and unending determination to make your partner and your relationship as perfect as you think they should be. And of course, many a relationship never gets that far.

"He said I was too perfect," Rebecca declared indignantly after the most recent man in her life announced that he did not want to see her anymore. "Can you imagine that? How can anyone be too perfect?"

Rebecca's boyfriend, like most mere mortals, felt extremely uncomfortable in the presence of a perfect person, someone who seemed too good to be true. How could someone with no flaws understand or accept an imperfect person like himself? What could he possibly offer someone who had it all? And if she actually cared about him, wouldn't she have let her guard down at least a little bit by now? After two months, he really did not know much more about Rebecca than he did on their first date.

"There I was bending over backward to make him love me," Rebecca told me, "and he had the nerve to say I had given him the impression that I wasn't all that interested in the relationship anyway. How could he possibly think that?" He could think it because Rebecca's effort to have her cake and eat it too had backfired. The mask she wore to conceal her vulnerabilities had become a wall that kept people at a distance.

THE CARETAKER MASK

■ PAMELA

Remember Pamela, the woman involved in a come here/go away pas de deux with Josh? She was convinced that love would be withdrawn from her as soon as she let her guard down. She could not trust anyone enough to have a truly intimate relationship, because as a child her trust had been betrayed so many times by her mentally ill mother.

As you may recall, because of her mother's manic-depressive mood swings, Pamela had learned to "roll with the punches," accepting love and affection from her mother when it was offered and going without it when her mother was either too depressed or too keyed up to provide it. However, Pamela's instantaneous attitude adjustments did not alter the fact that her mother's behavior was unpredictable or that not knowing what kind of mood her mother would be in from one day to the next made Pamela extremely anxious.

Worrying about what she would find when she got home and anticipating the worst, the afternoon bus ride home from school was a nightmare for young Pamela—until she became a bus monitor. "I was responsible for keeping all the kids under control," she recalled. "It was a thankless task, but it took my mind off other things." So did mothering her younger siblings who had an even more difficult time weathering their mother's constant changes than she did. "When I was home, I had to be strong for them," Pamela said. "If they saw me fall apart, then they really would have been terrified. And they wouldn't have had a hot meal at dinnertime or clean clothes to wear if it wasn't for me."

Pamela became her siblings' substitute mom, a caring, responsible one who would not let them down the way their real mother had. Each time they turned to her for support, encouragement, or advice, Pamela felt good. "At least I was doing something," Pamela explained. "I had always felt so powerless and afraid, but once I knew they depended on me I didn't feel so out of control. I could handle things better. I had to—for their sake."

Of course, it did not hurt that Pamela's father praised her for taking care of her siblings and their home. Nor was it surprising that Pamela's friends came to her with their problems, that her fondest college memories were attached to the volunteer work she did on a suicide prevention hot line, or that she chose a helping profession—physical therapy—as her career. By the time she reached adulthood, all positive feelings about herself were linked to soothing others, and Pamela felt safe and secure only when her caretaker mask was in place.

If you wear a caretaker mask, you present yourself as a veritable Rock of Gibraltar, someone who is always ready and willing to help anyone who needs assistance. You, on the other hand, never seem to need anything from anyone. You create the impression that you are strong, capable, and compassionate, and this is not necessarily a false impression. You are truly qualified to be everyone's therapist. You have been taking care of people for years. The problem is that living inside of you is a meek, frightened child who remembers all too well the terror and powerlessness you felt because you could not control the chaos that occurred in your childhood home.

Your mask is designed to keep people from seeing that anxious, insecure side of you. Your if/then equation is: "*If* people knew that I needed them, *then* I would be at their mercy." You feel in control of others only when they need you. Your effort to simultaneously meet your need for intimacy and ward off your fears about it requires that you be strong, giving, and helpful at all times.

If you wear the caretaker mask, chances are that as a child you played the hero role in a dysfunctional family. Back then, being the responsible caretaker helped you survive in the midst of chaos. By becoming the strong one, by focusing on what other family members needed and helping them feel safe and comfortable, your truly out-of-control situation seemed controllable, and your runaway emotions could be kept in check. In addition, doing *for* other people may be the only source of self-esteem you have ever known. You have few memories of being nurtured, and those that you do have are tainted—by the disappointment and betrayal you felt when love was withdrawn; by the resentment that your parents seemed to convey when they did take care of you; by the fearful contradiction of being loved by someone who also abused you. On the other hand, you have many pleasant memories of being praised for nurturing others—feeling competent when you successfully assumed adult responsibilities, and attracting friends by being compassionate and understanding. You donned your caretaker mask to get less of what hurt and frightened you—being aware of your needs and expecting others to attend to them—and to get more of what made you feel good and in control—focusing on and attending to other people's needs.

You may wear the mask of the reluctant caretaker, bemoaning the fact that you always seem to end up with men who are looking for mother substitutes or helpless women who fall apart at the drop of a hat. Yet, you are the one who feels the first spark of attraction to that sad-eyed, troubled soul or that adorable ditz. And you are the one who subtly and perhaps unknowingly encourages that man to pour his heart out or offers to rescue that woman from the drunk who is harassing her. You can spot untapped potential from a mile away and instinctively recognize that you could be the one to bring out the best in that person.

You may wear the mask of the insecure caretaker, who helps out and tries to make others feel better because *you* need to be reassured that everything is all right. "There now, the problem's taken care of," you announce and wait expectantly for someone to confirm your perception, repeating some variation of that statement until you get the response you want. "You're sure you're okay?" or "You're not still upset, are you?" you ask (and ask and ask) until your partner says, "Yes, I'm fine," often adding, "so will you please stop bugging me?!"

As your helpful mask hardens, you may seem more meddlesome than concerned and more overbearing than compassionate. Extremely sensitive to circumstances that could get out of control, you step in quickly to make sure that does not happen. You do not just assist people who are struggling, you take over—assuming their responsibilities for them. You do not just offer suggestions, you give "foolproof" advice and expect it to be followed. You sincerely believe that you are only trying to help, but you are in fact trying to control people and situations in hopes of controlling your own anxiety.

Because you believe that letting other people know about your needs puts you at their mercy, you act as if you do not have needs and feel extremely uncomfortable whenever anyone attempts to take care of or give to you in any way. Eliminating the potential for interdependence, your relationships can never be truly intimate. What's more, like all masks, yours comes with its own paradox. Because you are prone to take on more responsibilities than it is humanly possible to handle, you eventually overdraw your account at the bank of giving and begin to resent the fact that everyone *"expects" you to take care of everything.* When you can no longer contain your resentment, it rises to the surface, and the resulting explosion rocks your relationship. Your partner receives the message—you need some tender, loving care—but when he or she tries to provide it, you become anxious and slap on your caretaker mask again.

Your approach irritates and frustrates healthy individuals, who ultimately distance themselves from you. You are left with the "wounded birds," men and women who desperately need you.

Unfortunately, if you are good at what you do—and since you have been doing it for so long, you usually are—your wounded bird will heal and fly away. That may be why, after years of relating to people with your caretaker mask in place, you end up breeding dependency in others, unwittingly teaching them that they do not have to take responsibility for their actions (because you will take it for them) and thereby preventing them from getting "well" (and leaving you). You may even end up in self-destructive, codependent relationships, like those I will describe in Chapter 7.

THE "ME, ME, ME" MASK

■ JEFFREY

"I went out with Jeffrey for six months," Kate said. "And the whole time, I felt like an accessory, a Chatty Cathy doll he trotted out to show his friends. Before we went anywhere important he'd want to know what I was going to wear, how I was going to do my hair. He had a set idea about how he wanted me to look, and he could be very pushy about it, cruel even. When we got to wherever we were going, we'd make this grand entrance and do a quick turn around the room to 'touch base' with people he wanted to impress. I could have met these people a dozen times, even been to their homes, but he'd always introduce me as if it were the first time I'd been anywhere with him. It was really odd."

There were plenty of other things about Jeffrey—the professional baseball player you met previously who was looking for a "perfect" woman—that Kate thought were odd. For instance, he insisted that she tell people that she was in sports medicine and not *just* an aerobics instructor. He seemed to be obsessed with his body, exercising for ninety minutes twice a day every day and consulting his physician about any minor ache and pain. "If he so much as sneezed, he was convinced he had a terminal disease," she said. "He subscribed to medical journals and owned every vitamin ever manufactured."

Jeffrey's home had at least one mirrored wall in every room, and he generally sat so that he was facing it. Kate often caught him looking at his reflection and not at her while they conversed. "The thing that finally did me in was that he was just so demanding," Kate explained. "If I didn't tell him how great he was every five minutes, he'd start pouting. It was perfectly all right for him to make plans that didn't include me and not even tell me until I was about to walk out the door to drive to his house, but he expected me to be there for him whenever he snapped his fingers."

One particular incident stood out vividly in Kate's mind. It had occurred after her car broke down while she was on the way to Jeffrey's house one night. She walked for miles along a dark deserted highway before finding a telephone and calling a tow truck. Then she called Jeffrey. "He started yelling at me," Kate said, shaking her head as if the shock caused by his response still had not worn off. "He called my car a piece of junk and me a 'bimbo' who probably forgot to put gas in it. He kept insisting that he had told me this would happen and kept asking what he was supposed to do while I was out fiddling around with my car. I swear he made it sound like I *made* my car break down just to inconvenience him. That was how self-centered he was. Everything was 'me, me, me.'" And that attitude was what ultimately convinced Kate to end her relationship with Jeffrey. "It was a losing proposition," Kate concluded. "I couldn't compete with the person he *really* loved—himself."

Although Kate's assessment of Jeffrey may sound harsh, it is entirely accurate. Jeffrey, whose parents elevated him to royalty status and who received special treatment and attention from his teachers and his peers, had developed a narcissistic personality.

Like the mythological Narcissus who fell in love with his own reflection, modern-day narcissists have fallen in love with themselves. They have an inflated sense of self-importance and view other people not as separate and distinct individuals, but as suppliers of the approval and praise for which they have an insatiable need. Some narcissists were only children, frail or sickly during their early years, born after the death of another child, or gifted in some way. They were also the center of their parents' universe and later became the center of their own. Others had parents who, because of their own insecurities or fragile psychological states, ignored, rejected, abandoned, or refused to encourage them. They may have been treated as if they existed only to reflect positively on their parents. Having no opportunity to develop a sense of themselves, they grew up feeling empty and dead inside, with no one they could depend on to meet their needs or set limits on their impulsive behavior. They compensated for this truly terrifying state of affairs by imagining that they were omnipotent. To this day they believe that they are special and entertain fantasies of attaining unlimited success, power, beauty, and ideal love.

Narcissists lack empathy and understanding for others, and simply cannot comprehend that their actions might cause other people pain or heartbreak. They need people desperately but only for the attention and admiration they can provide. They will dominate, manipulate, and exploit people ruthlessly in order to get ahead professionally and keep the spotlight on themselves at all times.

You are more likely to encounter people wearing this mask than to wear it yourself. I say this because, even though being in love with oneself makes it virtually impossible to be intimate with others, a narcissist does not know that or want to know it, and hence would probably not be reading this book.

When you first meet someone who wears the *me, me, me* mask you see someone who is personable, charming, exciting, and fun. With impeccable social skills, comic flair, impressive personal and professional credentials, the narcissist looks exactly like the man or woman you have always dreamed of meeting. Unfortunately, as time passes that dream becomes a nightmare.

From the outset, narcissists are interested in how you respond to them rather than who you are. The more doting and malleable you seem, the more appealing to them you will be. Since they hope that you will enhance the impression they make on other people, you must look good, and, as Jeffrey did with Kate, they will give you pointers on how to look better. People who wear the *me, me, me* mask are apt to sweep you off your feet. Then, once they have, they expect to be praised and magnificently rewarded for the smallest thoughtful gesture. For instance, according to Kate, whenever Jeffrey asked her about her day and actually listened to what she had to say, he would immediately ask, "Did you notice that I didn't interrupt once?" or "I thought I was very supportive just now. Didn't you?"

These are the realities of being in a relationship with a narcissist, and it is up to you to decide whether or not you can live with those realities. You are not going to single-handedly change someone who wears the *me, me, me* mask, and that person is not going to remove the mask. Narcissists are welded to a facade that they do not realize is a facade. They have no insight into their own behavior or its effect on you. People and relationships are only fuel for their egos, and if one oil well runs dry, they simply go out and find another.

MASKS GALORE

There are dozens of other fictional selves that impression managers can perpetrate in hopes of obtaining the closeness they want while protecting themselves from the consequences they fear. Some of the more common ones include:

- the Self-Sufficiency mask—that combines aspects of perfectionism and caretaking to give other people the impression that you are an island unto yourself, needing no one. It is the favored mask of those of you who use the intimidator approach to life and relationships.

- the Everything's Fine, Fine, Fine mask—that relies on a facade of unending cheerfulness. If you wear it, no one ever sees you without a smile on your face and no matter what happens, you shrug it off and look on the bright side.
- the Secret Agent mask—that makes you look as if you have taken a sacred oath to never reveal more than your name, rank, and serial number. You would swallow a cyanide capsule before you admitted that you loved or needed someone—although you may assume that the person you love knows it without having to be told.
- the Whirling Dervish mask—that is used to meet your need to be constantly reassured that you are loved. You test your partner's commitment by stirring up jealousy, being sarcastic, pouting, or instituting the silent treatment. You rarely come right out and say what is on your mind because you believe that if your partner really loves you, he or she will know what you need and supply it.
- the Gut Spiller mask—that leads other people to believe a close connection exists when it may not. Substituting self-exposure for self-disclosure, you discuss personal and private matters with virtual strangers or use your partner as a sounding board, without any intention of returning the favor when he or she needs to unload.
- the Entertainer mask—that uses humor as a distancing device, keeping other people happy and amused, cracking jokes when someone makes an intimate gesture, and concealing insecurities by laughing them off.
- the Siren or the Stud mask—that is the facade you prefer if you have learned that being attractive and sexy are your most reliable strong points and that being easy and available are prerequisites for being loved.

FROM IMPRESSIONS TO ILLUSIONS

Perhaps the most tragic side effect of impression management is that by wearing a mask, or masks, designed to hide your flaws from others, you never get a chance to learn that you are lovable even *with* those flaws. You continue to believe that you are not good enough the way you are and feel compelled to continue pretending you are someone else. And even though you sincerely believe that doing this will *help* you get the genuine intimacy you want and need, it won't. At best you will have relationships that look intimate and sometimes even feel intimate, but in reality, are not.

Ben, a thirty-four-year-old advertising executive, found himself in that kind of *pseudo-intimate* relationship.

■ BEN

Even before he began having an affair with Margo, the married president of the advertising agency where he worked, Ben felt extremely close to her. "Margo always confided in me," he said. "From our very first meeting, it felt like we had known each other all our lives. And less than a week after I started working for her, she was coming into my office, and we were talking for hours like two old friends." Margo did most of the talking—about everything from her exploits in the business world to her dismal sex life with her stockbroker husband, Mario. But Ben did not mind doing most of the listening. He could hardly believe that someone as beautiful, successful, and sophisticated as Margo had chosen him as her confidant.

Once they began their affair, it was not unusual for Margo to call Ben in the middle of the night and "pour her heart out" because she and Mario had a fight, or "bounce ideas off him" because she was worried about an upcoming meeting and too keyed up to sleep. This too made Ben feel special and important. Margo needed him, and he accepted the fact that, having chosen to become involved with a married woman, he could not place a similar call to her home—no matter how distraught he might be. Under the guise of preventing office gossip, Margo managed to be emotionally unavailable to Ben during the work day as well. She absolutely forbade Ben to come to her office without an appointment and would not accept his calls unless he told her secretary the specific reason he wanted to talk to her. Even so, Ben got his first inkling that something was amiss only after his mother died suddenly, and he turned to Margo for comfort. She offered none.

Arriving at Ben's apartment for their usual Wednesday-night "date" and hearing what had happened, Margo turned tail and ran. "I can't handle this," she said. "I'm going home. Take as much time off as you need and I'll see you when you get back." For weeks afterward, Margo was "too busy" to see Ben after working hours, and her impromptu visits to his office ceased. "I thought it was all over between us," Ben said. But when the advertising agency lost a client, and Margo needed a shoulder to cry on, she once again turned to Ben. They picked up where they left off—having a subtly but profoundly unequal relationship in which Margo controlled both the amount of closeness and the communication channels.

In pseudo-intimate relationships, communication is calculated, and at least one person cannot or will not reveal his or her real self. *Illusions of intimacy* are created in order to fortify the masks that one or both partners are afraid of removing. Since your partner's cooperation is required to maintain the illusion, you may subtly "reward" behavior that reinforces your perception of yourself and the relationship or "punish" behavior that does not. You unknowingly strike an unspoken, *collusive* bargain with your partner so that each of you will relate to the other with your complementary masks in place.

For instance, Carrie and Carl, who have been married for ten years, met when she was a twenty-three-year-old graduate student enrolled in a class he was teaching. Captivated by Carl's charismatic presence, in awe of his "brilliant mind," and enthralled by the special attention he paid to her during classes, Carrie asked Carl to be her academic adviser. He ended up advising her on a good deal more than her schoolwork. In scenes that could have come straight from *Pygmalion,* Carl molded Carrie into his image of the perfect woman. He gave her books to read and took her to plays so that she could "improve her mind." He taught her social graces and his philosophy of life, ways to save money and organize her kitchen cabinets, how to dress, and how to be a good lover. Carrie absorbed every pearl of wisdom Carl bestowed upon her and followed his instructions to the letter. She sincerely believed that he knew what was best for her and lived for the moments when his usually stern face lit up with an approving smile.

The happiest day of Carrie's life was the day Carl proposed. She had lived up to Carl's expectations and "passed the final exam," she thought. Little did she know that there would be more tests to come and that neither she nor Carl would ever be or share their real selves with one another. A lifelong impression manager, Carl had no inclination to do that, and he had "trained" Carrie not to. For the next decade this couple related to one another exactly as they had during their courtship—never deviating from their respective roles as all-knowing Henry Higgins, who taught and decided what was best for both of them and malleable Eliza Doolittle, who learned and went along with the decisions that were made for her.

Having started out believing that they could not have genuine intimacy without suffering painful consequences, some people may even end up convincing themselves that they do not need the "real thing" at all. Indeed, they may conclude that they would be safer and happier *without* intimate relationships and that they much prefer social contact that enables them to have sex, feel important or powerful, and impress people they admire, to collect "trophies" that confirm their self-worth and enhance their self-esteem. They may become master manipulators who resort to trickery in order to get something other than the closeness they lead others to believe that they want.

For instance, Paul, a forty-two-year-old psychologist, takes his therapeutic skills with him wherever he goes. Deftly he draws women into conversations, encouraging them to tell him about themselves, then responding the way any well-trained therapist would. His sensitivity and understanding are like a breath of fresh air for many women, especially those who have recently ended relationships with cold, uncommunicative men. They are thrilled to meet someone so supportive, someone who seems so unafraid of intimacy. Taken in by Paul's interest and compassion, they do not notice that while pumping them for information and responding to it so well, Paul reveals very few details about himself. Not until their whirlwind romance abruptly ends—two weeks after it began—does it dawn on them that Paul had never intended to have a close, lasting relationship. He was not the person he appeared to be and did not want what he led them to believe he wanted. He had simply found a foolproof way to seduce them.

YOU CANNOT HAVE YOUR CAKE AND EAT IT TOO

Truly intimate relationships can only develop if both partners spontaneously express honest emotions, feel free to share their innermost thoughts, and can be who they really are with one another. Consequently, wearing masks, censoring yourself, and "tricking" other people into accepting you, *always* creates an impenetrable barrier to the very closeness you were hoping to find. There is no way around it. If you are unwilling to risk being and sharing your real self with another person, you will not fulfill your need for intimacy. What's more, by keeping yourself at a safe distance from other people, you never get the opportunity to confront your fears and discover that close relationships are not as dangerous as you imagined they would be. In fact, as one pseudo-intimate relationship after another falls by the wayside or the pressure to keep up appearances builds, intimacy seems all the more threatening, and you will go to even greater lengths to avoid it. Your needs go unmet and your fears are realized. You are lonely, anxious, frustrated, depressed. Instead of having your cake and eating it too, you end up hungry and empty-handed.

To remove this barrier to intimacy and clear a path leading to the close, nourishing relationship you want and need, you must go back to basics, replenishing the intimacy prerequisites that you have been compensating for by creating impressions and intimacy illusions. The four predominant sources of conflict and confusion for impression managers are:

1. Courage. You need to get out of your own way in this area and learn to assess objectively the risks involved in being and sharing your real self *today*. Many of the fearful consequences that you conjure up in your mind are attached to unfinished business from your past and not what is actually going on around you now. You may be protecting yourself from consequences that you will not suffer today; you may be afraid of encountering emotions which you are better equipped to handle as an adult than you were as a child. Of course, no matter how objective you become, taking risks will still stir up a certain amount of anxiety. Consequently, you must also learn techniques for reducing anxiety that are more effective than pretending that you do not feel it.

2. Self-Worth. Believing that you are not good enough the way you are is the reason you began wearing masks in the first place. And you will continue making impressions and settling for pseudo-intimate relationships unless you stop focusing all of your attention on improving your packaging. You need to look inward and reacquaint yourself with you, learning to appreciate and use your strengths as well as accepting the fact that you have flaws and weaknesses. Being imperfect does not mean you are unlovable. It means that you are human. By coming to accept your humanness and love yourself, warts and all, you will finally be able to let down your guard and let genuine intimacy into your life.

3. Self-Disclosure. In addition to learning to accept yourself, you must learn to reveal yourself, to say what you mean and not just what you think other people want to hear; to ask for what you need instead of trying to trick people into giving you what you want. This does not mean that you should yank off your mask, toss it into a dumpster, and go around "being real" with everyone you encounter. Self-disclosure is a skill that you must develop slowly. You have had almost no experience with it in the past and are going to have to practice it, learning—sometimes through trial and error—when and with whom to share and how to communicate your true thoughts and feelings effectively.

4. Positive Regard for Others. As a longtime impression manager, you have undoubtedly developed the habit of judging books by their covers, of being impressed with people as well as trying to impress them. Attracted or repelled by the packaging other people come in, you have not given enough credence to or even noticed who other people are on the inside. You have treated

them like objects, placating, manipulating, and dumping on them, pretending to be enthralled by them or attempting to control them. You must now learn to accept them, to empathize with them and be sensitive to their needs and feelings, paving the way for the interdependence and mutual sharing that has been missing from your relationships in the past.

I FOUND SOMETHING ELSE
TO TAKE AWAY THE EMPTINESS:
Addictions and Compulsive Behaviors
as Barriers to Intimacy

- "Food was my first love, my best friend. It was what I turned to when things went wrong and when they went well, and especially when I couldn't tell how they were going. It was always *there for me.* There just wasn't anything as *comforting and satisfying* as eating peanut-butter-and-banana sandwiches or a bowl of chocolate ice cream smothered in hot fudge sauce."
- "Alcohol was the great equalizer. I'd go to a party and there'd be people there who I was usually too intimidated to talk to. But after a few drinks I'd loosen right up and *be myself with them.* I'd get this *warm feeling inside* and know that I *could handle anything that was thrown at me.*"
- "I only pick up women whom I feel a *special connection* with. If we're *on the same wavelength* the sex will be better because we'll *feel close.* Then, even if I never see them again, I know I *mattered,* you know, meant something special to them, just like they meant something to me."
- "I got involved with my guru five years ago when I went to a meditation session in the big, old house where he lived with some of his followers. As soon as I walked in and met the other people there, I *felt at home with them,* like I'd finally found a place where I *belonged.* Right away I knew that if I followed the guru with all my

119

heart, I *wouldn't have to feel like I was all alone in the world* ever
again."

The italicized passages in these quotes from present and former
patients of mine are virtually identical to the benefits of intimacy
I described in Chapter 1. However, these four individuals turned
to something other than intimate relationships to obtain those
benefits. Like millions of men and women, they dealt with the
intimacy paradoxes in their lives by using food, alcohol, sex,
religion, or other substances and activities as substitutes for genuine
intimacy.

If you find that working out, shopping, gambling, watching
sporting events on TV, smoking pot, or other activities are far more
appealing than relating to other human beings, then you may be
doing this also. If you are struggling with or recovering from a
dependency on addictive substances or compulsive behaviors, there
is no doubt about it. Believing that you could not get the "real
thing," you got what you could and unwittingly engineered what
author Anne Wilson Schaef calls the "escape from intimacy" that
all addictions provide.

Of course, you never said to yourself, "I want love, but I'll snort
cocaine instead," or "I need companionship, but if I go on a
spending spree I won't feel that need anymore." You simply stumbled upon something that produced feelings which *seemed* as good
as, and sometimes better than, those close, caring relationships
could provide. Or you found a way to anesthetize the anxiety and
other unsettling emotions that churned inside of you whenever you
attempted to get close to other people. Or while you were under the
influence of certain substances or absorbed in certain pursuits, you
did not notice the inevitable emptiness of a life without intimate
relationships. Your choices were made unconsciously, and your
continued use of substances or activities as intimacy substitutes
became a reflex action, a habit.

Unfortunately, intimacy substitutes are quick fixes and nothing
more. They do not eliminate your need for intimacy or your fears
about people and relationships. In fact, relying on quick fixes to
provide the "good stuff" and bury the "bad" can net you precisely
what you were hoping to avoid—a lonely, isolated existence, emptiness and despair.

This chapter describes the path we take whenever we expect
something "out there" to fill the empty spaces inside ourselves or
compensate for the intimacy prerequisites we lack. It also explains
why that path always circles back to the original source of conflict
and confusion and how replenishing certain prerequisites enables

you to restore not only your sanity but your capacity for genuine intimacy as well.

BORN TO RUN

■ *SYLVIE*

"I met someone," Sylvie announced. "Months ago actually. I didn't mention it before because I didn't know if it would amount to anything. But it has. Last night he asked me to marry him."

Sylvie now had the rapt attention of the other members of my therapy group for women recovering from addictions and compulsive behaviors. With eight sets of eyes trained upon her, the thirty-four-year-old pediatrician continued, "Except for being a few years younger than me, he's everything I've been saying I wanted. Attractive, smart, funny, not looking for a mother substitute, not intimidated by my career or my bank statement, a good lover, an even better friend—and sane. He's never done drugs, doesn't like to get drunk. As far as I can tell he doesn't have any compulsive behaviors and believe me, I've looked for them."

The longer Sylvie talked, the more incredulous she sounded. She paused, running her fingers through short-cropped dark hair streaked with strands of premature gray. Glancing briefly at various group members, Sylvie's cat-green eyes gauged their reactions (curiosity, skepticism, concern) and conveyed her own bewilderment. Taking a deep breath, she went on, "Ever since I cleaned up my act, I've been talking about finding a real relationship, settling down, getting married, the whole package deal," she explained. "But now that I've got a shot at it I'm *scared to death*. I want to pack my bags and buy a one-way ticket to the nearest deserted island."

Sylvie had come a long, long way since her days of swallowing amphetamines and snorting cocaine to pick herself up and then drinking or taking tranquilizers to bring herself down. She no longer reached for cheeseburgers or strawberry cheesecake whenever anything good, bad, or unexpected happened to her. With her body at its ideal weight and well-toned from daily workouts, Sylvie was physically healthier than she had ever been. Her thriving medical practice kept her busy, but not so busy that she felt overwhelmed or exhausted. She had a well-balanced life-style that included time for friendships and other interests as well as work. On the outside, she was a living, breathing example of the miracle of recovery. However, on the inside, she continued to struggle with the feelings that started her on a downward spiral to the "bottom" she had hit three years earlier. Some days her urge to use a quick fix to escape those feelings was as powerful as it had been when she first experienced it as a child.

FINDING A QUICK FIX

"I was eight when they finally figured out something was physically wrong with me," Sylvie explained during her intake interview for the therapy group. Born with a hip abnormality and after a period of rapid growth at age six, Sylvie began to complain of pain when she walked or sat in certain positions. "But no one believed me," she recalled. "My mother took me to one doctor who said he couldn't find a problem and from then on everyone acted like I was faking. If my father caught me limping, he'd yell at me to stop. My teachers and the housekeeper who took care of us while my mom was off doing her volunteer thing constantly hassled me about not wanting to go outside and run around like other kids. I felt like I had to at least try to do what they said, even though it hurt like hell when I did."

When the real problem was finally diagnosed, Sylvie received several weeks of physical therapy and then was confined to bed. "I guess I had watched a few too many episodes of Dr. Kildare," she recalled. "Because I was sure I was going to die and they were just trying to make me comfortable until I did." When Sylvie voiced her fear, the doctor and her mother laughed. "Maybe I would have too if I was in their shoes," she said, "but they never did tell me I *wasn't* going to die or what was really happening.

"So there I was," Sylvie continued, "in physical pain, terrified, stuck in bed for three months, with no one taking me seriously or reassuring me that whatever I had wasn't terminal. My parents went on with their lives as usual. My brothers and sister were too young to understand anything, and our housekeeper was too busy with them to bother with me. When no one was around I'd sneak downstairs and get junk food to bring back to bed with me. Then I'd eat and read, or eat and watch TV, or just eat. I wasn't hungry. I wasn't anything. Now I know that was the point—to not feel anything. But back then, I just did it."

In eating Sylvie had discovered what Stanton Peele in his book *Love and Addiction* described as an "experience that absorbs a person's consciousness, relieving their sense of anxiety and pain." She had responded to the internal message behind all quick fixes: *I feel frightened (sad, angry, frustrated, confused) and that feeling is threatening to overwhelm me. Therefore, I must Do Something to get away from or get rid of it.*

This desire to escape from frightening or confusing experiences is a normal impulse, and most of us have, at one time or another, acted upon it, releasing tension by engaging in activities that were completely unrelated to what was actually bothering us (swimming laps to relieve job stress, for instance, or cleaning closets to take our minds off the blood test results we are waiting to receive). However, these temporary stopgap measures are taken to extremes by those of us who learned that it was wrong or pointless to express or even feel certain emotions, especially "bad" ones such as anger, sadness, neediness, or even physical discomfort.

Although she would not realize it until many years later, Sylvie got that message loud and clear from her parents, both of whom were emotionally and physically unavailable most of the time. A coldly rational man, Sylvie's father paid little attention to his offspring and had little tolerance for their "childish" behavior. "We were just kids and couldn't help it," Sylvie explained. "But he wanted little adults, smart little adults, so in a way I got off easy with him because I was the best at acting like an adult, and I was the smartest." But she did not "get off" *that* easy. Whenever she verbalized an emotion, Sylvie's father told her that she was "too smart" to feel that way. In her young mind the implications of this message seemed clear: Since it was good to be smart, but not smart to feel, to be good she must not feel.

In addition, during Sylvie's childhood, her father (unbeknownst to Sylvie) had a series of extramarital affairs, of which her mother was painfully aware but chose not to face, for fear of being left alone with four children to raise. She buried herself in community service work and when she was at home seemed far more concerned with how things looked than how they actually were. Obviously adept at shutting down her own emotions and also convinced that she was keeping the marriage together for her children's sake, Sylvie's mother responded to her youngsters' expressions of sadness, anger, or discontent by reminding them of all the nice things they had and insisting that they "had no right to complain." All four siblings, each in his or her own way, learned not to.

If you too were discouraged from feeling or expressing emotions, chances are that you also observed behaviors that reinforced that message. Like Sylvie's mother, one or both of your parents may have been "activity addicts" who filled their waking hours with work, hobbies, household chores, and numerous other pursuits that kept them too busy to face or solve the problems in their lives. You may have watched people who mattered to you get drunk whenever anything went wrong. They may have overeaten or offered you food or presents as the only means of rewarding, consoling, or showing that they loved you. Since you saw them "doing things" instead of talking about or otherwise dealing with emotions, it seemed wise and natural to take the same approach yourself.

In addition, quick fixes are particularly appealing to those of you who lacked close, nourishing relationships that would have provided you with a solid sense of security and self-worth. When you do not feel good enough on the inside, you invariably look for something on the outside to make you feel better. If you stumbled upon something that seemed to do that, you were apt to stick to it, especially if it also appeared to fill the gap that was left by the absence of intimate relationships in your life.

FILLING THE VOID

"As you can see, my hip problem didn't kill me," Sylvie chuckled before biting her bottom lip and turning serious again. "Not physically anyway. But it definitely took its toll on me emotionally and socially. I'd never been the most popular kid in the world, but when I got back to school after those three months in exile, I had 'loser' stamped all over me. I was smart. I still limped, and thanks to all that junk food, I was a little walrus. Nobody wanted me on their team during gym class. The 'cool' kids didn't want to hang out with me. I had gotten locked out of life and didn't have a clue about where to look for the key. Mostly I looked in the refrigerator. I was hungry all the time."

Actually, Sylvie was lonely, hurt, confused, and frightened. But all these emotions felt like hunger to her and all were silenced by eating. "My mother, the queen of denial, kept saying I just had a healthy appetite," Sylvie recalled. "My father called me 'the bottomless pit.'" Although neither he nor Sylvie knew it at the time, Sylvie's father was right on target. "I was empty inside," Sylvie said. "I ate because I was empty. I ate to fill the void."

Perhaps you are familiar with that void, that hollow feeling in the pit of your stomach or what another one of my patients calls the "black hole of nothingness." It is a feeling of being adrift and disconnected from the world around you, a yearning for the presence of someone familiar and comforting. This empty space inside of you has existed since infancy when you first recognized that you were not one with your primary caretakers but separate from them. Some of us barely notice it, becoming aware of it only when something about our immediate circumstances leaves us feeling rejected, lonely, bored, disappointed, or drained. For others, it is a constant presence.

If it is eaten away from the inside by the fundamental beliefs that you are unworthy or a "loser," powerless or unable to trust people, the empty space becomes a bottomless pit. Those same beliefs—

which point to at least two missing intimacy prerequisites—are apt to make you feel inadequate in the presence of other people. Anticipating only negative outcomes from your efforts to share yourself with others, sometimes going so far as to view all intimate relationships as dangerous, you tend to avoid them and feel lonely and disconnected almost all of the time. The bottomless pit becomes an endless abyss echoing with the sound of a small frightened voice calling, "Fill me up, fill me up."

If you already learned to do something about distressing emotions rather than dealing with them, you will respond to this voice the same way Sylvie did—by stifling, stuffing, or anesthetizing your feelings and looking for something outside yourself to fill the void. It is not difficult to find. Our society provides a veritable cornucopia of emptiness fillers from which to choose. There are substances—alcohol, tranquilizers, diet pills, cocaine, marijuana, caffeine, nicotine, and sugar to name a few. And there are processes—work, gambling, overeating, spending, sex, exercise, religious fanaticism, and many more. Both are mind-altering and short-circuit your internal information system, with substances producing chemical changes in your brain and the more subtle and tricky processes absorbing your attention so completely that your emotional state and interpretation of events get turned upside down and inside out. They do indeed relieve anxiety, enable you to avoid the full impact of unpleasant situations, produce pleasurable sensations and create the illusion that you are in control and your life is proceeding without a hitch. These results are only temporary, however.

Every quick fix is followed by a letdown which generally leaves you feeling worse than you did before. The void is back and its specter of loneliness and disconnectedness looms larger than ever. The very thing you turned to in order to relieve the pain causes more pain—which you relieve by doing more of the same. This is not necessarily stupidity or willful self-destructiveness on your part. The substances and activities themselves are incredibly seductive. They produce an initial feeling of comfortable numbness, euphoria, or excitement—a "high" that draws you back to them again and again like a moth to a flame.

What's more, when you discover a substance or activity that kills pain or takes away the emptiness, you make a mental note of it. *This is the ticket. This fills the void. This is exactly what I've been looking for,* you believe, and you are sure that you have found that perfect something that will "do the trick" and cure whatever ails you. As soon as this idea registers in some corner of your mind, magical thinking takes over, convincing you that when you smoked pot, had a one-night stand, ate peanut-butter-and-banana sandwiches, or did exactly what your guru told you to do, you felt good and your bad feelings disappeared. *Therefore, whenever you want to feel good or avoid feeling bad, you must do that thing again.* You literally create a superstition and with it the false hope that if you continue to use that substance or engage in that activity, you can feel good all of the time or get rid of your anxiety and loneliness entirely. Largely unconscious, these happen to be the core beliefs behind addictions and compulsive behaviors—which any intimacy substitute has the potential to become.

Having learned how to feel good or avoid feeling bad, you practice that behavior and, like anything you do over and over again, it becomes a habit. By the time you realize that your quick fix has outlived its usefulness, you find it practically impossible to break the habit. It has you. You are hooked.

GOING DOWN, DOWN, DOWN

"Once I hit my teens, the 'it's just baby fat' line didn't wash anymore," Sylvie continued her story. "I'd always wondered why they let things slide for so long. I mean, when my mother went grocery shopping one day and saw that the chips, the cupcakes, and most of the ice cream were gone the next day, why didn't she say anything? Didn't anyone hear me in the kitchen less than an hour after dinner or notice the sound of Cheetos crunching while I was doing my homework? Maybe they didn't think it was their responsibility and maybe it wasn't, but boy when they decided it was, they got on me with a vengeance."

Like many parents of overweight youngsters, Sylvie's parents begged, pleaded, and bribed her. Her father teased her unmercifully, and her mother, buying dozens of diet books, prepared special meals for her. "They accused me of not caring about my appearance or my health," Sylvie said. "But that wasn't true. I cared. I hated myself for being fat. I hated myself for not being able to stop eating so much. Before I'd go to sleep at night I'd pray, no, I'd beg God to make me stop eating. But he didn't."

Everywhere Sylvie turned she got more rejection. She had not made any headway with her peers and had only two friends, one of whom was an overeater like herself and the other, rather ironically, an anorexic. Her parents' efforts to get her to slim down felt like rejection also. "They couldn't accept me the way I was," she sighed. "It was like they were telling me that they would only love me if I lost weight." Even God had abandoned her, she thought at the time.

"I was a complete mess," Sylvie said. "There are things I did then that may pale in comparison to what I did later, but they were still pretty despicable. Like taking money from my mother's purse so I could buy candy from the vending machines at school. Or sneaking junk food out of my friend's houses and hiding it under my bed so I could have it to eat if I woke up hungry in the middle of the night. And lying. I was constantly lying."

Since all they saw Sylvie eat was lettuce and carrot sticks, no one could understand why she didn't lose weight. Naturally she pretended to be just as baffled as they were. "I felt worse than ever," Sylvie sighed. "I wasn't just eating myself into oblivion anymore. I was also a liar and a thief."

STARTING A VICIOUS CYCLE

The most self-defeating aspect of using intimacy substitutes is not that you are using them but that you end up violating your own ethics to "protect your supply." You lie, sneak around, and use the "best defense is a good offense" ploy—vehemently lashing out at others to keep them from criticizing your behavior (or worse yet, making you actually give it up). You run "cons" on people who care about you, break promises, even steal. You become more and more dishonest, and your lies—in whatever form they take—are designed to deceive you as much if not more than they deceive others.

Whether you are filling the void by drinking, binge eating, having sex with virtual strangers, shopping until your credit card balances are sky-high, or gambling away your life's savings, when you allow yourself to think about what you are doing, you certainly are not proud of your behavior. Indeed, like Sylvie, you may hate yourself for engaging in it. You must contend with the *guilt* that results from doing something that you think is wrong in the first place and the *shame* that comes from believing you are a bad person, weak-willed and worthless because you cannot seem to stop doing it. Both are extremely uncomfortable feelings and naturally, having gotten into the habit of stuffing, stifling, and anesthetizing your discomfort, you are compelled to do that with your guilt and shame. Not only do you return to the very behavior that is stirring up those feelings, but you also develop a new habit of concealing and denying that behavior. If other people do not know what you are doing or you can convince them that your actions are not as much of a problem as they are making them out to be, you may be able to convince yourself of this as well and avoid the self-reproach that makes you feel "worse than ever."

Of course, your deceit and dishonesty only increase your guilt and shame, creating a feedback loop in your internal information system that looks something like this:

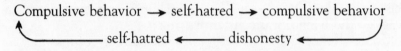

Periodically you will get so fed up with yourself or so alarmed by some side effect of your quick fix (weight gain, for instance, financial debts, the threat of sexually transmitted diseases, or an automobile accident resulting from drunk driving) that you will make an effort to break the cycle. However, because you do this by trying to discontinue the compulsive behavior without examining the fundamental beliefs about yourself and intimacy that are motivating it, your chances for success are minimal. You simply end up in a different, but no less self-defeating, cycle.

MAKING QUICK FIXES AND ESCAPES
A WAY OF LIFE

At sixteen Sylvie discovered diet pills and recognized right off the bat that they not only curbed her appetite but also got her high. That old, *"This is it. This is what I've been looking for"* thought took hold and she was off and running.

"I got the pills from a diet doctor *at first,*" she explained. "The weight was coming off because I wasn't hungry, and I was using my excess energy to exercise fanatically."

The weight loss, and even more so the diet pills, boosted Sylvie's confidence. Indeed, when she was high on amphetamines, she felt like she was "a terrific person, the best." Other people *appeared* to think so also. In retrospect, however, Sylvie realized that those other people—all drug users—may have seen life and each other with an even more distorted vision than her own. "I felt like they were my friends, that we were kindred spirits," she said. "But the truth was that all we did was sit around and get high together."

Sylvie's new "friends" introduced her to marijuana which she took an immediate liking to. "It took the edge off when I was 'speeding,'" she explained. Soon she was not just using it when someone offered her a joint at a party, but also buying it and smoking it when she was alone. "I used to roll a joint right before bedtime," she said, "and in my pajamas sneak down to the garage to smoke it. I really couldn't get to sleep otherwise, and I hated it when my mom had people over or our housekeeper was still up and walking around, because that meant I had to wait or maybe not even do it that night, which I really couldn't stand."

Sylvie tried other drugs during this time, but never drank. "Booze had too many calories and by then I was obsessed about gaining back the weight I had lost. I weighed myself literally dozens of times a day. If I felt fat, I'd get up in the middle of the night to ride the exercise bike, sometimes for an hour or more. The diet doctor wouldn't give me pills anymore, so I started buying them on the street. When I couldn't get my hands on them, I'd take laxatives and use ipecac to make myself vomit after I ate."

Purging became a new *this is it. This is what I've been looking for* experience for Sylvie. Several times a week, especially after a tough day at school or an argument with her parents, she would go to a convenience store and stock up on junk food. Then she would drive to a secluded spot and eat it all in her car. "I had this whole routine where I'd eat a certain amount of one thing, then some of another, then some of the next, then go back to the first. It had to be in that order, as if something horrible would happen if I broke the pattern." When she was finished eating, Sylvie drove to a different spot and vomited. Then she found a third location to dump her trash. "It was incredibly time consuming," she explained, and that was one of the reasons she gave it up. The other was that she found a boyfriend.

John was not the first boy Sylvie had dated, but he was the first she dated steadily and provided her first opportunity to have the kind of close relationship she had been longing for. By her own admission she "blew it."

"John was a nice guy," Sylvie said. "In fact, at the time I was always saying he was too nice. He would do absolutely anything for me, and I couldn't deal with that. Maybe I hated myself too much to believe someone would *want* to do things for me. I don't know, but I do know that I was always testing him to see how much he would put up with. I'd start arguments for no reason. I'd be coming down from an amphetamine high and take all of my rotten feelings out on him. He was adamantly against drugs, and I'd go to parties with him and make sure he knew that I was going upstairs to smoke pot. I couldn't let him care about me, I guess. In fact, after a while just being around him made me tense." After six months Sylvie managed to convince herself that she was happier alone than she was with John, and they stopped seeing each other.

During the period of time Sylvie just described, she went for long stretches without engaging in the *behavior* of overeating, but she never once discontinued the *process* she had been using to escape from intimacy and squelch her anxiety. Whether she was overeating or dieting, taking amphetamines or smoking pot, exercising fanatically or "testing" her boyfriend, she repeatedly used the same methods to cope with the stresses and strains of her daily life.

Sylvie's mind was always *preoccupied*—focused on her weight, where she could get more diet pills, what she had eaten after she had already consumed it. Although these thoughts may have been troubling in and of themselves, they kept her mind off more unsettling ideas including how worthless and empty she felt and how confused she was about intimacy. She had certain *rituals*—getting into her pajamas, rolling a joint and smoking it in the garage before going to bed, and buying junk food, parking her car, eating it in a certain sequence, and then driving to a secluded spot and purging. She derived a certain comfort from these routines and became agitated if they were interrupted. Sylvie's quick fixes were *compulsive behaviors* which, try as she might, she could not discontinue once they were triggered by emotions that may have never reached her conscious awareness or by obsessive thoughts that would not "go away" until she did something about them.

All three habits—as self-defeating as they repeatedly proved to be—were part of the repertoire of preferred strategies and tactics for dealing with life that had been incorporated into Sylvie's personality. They, along with the *despair* or letdown that inevitably follows the use of such strategies, are the hallmarks of an addictive personality, as are the grab bag of *distancing behaviors* Sylvie used with John, and which are also used to conceal your actions and protect your "supply" of quick fixes.

Obsessions and compulsions first and foremost distance you from yourself. They distract you and blind you to experiences that might cause real upheaval and unbearable pain. However, they also prevent you from knowing and accepting yourself which, as you know, is essential for getting close to other people.

Of course, closeness may not be one of your top priorities. Indeed, because the pursuit of quick fixes takes precedence over all else—including relationships—you tend to isolate yourself physically and emotionally. Your dishonesty, manipulations, and hostility virtually guarantee that other people will stay at arm's length. Indeed, anyone who might have the potential to form a truly intimate relationship with you makes a hasty exit from your life. And, like Sylvie, you may find that your circle of friends is populated primarily by other "addicts."

However, *nothing you have done or will do eliminates your need for intimacy,* and your fears about it actually increase. While you are busy with your substances or activities and becoming an expert at distancing yourself from others, you are not developing skills for relating to people. You are apt to feel more anxious and inadequate in social situations and, because you have gotten almost no practice feeling or dealing with them, you have less tolerance for those unsettling emotions. That gaping hole in your solar plexus gets bigger and your awareness of it more painful, so that you need even more of your intimacy substitutes to fill it.

You are now in the grips of a deadly disease, an addiction to a substance or activity which you pursue at any cost, denying the consequences to yourself, others, and whatever releationships you have managed to form and hang onto. You become progressively more preoccupied, dishonest, self-centered, isolated, suspicious, devoid of feelings, controlling, blind to your own behavior, and dysfunctional. Your capacity for intimacy diminishes and eventually disappears. *You simply cannot be in your disease and in a relationship at the same time.*

"ADDICTS" IN RELATIONSHIPS

Over the next twelve years Sylvie was dragged down further and further by her seemingly insatiable need for quick fixes. She had several more relationships with men like John whose "niceness" somehow made being with them intolerable. Sylvie can say in retrospect that the problem was within herself. While she was with these men, however, she saw *them* as the problem. "I thought they were all amateur psychologists with rescue fantasies. It seemed like all they wanted to do was change me." In other words, they were coming between Sylvie and her "supply."

Each time Sylvie entered into a relationship, she initially felt better about herself. At least part of the void was being filled by the other person and the intense togetherness that comes during the beginning, romantic phase of any relationship. She automatically "let go" of some of her compulsive behaviors. For instance, she never binged and purged while she was in a relationship. She might give up or cut down on her drug use and become less obsessed with her weight. But then, when the "honeymoon" was over, and genuine intimacy became a possibility, Sylvie got anxious again. "I felt that at any moment the guy was going to see through me—see me the way I saw myself, which definitely was not a pleasant sight." She began testing, the way she had tested John, being "impossible" and acting as if she was trying to see how far she could push these men before they rejected her as she expected them to. Since this made her even more anxious, her obsessions and compulsions returned. "At that point all hell broke loose," Sylvie said. "They thought I was changing in ways they didn't like, and I thought they were trying to control me and make me into something I wasn't."

Somehow, in the midst of all this chaos, Sylvie managed to get through college and medical school, complete her internship and her residency, and begin a medical practice. "I was high the whole time and although I now know that plenty of people knew I was or at least guessed I was, I was absolutely convinced that no one had a clue. I got good grades. I took care of my patients. I got by somehow, but I didn't do anything as well as I could have, and there were dozens, maybe even hundreds, of times that I caught myself or someone else caught me right before I made a crucial mistake. I was skating on paper-thin ice, but I was functioning—until I got involved with Mark."

Sylvie's relationship with Mark was her first and only romantic relationship with someone who was also using drugs. "We did them together," she said. "It was just about all we did. That and tell each other how what we were doing wasn't so bad, that we had it under control and were living the good life. Mark was a doctor too, already past the paying-back-his-student-loans stage and making tons of money, which we spent as quickly as it came in. The amount of cocaine we could consume in one weekend was mind-boggling. We drank enough to support at least one distillery all by ourselves. And then there were our fights."

Whenever they were together Sylvie and Mark had at least one argument. They would argue over drugs, over their schedules and why she could not manage to get hers to match his, over television sporting events, and especially over any statement one of them made that the other perceived as criticism. In a way they were both "testing" each other, seeing how far they could push—as Sylvie had done with her previous lovers. Only this time the other person pushed back. In a matter of moments they were smashing china, overturning furniture, and assaulting one another. "Then we'd make up, do some coke, and have sex or take some downs and go to bed. It was like that almost every day." Sylvie shuddered as she remembered what she now calls her "descent into hell."

"There was never a question of one of us leaving," she continued. "We were constantly telling each other how much we needed each other. And Lord knows no one else would have put up with either one of us." The couple continued to argue and reconcile, argue and reconcile. Sometimes neighbors would call in the police. Sometimes Sylvie would be so battered that she couldn't go in to work. She was not functioning anymore.

As Sylvie's account so clearly demonstrates, as your dependency on addictive substances or compulsive behaviors grows, your life becomes more and more unmanageable, and you become less and less likely to have anything approximating intimacy in your life. Indeed, Sylvie's relationship with Mark had no real intimacy, just codependency—an excessive, insatiable need for a relationship or another person to supply you with a sense of self-worth and to help you maintain your illusions about yourself and your life. Codependency, which you will read more about in the next chapter, is itself a type of addiction, one that you—like Mark and Sylvie—add to your ever growing list of dependencies.

Intimacy and addictions of any kind cannot coexist for several reasons. First of all, to be intimate with another person you must know yourself, and if you are in the grips of an addiction, you do not. Your addiction has short-circuited your internal information system so that you have only the vaguest notion of what you are thinking, feeling, wishing, or fearing at any given moment and almost no data about who you really are. What's more, you do not *want* to know any more than you do. Any addiction is a desperate attempt to avoid such awareness, and if data about yourself surfaces, you will quickly bury it again.

Secondly, because you have been anesthetizing yourself for so long, you truly do not notice when you are angry, afraid, lonely, needy, or satisfied. You have one and only one response to everything you encounter—do something (get high or engage in a compulsive behavior). This is not exactly an ideal foundation for closeness or communication. Indeed, the stress of trying to be in the relationship is apt to drive you further into your disease.

To be intimate is to be with another person, to be present in the relationship, and you cannot be. You are kept so busy with your addiction that you are "someplace else" most of the time. Or as one of my patients put it, "You live your life in your head and nobody can get in there with you." Even if you are in the same room and sharing the same bed, you are emotionally unavailable to your partner. There is a third party with you at all times—your addiction—and it definitely gets more time and attention than your real, flesh-and-blood spouse, lover, or friends. Sometimes it gets more attention from both of you. Like a problem child in your family, it is, in one way or another, the focus of all of your interactions.

Finally, if you are dependent on an addictive substance or compulsive behavior, you will do anything and give up anything to protect your supply; you are by now convinced that to continue to use or do is essential to your survival. You need "it" to feel normal, and you are plagued by the notion that other people want to deprive you of "it." Your perception of the people in your life is based entirely on this premise. Everyone is defined by the role they play and whether they, in their assigned roles, are for you (willing to help you meet your need) or against you (likely to try and prevent you from getting what you want).

Some people are useful as "connections." The bartender, prostitute, blackjack dealer, guru, or baker fall into this category. They are the source of your "supply." Other people are valued because they play the role of enabler. They need to be needed, are compulsive people pleasers, as addicted to you as you are to your "supply," or they simply do not know they are helping you out. These people—who you have an uncanny knack for attracting—cover up your behavior, protect you from the consequences of it, and attempt to remove the "pressures" that may be prompting you to do what you are doing. Their every move, no matter how well intentioned, enables you to get what you want without being obliged to supply anything in return. Often the person you marry, enablers can also be bosses, friends, parents, children, clergy, therapists, or almost anyone who feels sorry for you or thinks that he or she can "save" you. In addition, two addicts can enable each other to continue their separate or shared addictions, as was the case for Sylvie and Mark.

With the exception of "partners in crime," (largely interchangeable drinking buddies, X-rated movie aficionados, fellow gamblers, and so on) everyone in your life who is not a connection or an enabler falls under the general heading of "the enemy." Although their actions may be intended to help you, these people have the potential to come between you and your supply. You resent them and play what psychiatrist Eric Berne called a hard game of "see if you can stop me"—lying, hiding things from them, manipulating, blaming or threatening them and, if pushed far enough, exploding angrily, becoming violent or simply cutting them out of your life completely. You have the least tolerance for people who have the audacity to change camps as connections tend to do when you do not pay for your "supply" or enablers do when they reach the end of their rope.

JUST AROUND THE CORNER FROM
THE LIGHT OF DAY

Three years ago, an argument that began while Mark and Sylvie were driving home from Thanksgiving dinner at Mark's parents' house got out of control. With Sylvie screaming for Mark to stop the car and let her out, Mark furiously slammed on the brakes. The car skidded and plowed into an embankment. Mark ended up in an intensive care unit. "I walked away with a few bruises," Sylvie said. "But something told me that I'd used up the last of my nine lives. It was only a matter of time until I got myself killed or killed someone else with my carelessness." She checked into a rehabilitation center immediately and has been clean and sober ever since.

"For a while I was high on sobriety," Sylvie explained. "I felt terrific. There was this whole world that I hadn't seen in years, and I was sure I'd gotten through the hardest part of recovery. I was going to twelve-step meetings regularly, making phone calls whenever I felt like I couldn't handle things on my own. I was working my program—for the booze and drugs. But I was back into the food."

One year and fifty pounds later, Sylvie was "sober but as miserable as ever." Although she found it difficult to believe that anyone could be addicted to food, she took her AA sponsor's advice and began working a twelve-step program for compulsive overeaters. Giving up her original quick fix proved to be far more difficult than giving up alcohol or drugs. Because she could not stop eating completely, Sylvie had to face herself at every meal. But more importantly, she was stripping away her last and oldest defense against her real feelings and her unmet need for genuine intimacy. "I was an emotional minefield," she recalled. "Every time I turned around, something sent me into a tailspin. I'd remember things I hadn't thought about in years. I couldn't stand to see or even hear about happy couples. When I did, I felt like someone had punched me in the stomach and knocked the wind out of me. But the worst was trying to have relationships with men. I'd meet someone whom I found attractive or interesting and get flooded by feelings I'd never felt before, at least not consciously. They'd scare the living daylights out of me, and the next thing I knew I was back into the food. Sometimes I'd get past that first wave of emotion and actually try to get closer to the man I'd already decided was *the* one for me, the one I'd been looking for. Either he turned out not to be or didn't feel the same way about me, and I was horribly disappointed." Again Sylvie sought comfort from her oldest and dearest friend—food.

"I guess I'd gotten smarter," Sylvie concluded. "Because it didn't take me very long to recognize the pattern. But I hadn't gotten smart *enough* because I decided that what was happening had to mean that I wasn't cut out for relationships." Sylvie came to believe that the only way she could stay "sane and healthy" was to stay away from men.

But the need for intimacy kept coming back to haunt her. "I was sober, but I wasn't happy," she explained. "I was thin, but I wasn't well. I kept wondering if being in recovery was worth the price. If it meant I had to be alone and lonely for the rest of my life, what was the point?" If you are recovering from an addiction or compulsion, you probably know where that line of thinking can lead you—right back into your disease.

RECOVERY AND RELATIONSHIPS

As Sylvie discovered, getting clean and sober or abstaining from compulsive behavior is not the same as being healthy and happy. Or to quote another one of my patients, "Sobriety is just sobriety. You still have to get a life." Getting a life includes forming and participating in close, nourishing relationships—in other words, taking another stab at intimacy. Although recovery from addictions and compulsions clears a path for intimate relationships, it does not necessarily prepare you to be in them.

The first problem you encounter may be the recovery process itself. Finally being able to "put down" a substance or let go of a compulsive behavior may be such a relief and seem like such a miracle, that you may take your twelve-step program's advice to "go to any lengths" a little too seriously and end up going to extremes. Rather than repairing your relationships with family and friends, you may distance yourself from them further, making your program and the people in it the center of your life. You may find yourself as preoccupied with your recovery as you were with your addiction and putting the same single-minded effort into it. Becoming "addicted to recovery" is a sure sign that you are still hiding from the source of conflict and confusion that led to your previous dependencies.

A second stumbling block to recovering your capacity for intimacy along with your sanity is the tendency to believe that all of your relationship problems can be blamed on your disease. "Now that I am in recovery," you think, "I won't have those relationship problems anymore." You had better brace yourself, because you are in for a rude awakening.

If your spouse or lover is a codependent who is not in his or her own program of recovery, that relationship will not improve. Indeed, it may flounder and fall apart without your addictive behavior to hold it together. Or it may simply be a struggle, the sort of struggle you never learned how to handle because you were too caught up in your disease. Believing that the relationship is getting in the way of *your* progress, you may direct your energies toward working on yourself instead. As a result, your relationship begins to die from neglect. Recovery gives you the willingness to be in an intimate relationship, but it does not necessarily give you the skills. You are going to have to learn them and find the patience and tolerance to wait out the storm until you do.

Recovery does not give you a clean slate. It gives you your original issues back. If you deal with specific addictive or compulsive behaviors but not the conflict and confusion from which you were using them to escape, you are apt to *find new ways to hide*, picking up new intimacy substitutes or returning to old activities that you did not realize were part of your "escape plan," the way Sylvie did. You may even *make relationships your new quick fix*, replacing your substance or process addiction with relationship addictions similar to the ones I will describe in the next chapter. The reassuring presence of another person gives you what you used to get from your compulsive behavior—a way to avoid paying attention to what is really going on inside and around you. That is not intimacy. Or you may go to the opposite extreme. Discovering that any effort to form intimate relationships brings a resurgence of anxiety and self-doubt, you may *come to believe that intimacy threatens your recovery and back away from it*. None of these options works. They not only undermine your happiness, they sabotage your recovery. You need intimacy. After all is said and done, it is that need which remains and which you must fulfill if you are truly to break the cycle of addiction.

GETTING BACK ON TRACK

Again and again Sylvie "relapsed." She went back to compulsive overeating, and at one point even resumed her bingeing and purging habit. She kept attending twelve-step meetings, however, and finally hit upon the core issue that was getting in her way. "I wanted love, marriage, a family, a friend for life," she said. "But I was sure I couldn't have those things, that I didn't deserve them because of the way I had screwed up my life. I don't really know why, but I was sitting in a meeting, and it suddenly dawned on me that there was more to it— that I had hated or at least disliked myself long before I had my disease to blame it on. Deep down inside I believed I had *never* deserved to really be loved and accepted."

Sylvie shared this thought with the group and after the meeting someone came up to her and said, "*That* is why you became an addict. And unless you go back to the source and figure out what happiness means and truly believe that you deserve all the happiness you can find, you will always be an addict, and your life will always be unmanageable." Those, Sylvie told me as her intake interview drew to a close, were the most valuable words ever spoken to her. I advise you to read them again. If you are attempting to recover from addictions or compulsive behaviors, they may be just as valuable to you.

The source to which you must return is yourself and to the areas of conflict and confusion that led you to look for quick fixes in the first place. Please note that I am not minimizing the importance of physical and spiritual recovery. Acknowledging that you have a problem and that your life has become unmanageable, seeking help and "putting down" substances or discontinuing compulsive behaviors is imperative—as is making peace with your higher power.

But to truly recover and finally stop running, you must learn from the past. If you do not or if you talk about it endlessly without understanding and accepting it, you are doomed to repeat it. You must break the negative *emotional* habits that you developed along with your addictions and compulsions. You must stop simply moving away from something (your addiction) and start moving toward something—and that something is intimacy.

Here are the five prerequisites for intimacy that are most likely to be missing from your life, the sources of conflict and confusion you need to return to and resolve.

1. Self-Worth: The fundamental belief that no one would want to know or love the real you was what prompted you to seek out intimacy substitutes in the first place. It is also the core belief behind all addictions and compulsive behavior. Whether you received praise for only one specific attribute (like being smart), encountered excessive criticism, or felt completely negated by the people who mattered to you, your feelings of unworthiness can almost always be traced back to childhood. Even if a lack of self-worth was not apparent earlier, once your addictive and compulsive behavior patterns emerge, you cannot help but damage your sense of self-worth. The vicious cycle of compulsiveness, dishonesty, guilt, and shame always leads to self-hatred.

2. Tolerance: No one dies from having feelings, but you have never been completely convinced of that. Anxiety and other unsettling emotions always seemed on the verge of overwhelming you, and you stifled, stuffed, or anesthetized your feelings because you could not *tolerate* them. The longer you practiced this psychic numbing, the lower your tolerance for the unpleasant and the unexpected became. As a result, your capacity to handle the ambiguity, conflict, and imperfections of intimate relationships is extremely limited and will keep you on the run unless you increase your tolerance for feelings. ᛫

3. Positive Regard for Others: You may have had enough of this prerequisite prior to the onset of your addiction, but invariably lost it while pursuing intimacy substitutes. Self-centeredness is the inevitable by-product of addictions and compulsions. Committed only to your supply of quick fixes, you came to view people as "for or against you," useful because they helped you get high, or in your way because you believed they were trying to deprive you of your supply. You tended to be as insensitive to their needs and feelings as you were to your own and perceived the responsibility to be there for them as an unpleasant obligation that was best avoided. All of these attitudes and negative emotional habits must be replaced by positive regard for others if you wish to have genuine intimacy in your life.

4. Trust: If you could have trusted people, you would have turned to them instead of substances and activities. But you could not. You became even more mistrusting and untrustworthy as your disease progressed. You must start from scratch on this prerequisite, slowly learning to trust again and demonstrating—especially to people who lived through your addiction with you—that you can be trusted.

5. Dependency: This is, of course, the crux of the matter. The perception that *this is it. This is what I have been looking for,* and the expectation that one substance, activity, or person can meet all of your needs has "done you in" repeatedly. Your intimate relationships cannot cure all that ails you, anymore than anything else has ever been able to. Excess has been the password in the past. Balance is the key to the future.

I DON'T WANT TO LIVE
WITHOUT YOU:
Is It Intimacy or Dependency?

■ ALISHA

"I swear I read every romance novel in the public library," Alisha chuckled as she recalled the major pastime of her youth—fantasizing about the all-encompassing, everlasting love she hoped to experience one day. Alisha was the forty-five-year-old schoolteacher to whom you were introduced much earlier in the book. When she first came to see me she had just left her alcoholic husband of twenty years. "I'd cry my eyes out at movies about star-crossed lovers," she continued. "I replayed every scene, imagining myself as the heroine. I would be swept off my feet by a man I immediately recognized as my soul mate. We would go through all sorts of trials and tribulations to test our devotion to each other. And we always passed the test. He proposed. We got married and stayed together until the end of time." Although Alisha was not naive enough to think that reality would ever be exactly like her fantasies, she was completely convinced that love conquered all. She truly believed that once she was in an intimate relationship, she would never feel lonely or empty or worthless again. At sixteen she set out to find this miracle cure for all that ailed her.

Unfortunately, Alisha fell head over heels in love with any man who showed the slightest interest in her and got involved with a series of dreamers and drifters who did not respond to her love and devotion in quite the way she had hoped. Whether she supported them financially, catered to their every whim, or smothered them with affection, they always left.

"I was twenty-four," Alisha recalled, "and I was desperate. All I wanted was someone to love, someone to be with so I wouldn't have to be alone for the rest of my life. I kept asking myself, 'What's wrong with me? Why can't I find someone who won't leave me?'" Then she found Frank.

Ten years her senior, sporadically employed and a heavy drinker, Frank bore little resemblance to the dashing young men Alisha had fantasized about during adolescence. On the other hand, since he was down on his luck and needed someone to take care of him as desperately as Alisha needed someone to love, he was not about to reject her. Within a month he had moved into Alisha's apartment and soon after that they were married. "I knew Frank was a mess," Alisha explained. "But he needed me and I thought, well I guess I thought that if I loved him enough he'd get better." He never did.

Frank was an alcoholic who loved his "supply" more than he would ever love Alisha. He rarely held onto a job for more than six months, disappeared for days on drinking binges, regularly got arrested for drunk driving, and wrecked so many cars that no insurance company would insure them. Alisha occupied the bar stool next to Frank in countless seedy taverns while he drank and talked more to the bartender than to her. More times than she cared to remember, she helped him stagger into the house and put him to bed. Year after year, Alisha's love failed to transform Frank, *but he did not leave her*. And for almost twenty years that was enough to convince Alisha to keep on loving him, devoting herself to him and hoping he would change.

She had found something that could "last until the end of time," but it was not intimacy. In fact, Alisha had encountered the fourth barrier to genuine intimacy—an overwhelming desire to be in and stay in a relationship *at any cost*.

ALL I NEED IS YOU

Built upon the fundamental belief that *you are nobody until some-body loves you*, this tenacious obstacle to intimacy leads you to believe that you are getting close to other people when you are actually becoming *overly attached* to them. Unhappy with your real self, you latch onto someone you believe can provide you with happiness and then live in fear of losing that person. Because you depend on your relationship to provide you with a sense of self-worth, no matter how unsatisfying that relationship may be, you cling to it.

You are caught in the grips of one of the most mind-boggling of all intimacy paradoxes: Your desperate need for love triggers the fear that you do not deserve it, and the fear that you may never find intimacy, in turn, intensifies your need. And so, like Alisha, you wait, hope, and keep trying to find love and make it last forever.

This barrier to intimacy is operating in your life if you:

- *find yourself attracted to somewhat tragic or troubled individuals,* feel a strong urge to help them reach their "true potential," and are willing to make sacrifices in order to achieve that end. Those drifters, dreamers, escape artists, and addicts who draw you to them like magnets confirm rather than disprove your belief that you are unlovable, and so you feel compelled to try harder to earn their love.

- *worry about other people's opinions of your partner and your relationship.* If you sense that your friends and relatives do not approve of your relationship and think as highly of your partner as you do, you become anxious and then—much like the impression managers described in Chapter Five—you try to cover up your partner's flaws and present your relationship in a positive light at all times.

- *are preoccupied or obsessed with your partner and your relationship.* You endlessly worry about saying or doing anything that might prompt your partner to love you less or leave you. Talking incessantly about your partner's problems and how you can solve them for him, you are obsessed with knowing his whereabouts at all times, checking up on him or trying to catch him "misbehaving."

- *live through and for another person instead of with him or her.* Centering your life around your partner, you lose interest in your own life, put your own dreams on hold and sever ties with your friends and family. Statements like "He [or she] is my whole life" or "I would be nothing without him [or her]" are ones that you make often—and mean.

- *believe everything your partner feels or does is either directed at you or caused by you.* For instance, if your wife bought an expensive appliance without consulting you, you would assume that she either had no respect for you or was getting back at you for something you did to irritate her. Or if your lover knew that you wanted him to stop taking drugs but snorted cocaine right in front of you at a party, you would conclude that he was intentionally trying to upset you or that you had done something to upset him and he had turned to cocaine for consolation.

- *live in a state of emergency preparedness,* waiting and watching for your partner's actions so you can quickly react in a way that will avert a crisis or control the outcome of an interaction.

• *are convinced that anything is better than being alone*—including staying in an unfulfilling relationship with a disinterested, physically or emotionally abusive, addicted, or unfaithful partner.

ADDICTED TO LOVE

The telltale signs of *overattachment* that I just listed are the exact opposite of the addictive behavior I described in the last chapter. Addicts find a substance or activity that produces feelings which resemble those they might derive from close, nourishing relationships and become so attached to their "supply" that they cannot form attachments to other people. On the other hand, if you are an overattacher, you not only connect with other people quickly and easily, but go out of your way to make sure that bonds, once formed, are not broken. You seem to have no fears whatsoever about getting close, making commitments, or sharing yourself with others. You do not deny your need for intimate relationships. In fact, your need to love and be loved is a compelling, ever-present force in your life.

Yet, you too are hooked on an intimacy substitute. Deep down inside you do not believe that you stand a chance of finding genuine intimacy. Instead you settle for sympathy, attention, approval, or other "strokes" that temporarily produce positive feelings but must constantly be replenished. You become dependent on an external source to supply you with feelings of self-esteem, fill the empty spaces inside yourself, and keep you from paying attention to your own doubts, fears, and painful feelings. Your "drug" of choice just happens to be another person and your relationship with that person.

Like the alcoholic, the compulsive eater or gambler, and the sex addict, *filling the void and obtaining your "supply" becomes your top priority.* "If Gary told me to jump off a cliff, I'd probably do it. That's how much I love him," Ellen said. "From the moment I laid eyes on him, I knew he was the man I'd been waiting for all my life and that I had to find a way to make him love me too. I wanted to send the rest of my life with him. I wanted to make him happier than he had ever been. Right then and there I promised myself that if Gary fell in love with me, I'd make our relationship last forever— no matter what it took."

You deny the negative repercussions of your "addiction," coming up with justifications for staying in unfulfilling and sometimes even dangerous relationships. "I probably should have left my husband sooner," Elizabeth explained. "I told myself that I couldn't afford to, but I had a decent job. I told myself that the kids needed a father, but in my heart I knew they'd be better off being raised by a single parent than living with Howard's rages. It was only a matter of time until he attacked one of them instead of the furniture. But still I couldn't leave. I felt like I *had* to stay."

You may become so dependent upon your partner and your relationship that *you will put up with any hardship, pay any price, and go to any length to hang onto them.* "I just went nuts," said a young man who was court-ordered to enter therapy after terrorizing his ex-girlfriend and her family. At first he merely made late-night telephone calls begging for another chance. But soon he was calling dozens of times each evening and hanging up as soon as someone answered the phone. He sent letters filled with threats. He left a decapitated Barbie doll on the front porch, slashed the tires and smashed the windows of his ex-girlfriend's car; spray painted the word *whore* on the front of her house, and finally broke in, holding the young woman at knife-point until the police arrived and talked him into giving himself up. "I couldn't live without her," he said. "I couldn't stand the thought of her being with someone else. If I couldn't have her, then I was going to make sure no one else could either."

Fortunately, most of you will never go to the extremes that this young man did. However, if you make other people and your relationships with them the central focus of your life, define yourself based on that relationship and feel compelled to hang onto it no matter what it costs you, you have indeed substituted dependency for intimacy and are hooked on your partner rather than involved in a truly close, nourishing relationship.

THIS TIME I'LL GET IT RIGHT

■ *ALISHA*

Alisha never knew her father. He abandoned his wife and children several months before Alisha was born. "I had a million questions about him," she told me. "And I may have asked them when I was very young, but I don't remember anyone answering them. There was this unwritten rule not to talk about him. Everyone acted like he had never existed at all." However, in Alisha's imagination, her father was very much alive. He was the stable, calm, reassuring presence that was so obviously missing from her childhood home, one in which her working mother barely made ends meet and was often too exhausted to provide her children with the affection and attention they needed.

"I know that my mom felt bad about not being able to buy us the things that we wanted," Alisha explained. "And I'm sure she wished she could afford to stay home with us and do the things other mothers did with their kids. But she couldn't, not unless she found a husband to support her. And Lord knows she tried."

On Saturday nights Alisha's mother would get dressed up and go out with her single friends from work. " 'Husband Hunting' was what she called it," Alisha recalled. "Every once in a while she'd meet someone and he'd be around just long enough for us kids to think he was going to be our new father. But then one day he'd be gone. You'd think we would have stopped getting our hopes up. But we never did. It was one disappointment after another." And with each disappointment Alisha withdrew further into a fantasy world, adding more details to her daydreams until her father became "a cross between Robert Young on 'Father Knows Best' and the pope."

In some of Alisha's fantasies her father had been in a car accident and was suffering from amnesia or had been imprisoned for a crime he did not commit, and she came to his rescue. Eternally grateful, he pledged his undying love and devotion to her. In other daydreams, the kind, loving man she believed held her happiness in the palm of his hand simply walked back into her life.

"My favorite fantasy was the one where my brothers and sisters and I were sitting around the dinner table when the front door burst open and our father walked in," Alisha said. "He was dressed up like Santa Claus and had sacks full of presents—everything our mom could never afford to buy us. He said he'd been away looking for work and had found a wonderful job. We were going to move to a big house in the suburbs with a gigantic yard, and he was even going to get me a pony. Somehow he just knew I wanted one. But the best part of the daydream was when he took me on his knee and said he loved me and would never, ever leave me. Naturally, we lived happily ever after, and I never felt lonely or afraid again."

By the time she reached her teens, Alisha's image of the perfect father had been replaced by a vision of the perfect lover, but the content of her fantasies never changed. She was still waiting for Santa Claus, still looking for someone to supply the joy, the meaning, and the sense of security that had been missing from her life for as long as she could remember. In spite of the richly detailed romantic fantasies she harbored, Alisha actually wanted just one thing—someone who would not abandon her the way her father had.

OVERATTACHMENT AND THE FEAR OF ABANDONMENT

If you are an overattacher, a fear that people you love will even-tually abandon you is apt to be the most powerful motivating force in your life. You may not be consciously aware of that fear, yet every time you bend over backward to please or accommodate your partner, sacrifice yourself for the sake of your relationship, or use various forms of emotional blackmail to hang onto someone you love, you are responding to that fear. You are attempting to avoid *reexperiencing* feelings of abandonment that are connected to un-finished business from your past. That unfinished business may be the result of actually being abandoned as Alisha was or of feeling abandoned because there was no one there to comfort and care for you when you needed such reassurance the most.

"Being molested by my stepfather was bad," Elizabeth com-mented. "But keeping it a secret was worse. It meant that I had to build these walls around me so that no one could see the pain or the fear. If they did, they might ask what was wrong and I might break down and tell them. Part of me wished they *would* ask, that they would see through the smoke screen, realize that I was hurting, and help me. But no one ever did." By keeping the sexual abuse a secret and maintaining a safe distance from others so that they would not inadvertently discover the truth, Elizabeth unwittingly engineered her own abandonment and did indeed feel abandoned. As she put it, "There just wasn't anyone to tell me that what he was doing was wrong, that it wasn't my fault, that I wasn't this horrible, helpless human being who had something so terribly wrong with me that I somehow drew my stepfather into my bedroom at night and made him do what he did to me. That was what really got to me, that feeling that I was completely alone without anyone to turn to or depend on or make me feel better."

You need not have been sexually abused to share Elizabeth's sentiments. If your parents were too caught up in their own prob-lems to be emotionally available to you, if someone you loved died, if you were given up for adoption, if you moved, leaving close friends behind, you too felt abandoned—painfully disconnected from people who mattered to you and could have provided you with a sense of security and self-worth. You were cut off from the positive input you needed. You were also left with an overabundance of sadness, helplessness, and self-doubt that you had no outlet for expressing. These private vulnerabilities became all the more ob-vious and frightening whenever you were by yourself, and consequently you preferred not to be alone. Indeed, having other people around you—especially people whose needs and problems could distract you from your own—became your primary method for coping with intolerable feelings of anxiety and loneliness, as well as the lack of love and acceptance you had missed out on in the past.

■ ELLEN

"I guess in the back of my mind I knew my family wasn't normal," Ellen said. "I didn't know any other kids whose mothers had heart conditions or whose fathers worked as much as mine did. We certainly weren't anything like the families on television. But I didn't really give it much thought. I just did what had to be done."

What had to be done was everything Ellen's chronically ill mother could not do—housework, cooking, child care, making her father happy—and it was much too much for a youngster to handle. "I was always one step away from disaster," Ellen recalled. "If I made one little mistake, it could start a whole chain reaction. My brothers and sisters would get out of control and that would upset my mother. She would tell my father what a trying day she had, and he would yell at me for shirking my responsibility. And what could I do except try harder to keep everyone happy and everything running smoothly?"

But try as she might, Ellen could not make her dysfunctional family function normally. "Something always went wrong," she said. "It was just one crisis after another. Someone was always in tears." And Ellen always felt as if she was to blame. "I just couldn't get it right," she sighed. And she never stopped trying. Failing. Trying once more.

OVERATTACHMENT AND THE NEED FOR CONTROL

If you grew up in a dysfunctional family, you could not control the chaos going on around you any more than Ellen could. You could not prevent your parents from disappointing and breaking their promises to you. And like Ellen, no matter what you did or how hard you tried, you could not obtain the consistent, loving attention you needed. But you could not stop trying either. If you did, you would be hit with full force by a sense of powerlessness, an awareness that you were at the mercy of people whom you could not influence and the certain knowledge that you were a helpless victim of circumstances beyond your control. Since this reality is simply too terrifying and painful for any child to accept, you came up with another way to cope with it.

Just as Elizabeth felt that she drew her stepfather's unwanted attention, somewhere deep within yourself you came to believe that you were responsible for what was happening to you; that something about you, some inherent deficiency in your real self, was to blame for your own unhappiness and everyone else's. As painful as this perception may have been, it restored your sense of control because you also came to believe that by altering your own behavior to accommodate the people around you, you could make your circumstances turn out the way you wanted them to. As a result of this belief, you got into the habit of keeping an eye on people who had the potential to hurt you and trying to anticipate their every move so that you could make *your* move first and influence the outcome of the situation. You hoped to ward off a tidal wave of unsettling emotions, intervene before disastrous consequences occurred, and please people or solve their problems so that they would provide the love and approval you needed. As Ellen discovered, no matter how hard you tried, you never seemed to "get it right."

INSTANT REPLAYS

At eighteen, Ellen married a man cut from the same cloth as her father. He worked fourteen-hour days, but used most of his wages to support his cocaine addiction. Like Alisha, Ellen thought her love could cure her husband. She sincerely believed that if she tried hard enough, she would make him happy enough to stop using drugs. Again she failed.

Ellen consulted a divorce lawyer with whom she became friends. While this eased the pain of separating from her husband, it only perpetuated her behavior pattern. Upon learning that the lawyer had an unhappy marriage himself, Ellen decided all she had to do was show him how happy she could make him, and he would leave his wife to marry her. Not surprisingly, it never happened.

Ellen drifted into her next relationship with a man who at some level must have reminded her of her mother. He was a hypochondriac, plagued by mysterious ailments that kept him bedridden for days at a time. Ellen nursed and supported him until the day she came home from work and found that he had left her. He knew he was going to die young, his parting note said, so he might as well live it up while he could. He was going to see the world and had drained their joint bank account to finance his trip. Still blaming herself for other people's actions, Ellen told herself that she should have seen this coming.

"Next time, I'm going to get it right," Ellen told a friend. "No more addicts, married men, or sick ones. I'm going to find someone who will really love me and appreciate the things I do for him." Only moments later, Ellen looked up and spotted Gary. He had already spotted her and over the next few weeks, as Gary heaped attention upon her, Ellen came to believe that her "prayers had been answered." But Gary was an escape artist and soon enough was neglecting Ellen, criticizing her, and seeing other women. As you will recall, Ellen viewed each of Gary's affairs or one-night stands as evidence of her failure as a wife and redoubled her efforts to make him love her and only her.

By now you may be shaking your head in disbelief and wondering what it was going to take for Ellen to figure out that she had been having essentially the same relationship over and over again. Surely she must've seen the pattern and realized that devoting herself to making other people happy was not producing the results she desired. But Ellen did *not* recognize this about herself, just as you may not recognize certain attitudes and habits of your own. Whenever unfinished business from the past is unwittingly carried into the present, you instinctively do what *feels* right and familiar to you—even though it turns out wrong and even though it seems as if you should have learned to do things differently by now. You use the very same methods for obtaining love that failed you in the past and, more often than not, use them with lovers or spouses who have many of the same character traits as the people who were unable to love you in the past. As a result, instead of "getting it right this time," something goes wrong again—and again and again.

OVERATTACHERS IN RELATIONSHIPS

As Robin Norwood explained in her book, *Women Who Love Too Much,* when you suffer from low self-esteem (as all overattachers do) and have a personal history that includes abuse, neglect, abandonment, or dysfunction, prospective partners with the potential to actually accept the real you and meet your needs for warmth and closeness seem bland and unappealing. You cannot put your finger on it, but they just are not "your type." Drifters, dreamers, addicts, and individuals who are about as stable as a nuclear reactor during a meltdown are more your cup of tea. Like Ellen, who from the moment she laid eyes on Gary, "just knew" that he was the man she had been waiting for all her life, you immediately feel as if you have found a kindred spirit, someone who fits you like a glove. You seem to "click" with this person and may even say, "We got along so well it was as if we had known each other all our lives." In a sense, you have!

If you take a close look at the people you tend to attach yourself to, you will often find that their personalities, their problems, or the way they treat you bears an uncanny resemblance to the attitudes and behavior of people who were vitally important to you in the past. At the very least, they will have been raised in families similar to your own and thus play by the same rules that you do. From your very first meeting, you will unwittingly begin to relate to one another in precisely the way you used to interact in your family or with previous lovers. Indeed, you would both feel lost if you did not. This tends to be true for any two people in an intimate relationship. However, when your family or your previous relationships were dysfunctional and you are an overattacher, "doing what comes naturally" invariably gets you into trouble—the same sort of trouble you have encountered before.

Of course you do not knowingly set out to repeat unsettling experiences from the past, and you certainly do not go looking for partners who are as cold and uncommunicative as your father, as emotionally unstable as your mother, as volatile as your ex-spouse, or simply so helpless and wishy-washy that you can easily push them around (and fulfill your need for control). In fact, you rarely see any of these character traits at the outset. As we all tend to do, you get caught up in the excitement of a new relationship. "High" on sexual chemistry and blinded by the glow of newfound romance, you idealize the other person and your relationship. However, because you so desperately need your partner to be the person who can supply you with self-esteem and fill all the empty spaces in your life, and because you are so desperately afraid that he or she will not, you hang onto your illusions long after the dust settles and reality begins to contradict them. You fall in love and remain in love with a dream, living in fear that, like all dreams, your partner and your relationship will evaporate into thin air. You also feel frustrated each and every time your partner or your relationship does not live up to your fantasy, and you feel compelled to tighten your hold in the hopes that he or she will be more like the man or woman of your dreams.

■ ELIZABETH

After her stepfather rather abruptly deserted his wife and stepchildren, Elizabeth's memories of his abuse began to fade. His nightly visits seemed like a bad dream from which she had finally awoken and like other childhood nightmares, she eventually forgot about it completely. All that remained was the loneliness and a terrifying sense that she was destined to be alone for the rest of her life. Elizabeth tried not to think about this and for a time did not have to. She transferred from parochial to public school and discovered something that was entirely new to her—having a best friend.

"Susie and I did everything together," Elizabeth recalled. "We had all the same classes, talked on the phone for hours, wore each other's clothes. I'd never been so close to anyone in my whole life, and I loved it." Elizabeth thrived on the undiluted closeness she experienced with Susie. *This is it. This is what I've been looking for,* she thought, echoing the exact sentiments of the addicted and compulsive individuals I described in the last chapter. She had finally found someone who was there for her, someone on whom she could depend, and having done without that sort of connection for so long, Elizabeth's thirst for it was insatiable. As long as Susie was in her life, everything seemed okay. She was not alone or lonely. Yet, Elizabeth could not stop worrying about losing Susie and being utterly alone once more.

Any slackening in the intensity of their friendship left Elizabeth feeling rejected. Whenever she saw Susie laughing with other classmates, Elizabeth felt jealous. If Susie called five minutes later than she said she would, Elizabeth felt compelled to ask if Susie was angry at her—not just once, but a dozen times during that conversation. Daily she made Susie promise that they would be best friends forever. "But then, one day, right out of the blue, she didn't want to be my friend anymore," Elizabeth said. "Or not my best friend anyway. She wanted us to be more a part of the crowd, and I didn't really want that."

Interpreting what was probably Susie's attempt to obtain some breathing room as a total rejection, Elizabeth found a new best friend, who also "abandoned" her, as did several other girlfriends and most of the young men she dated during high school and college. "Loyalty was like a four-letter word to them," Elizabeth sighed. "They were always moving on to greener pastures and leaving me behind." Actually these men and women were simply trying not to be swallowed alive by Elizabeth's possessiveness, intensity, and demands for constant togetherness. Elizabeth had become a *clinger.*

CLINGERS

Yearning for the closeness and companionship they believe will fill the ever-present void in their lives, *clingers* like Elizabeth form bonds quickly and then hang onto people and relationships as if they were life preservers. Convinced that without them they would drown in a sea of loneliness, clingers not only expect their lovers or spouses to meet all of their needs all of the time, but demand proof and more proof of their commitment to the relationship. Yet no amount of reassurance is ever enough to actually stave off their fear of abandonment.

If you are a clinger, you initially attract sympathy with your wistfulness—especially from people with take-charge personalities and rescuer tendencies. You appear helpless, inhibited, in need of direction, and you do in fact feel most comfortable when following someone else's lead rather than making decisions on your own. You have serious reservations about your ability to take care of yourself, which naturally intensify your fear of abandonment *and* your desire to be in and stay in a relationship at any cost.

Extremely sensitive to the slightest sign of rejection, your typical response is to cling more desperately to the object of your affection. Any time spent without your beloved is time spent in pain and anxiety. Any interest or attention your partner shows to others leaves you consumed by jealousy and self-doubt. Feeling inadequate and fearing that your relationship is doomed, you will use everything from flirting with a third party to shedding a river of tears in order to reel your supposedly straying lover back into your arms. If things really seem to be getting out of hand, you will fall apart. These dramatic, hysterical, emotion-fraught outbursts or physical breakdowns of one kind of another force your partner to pay attention to you. Of course, they can and often do backfire, driving away the person to whom you were clinging.

■ ALISHA

Alisha's alcoholic husband, Frank, was not just her partner, but also her "project," her life's work. In the name of love she hovered over him, giving unsolicited advice, trying to keep him out of trouble and ease the pressures she believed prompted him to drink. Each time he lost a job, she scoured the want ads and nagged him until he called for interviews. She gave him pep talks to boost his confidence. Then she checked up on him by phoning his prospective employer to ask if he had kept his appointment. She left AA pamphlets around the house, hoping he would read them. She begged and pleaded with him to quit drinking, and sometimes she tried to shame him into changing, rubbing salt in his wounds by listing in great detail all the ways he had failed her as a husband.

Alisha frequently promised herself that she would stop "bugging" Frank. But somehow she could not. He was always doing something or about to do something that required immediate intervention on her part. There were bills he would forget to pay if she did not remind him at least a dozen times, people he would offend if she did not interrupt him in midsentence, cars he would wreck if she did not drag herself out of bed at one A.M. and go from bar to bar until she found him and drove him home.

"I did everything I could think of to help Frank get better, Alisha explained. "But he never listened to me, never apprreciated any of it. He even accused me of driving him to drink. But he'd be lying in some gutter by now if it weren't for me."

And where would Alisha be if it weren't for Frank? What would occupy her mind if she did not have to worry about him? Could she have felt secure in a relationship with someone who was healthy enough to take care of himself? Probably not. Alisha was a coercer, and unlike clingers who look to others for direction, longing to be nurtured and cared for, coercers only feel comfortable when they are giving directions and doing the caretaking.

COERCERS

If you are a coercer, you try to mold and shape your partner into the person you want him or her to be. Since the people with whom you become involved tend to be, as Alisha put it, "a real mess," you have your work cut out for you. You are more than willing to rise to that challenge, however. Your need for control compels you to stay one step ahead of your partner, and you tend to create crises, turning problems into catastrophes and then charging in to save the day. For instance, one of my patients whose husband had been depressed for some time became convinced that he was considering suicide. Not only did she rearrange her schedule so that she could spend as much time with him as possible, but she decided not to take a college course she needed to complete her degree so that she and her husband could use the tuition to take a vacation that she thought would cheer him up (but that he could have lived without—the operative word being *lived*). Similarly, when a member of one of my therapy groups received an overdue notice from the electric company, he found it necessary to jump to the conclusion that his wife's sloppy bookkeeping and penchant for shopping had brought him to the verge of bankruptcy. After weeks of arguments, he took back responsibility for the family finances and put his wife on a strict budget, secure in the knowledge that his wife was damned fortunate to have him around.

If you are a coercer, you constantly assume other people's responsibilities and cover all contingencies so they will not have to suffer the consequences of their actions. Although you do this with the best of intentions and truly believe that you are helping your partner get better, you are actually ensuring that he or she does not. However, the longevity of your relationship is virtually guaranteed. As Alisha did, you can spend decades trying harder and harder to keep your partner out of the gutter, the unemployment line, prison, or a psychiatric ward.

■ ELLEN

"Plenty of people knew about Gary's flings," Ellen said. "All of my friends knew, and they would ask me how I could put up with it, why I didn't leave him. The truth is that I did think about leaving him. But whenever I did, I wound up feeling that I was being unfair, that I would be punishing him for something that wasn't really his fault. He had such an unhappy childhood, and all the women he had been involved with before me walked out on him at the first sign of trouble. I couldn't do that to him. I couldn't live with myself if I hurt him the way they did. I knew that he needed someone to hang in there with him, to stand by him no matter what he did. He needed unconditional love, and I told myself that once he realized I could give him that, he would stop running around."

Ellen believed that she knew exactly what her husband Gary needed and, as you've seen, was willing to do whatever it took to fulfill his needs. But what about her own needs? Didn't Ellen need to get something from her relationship as well as give her all to it? These questions never crossed her mind. Devoted to serving other people, making them comfortable and keeping them happy, it rarely occurred to Ellen that she might deserve some tender loving care herself. Self-sacrifice for the greater good of her family, and later her adult relationships, came as naturally to Ellen as breathing.

In Ellen's dysfunctional family, her chronically ill mother needed Ellen to assume the tasks that her own fragile health prevented her from completing. Her workaholic father always seemed unhappy, and Ellen believed he needed her to cheer him up. Her siblings needed Ellen to nurture them since their parents could not. With so many people relying on her, Ellen's own needs got lost in the shuffle—never to be found.

Whenever anything went wrong in the lives of the people she loved, Ellen felt responsible. She had absolutely no part in the cutbacks at a local factory that caused her brother to lose his job. It certainly was not her fault that her boss's mother died or that her friend's husband was divorcing her. Yet, Ellen felt bad for these people and made it her business to help them feel better. Even when other people's behavior—like Gary's many infidelities—hurt her, Ellen felt that she had to forgive and redouble her efforts to make them happy. Of course, Ellen was rarely happy herself. But then, she was a *martyr* and did not expect to be.

MARTYRS

As a martyr, you are unaware of—or at the very least undervalue—your own needs. You center your life around others and their problems. When they hurt, you hurt; when they are happy, you are happy. You live vicariously through them because you have only a vague notion of your own identity or doubt your own ability to get what you want out of life. You will tolerate enormous amounts of exploitation and pain in order to hang onto what little you have.

A lifelong people pleaser, your ultimate goal is to make other people happy, but just as important is never making them angry. You walk on eggshells, looking for signs of displeasure or disapproval, trying to be prepared for the unexpected at all times. An eyebrow raised in reaction to a question you have asked is enough to make you withdraw it. You block your thoughts and feelings or lie about them. No matter what you are really feeling, you always say that you are fine.

Because you try to "read minds"—guessing at what is bothering others and trying to make them feel better—you expect other people to read your mind as well. You believe that they should somehow "know" what you are feeling and show that they care.

They rarely do. In fact, with great regularity, other people treat you disrespectfully. They take advantage of your willingness to make sacrifices on their behalf so that it seems as if the more you give, the more they expect from you. You may feel angry, unappreciated, or used, but you also feel incapable of doing anything to change the circumstances that stir up those emotions. You simply try harder to please and do for others, hoping that they will magically "get the message" and finally provide you with some nourishment in return.

Thanks to your never-ending effort to meet everyone else's needs while neglecting your own, you also fall apart from time to time. You drop everything, too upset about your partner to follow your daily routines; or you literally make yourself sick with worry, so overwhelmed by your constant caretaking that you crumble from

sheer exhaustion. This temporarily nets you a modicum of attention and comfort from friends or relatives who sympathize with
your plight. You are so starved for warmth and closeness that you
are grateful for even these crumbs of concern and affection that are
tossed your way.

By now it must be obvious that clinging, coercing, and martyr-
dom are not conducive to establishing and maintaining truly intimate relationships. Indeed, as you can see from all three case
examples I provided in this section, the steps overattachers take to
hang onto their relationships often end up driving other people
away. Yet, most overattachers—Elizabeth, Alisha, and Ellen included—eventually manage to form attachments that last years,
decades, or even a lifetime. The basis of these long-term relationships is not mutual respect, interdependence, and the ability to
be and share one's real self with others, however.

Instead, the tie that binds overattachers to their partners is
codependency, an addiction to another person's dysfunctional behavior. Codependents try to derive a sense of self-worth from their
connection to other people. They also avoid their own feelings by
obsessively thinking about, and compulsively trying to control,
other people's actions.

CODEPENDENCY

Although the term codependency was originally used to describe
the attitude and behavior patterns of people caught up in someone
else's alcoholism, your partner need not be an alcoholic or a drug
addict for you to be a codependent. He or she is apt to be dysfunctional in some way, however—chronically depressed, physically ill,
obsessed with work, narcissistic, prone to violence, or for some
other reason, *incapable of giving you the love and approval you so
desperately want.* If you are an overattacher, you do not wind up
with such people by chance. Living through, and doing for, others
is how you learned to confirm that you are of value to them and
why you maintain your connections with them. Consequently, you
need someone with problems you can fret over and try to solve;
someone whose hidden potential you can nurture; someone who
can provide you with a mission in life and distract you from your
own pain, fear, and sense of inadequacy.

The people to whom you attach yourself need something also—
someone to assume the responsibilities they shirk and shield them
from the consequences of their actions; someone to help them
maintain the facade they present to the outside world; someone to

forgive them for every transgression or indulge them the way their parents once did, or serve as a scapegoat on whom they can blame their failures or excesses. Your needs and theirs fit together like interlocking puzzle pieces, and your relationship is like a business deal in which each of you agrees to fulfill the other's needs—and unfortunately, perpetuate each other's unhealthy behavior patterns.

To live up to your end of the unspoken and unrecognized agreement, you must *deny unpleasant realities*, including both the severity or unmanageability of your partner's problem and your own needs and feelings. You must be able to distort reality and completely convince yourself that your relationship is the way you wish it could be. Of course, you may admit to a few "minor" problems, but you are quite sure that you have them under control.

Your partner's dysfunctional behavior makes it possible for you to continue doing what is most familiar and comfortable for you. And your clinging, coercing, or self-sacrificing habits in turn *enable* your partner to remain dysfunctional. In addition, they serve to reassure you that you are not the one with the problem, while at the same time keeping you out of touch with your own pain, anxiety, and sense of powerlessness.

But just as the anesthetizing effect of drinking, overeating, gambling, or other substances and activities eventually wears off, creating a need to do more of the same, so does your compulsion to cling and control your partner. Because perpetually worrying about other people and watching for signs of impending doom is itself painful and anxiety provoking, you are left in a near constant state of emotional distress, rather than being fulfilled. Because the problems you try to fix are not your own and the circumstances you try to control are actually beyond your control, you fail to obtain the results you desire more often than you succeed. And even when you do succeed, you fail. In trying to control the uncontrollable—most notably, other people's thoughts, feelings, or actions—you actually end up being controlled, reacting to what is happening around you rather than acting on your own behalf. External circumstances and other people's behavior wind up influencing everything you do, instead of the other way around.

Frustrated and more terrified than ever of losing control completely, your need for control intensifies and compels you to try harder to hang onto your relationship and make it measure up to your expectations. Becoming more and more preoccupied with your partner and his or her problems, you further neglect yourself, your children, your other relationships, your work, and your social responsibilities. You find it extremely difficult to have fun or be spontaneous. You stand for behavior that you swore you would not tolerate, whittling away at what little self-esteem you had and making you all the more dependent on your partner and your relationship to supply you with any sense of identity at all.

In short, your addiction to your partner and your relationship progresses like any other addiction. You become progressively more detached from your own feelings. You become progressively more dishonest about who you are, who your partner is, what you like or dislike, and what is or is not going on in your relationship. And you become progressively more consumed with self-loathing and despair. Clearly, your compulsion to be in and stay in a relationship at any cost has neither netted you the love you need or lessened your fear that you are unlovable. Not only have you failed to find intimacy, you have sacrificed your own life to maintain your supply of an intimacy substitute.

BREAKING THE CHAINS

If you are an overattacher—whether or not you have crossed the line into codependency—the connections to other people that you hoped would ward off your fear of abandonment, enhance your self-esteem, and allow you to have some semblance of control over your life have become chains of bondage. You are not in control. You are not happy with yourself. You are, if anything, *more* fearful and anxious than ever, and you are indeed hooked on the person to whom you have attached yourself. Like the people I described in the last chapter, you will have to take steps to recover from your addictive disease before you can even entertain the notion of establishing a lasting, truly intimate relationship with your present partner or someone else. In Chapter 11 you will find a list of resources—including twelve-step programs for codependents—to help you do that.

Once you have begun to break the chains that are binding you to unhealthy relationships, you can prepare yourself to experience genuine intimacy by replenishing the intimacy prerequisites you are most likely to lack. They are:

1. Self-Worth: Your decidedly low opinion of yourself is at the very heart of your tendency to overattach, and it is absolutely essential that you learn to like and respect yourself. Once you come to view *your* life as worth living, you will be less inclined to try and "help" other people live theirs. You will have to take some time to look inward and, for perhaps the first time in your life, find out who you really are, recognizing that you are somebody even when you are not in a relationship.

2. Trust: You have almost no useful experience in this area. Your fear of abandonment and need for control has made the mere thought of trusting other people a terrifying one. And your lack of self-awareness has repeatedly led you to trust people who were actually untrustworthy. Consequently, you must start from scratch on this one, learning *how* to trust and *whom* to trust—starting with trusting yourself.

3. Tolerance: Because you tend to interpret any disagreement between you and your partner as proof that the relationship is over, you are apt to have little tolerance for conflict. You try to control people and events in hopes of avoiding it. Your own anger scares you to death and you repress it, crying, becoming depressed, overeating, or getting physically ill in reponse to circumstances that might prompt outrage in others. Consequently, you may be too tolerant of other people's truly inappropriate behavior, withstanding the abuse of angry, explosive individuals because you are afraid to respond—even believing that being battered or berated is still better than being alone. You must find a balance in this area and learn to cope with conflict and anxiety in new ways.

4. Interdependence: With the intimacy building blocks of self-worth, trust, and tolerance as a foundation, you must begin to develop the ability both to give and take, to share responsibility for solving mutual problems, to become detached enough to allow other people to live their own lives and make their own mistakes, and to view circumstances objectively enough to stop trying to control the uncontrollable. Then and only then will you be able to achieve the reciprocity necessary for a genuinely intimate relationship.

5. Intimacy Role Models: If you are an overattacher, you simply do not know what sort of behavior is normal, healthy, and appropriate in an intimate relationship. You probably did not observe intimacy in your home and bought into the idealized version of relationships you encountered in romance novels, movies, and television shows. You expect far too much of your partner and assume that satisfying relationships "just happen" through the magic of true love. You will have to reexamine your beliefs and discard those that are unrealistic, as well as learn how to be in a real relationship with a real flesh-and-blood human being.

8

THE INTIMACY PARADOXES
IN YOUR LIFE AND
RELATIONSHIPS TODAY:
Writing a Prescription
for Positive Change

> God, grant me the serenity to accept the things I cannot change, the courage to change the things I can, and the wisdom to know the difference.
>
> —anonymous

Recited at the beginning of every twelve-step recovery meeting, the serenity prayer offers sage advice for all of us. It's a reminder that our efforts to improve our lives are well spent on that which we can change—ourselves and the beliefs or behaviors that prevent us from having close, nourishing relationships—and wasted on circumstances that are beyond our control—most notably, other people, what they think about us, and how they operate in intimate relationships. It is often said, and my personal and professional experience has repeatedly confirmed, that *the difficult part is telling the difference.*

This chapter makes that task a bit easier. Focused entirely on *you,* it will help you identify how intimacy paradoxes affect your life and relationships today and decide what it is about yourself that you wish to change.

By the time you've reached the end of this chapter, you will have a better understanding of yourself and what is important to you, providing a solid foundation on which you can build relationships that are healthier, more satisfying, and more intimate than they have been in the past.

HOW TO WRITE A PRESCRIPTION FOR POSITIVE CHANGE

Regardless of the nature or magnitude of their problems, when individuals, couples, or families come to me for help, the first thing I do is conduct an evaluation. Together, my patients and I examine the problematic areas of their lives and relationships. We discuss what they would like to change, determine what they *can* change, and then come up with a treatment plan that details the steps they will take to resolve their difficulties. I have adapted this process to create the self-diagnosis and goal-setting exercises you will find in this chapter. By completing them you will be writing your own personal prescription for positive change—deciding what you and nobody else but you—need to, want to, and can do about the intimacy paradoxes in your life and relationships.

In the four chapters that preceded this one, you read about people whose problems may have seemed far more dramatic and debilitating than your own. With a sigh of relief, you may have said to yourself, "Succeeding in my career may be important to me, but it certainly hasn't done as much damage to my relationship as it did to Linda and Robert's" or "I prefer to make a good impression, but I don't go to the extremes that Rebecca, Pamela, or Jeffrey did." Although you may have recognized some of your own thoughts, feelings, and behaviors while reading about intimacy substitutes or overattachment, you may not have fit the description of an addict or codependent, and your life may not be as unmanageable as Sylvie's, Alisha's, Ellen's, and Elizabeth's. But, that does not mean that *your* intimacy or relationship problems are insignificant.

You may have picked up this book because *you* have difficulty establishing close, nourishing relationships or feel dissatisfied with the amount of intimacy in the relationships you have. Even if you are in less trouble than the people I have described thus far, your difficulties and your dissatisfaction are meaningful to you and in one way or another you suffer because of them. Try to avoid falling into the "It's not so bad; other people have it worse" trap that might convince you not to take action because your circumstances are not dire or life-threatening—yet. In fact, you are well advised to stay away from comparisons altogether. Your goal is not to obtain someone else's life or relationship, but to improve your own.

Another rule of thumb for writing prescriptions for positive change is to set *reasonable* goals—tasks you can actually accomplish over a period of, say, three to six months. Unrealistic goals, such as *never* feeling depressed, or eliminating *all* sources of frustration and resentment from your relationships, or getting over your last relationship by the end of the month only result in creating more anxiety by raising the stakes on your effort to change. You also increase the likelihood that you will fail to attain your lofty expectation. A goal such as finding a relationship that will not disappoint you (especially if you set a time limit) is also unreasonable because it involves too many factors that are beyond your control.

Here are several examples of realistic goals for change:

- Cutting in half the number of sarcastic or critical remarks you make over the next six months.
- Learning to communicate resentment or frustration when you feel it, instead of stewing for weeks and then exploding.
- Trying one new way each week for meeting people.
- Developing coping skills, like writing in a journal, calling friends, or meditating—and using them when you feel upset and might otherwise take a Valium or obsess about your spouse.

It is also important to know that when setting goals, you do not *have* to address your most painful or unmanageable problems first. Many of my patients find it helpful to start with their least unmanageable problems so that they improve the odds of experiencing a success. This, in turn, builds the confidence they will need to tackle more tenacious obstacles.

Keeping these bits of advice in mind, grab your pencil and a notebook, or several sheets of paper, and forge ahead on the first leg of your journey toward genuine intimacy—self-discovery.

ARE YOU CAUGHT IN A COME HERE/GO AWAY TUG-OF-WAR?

That which we need, we also fear. This is the most primal intimacy paradox and the source of many unproductive relationship patterns. Hoping to obtain your heart's desire without suffering consequences that frighten you, you do your own personal version of the come here/go away dance. And you do that dance to a tune composed by your own unique needs and fears. The following exercise will help you identify those needs and fears and how they influence your beliefs and behavior.

Take out a sheet of paper and draw a line down the center. Label the left-hand column "Come Here" and in it list the needs you are hoping an intimate relationship will fulfill. Here are some suggestions:

- a feeling of connection with someone
- security
- company (someone with whom I can spend time and share experiences)
- an ally (someone to be on my side and keep me from feeling utterly alone in the world)
- nurturing
- validation of my self-worth
- love and affection
- emotional support during times of stress
- acceptance and a sense of belonging
- someone with whom I can share my innermost thoughts and feelings
- pleasure, passion, romance, warmth, approval, or any other needs that come to mind

Label the right-hand column "Go Away" and in it list anything that you are afraid might happen if you let down your guard or fail to maintain a safe distance from other people. Here are a few suggestions:

- rejection or abandonment
- entrapment (getting stuck in the relationship)
- being boxed in (limiting the options in other areas of my life)
- losing control over myself and my life
- being controlled by another person
- losing my identity or independence
- failure
- being overwhelmed or drained dry by my partner's needs
- making a fool of myself
- making myself vulnerable only to be hurt or have my trust betrayed, or any other fears that come to mind

Go back over both lists and put a plus sign (+) beside the needs or fears that you believe work to your advantage in intimate relationships and a minus sign (−) beside those that seem to get in your way. To do this, try to keep in mind that what you think you need from an intimate relationship may not always work to your benefit. For instance, if your idea of an ally is someone who will never criticize you under any circumstances and will accept you no matter what, you may be seeking out partners who agree with you even when you are wrong or are behaving self-destructively. Likewise, your fears do not always work against you. A feeling of being overwhelmed or drained dry, for example, can actually provide the motivation you need to set limits on another person's truly unreasonable demands.

Next, give each need that you marked with a plus sign and each fear that you marked with a minus sign a weight (from 0 to 100) based on how powerfully it influences your approach to intimacy and your behavior in personal relationships. When all of the forces that pull you toward or drive you away from genuine intimacy have been weighted, tally each column and compare totals. If your fears significantly outweigh your needs, your determination to protect yourself from harm may lead you to deny your needs and not make intimate connections at all. If your needs are more influential, you may be driven by an overwhelming desire to fulfill them, negating your fears and clinging for dear life to relationships that are hazardous to your health and emotional well-being.

You are most likely to discover that your two totals are closer than you thought they would be and therein lies the source of your come here/go away dance—ambivalence. You want closeness and feel lonely without it, but feel anxious and want distance whenever you do get close. Pulled in opposite directions by compelling but contradictory forces, you may relentlessly pursue prospective partners only to turn tail and run as soon as you have "caught" them; give to your partners but feel uncomfortable being on the receiving end; or walk on eggshells and anxiously wait for the other shoe to drop and your relationship to end.

YOUR PRESCRIPTION FOR CHANGE

As you might expect, discontinuing your same old unproductive come here/go away dance involves finding ways both to conquer your fears and more effectively meet your needs. To set goals in this area, complete the following sentences:

Needs

- The need I would most like to fulfill is . . .
- In the past, I have tried to accomplish this by . . .
- Of these measures, I would like to continue . . . and discontinue . . .
- In addition, I would like to learn to . . .

Fears

- The fear I would most like to conquer is . . .
- In the past, I have protected myself from this fear by . . .
- Of these measures, I would like to do *less* . . .
- In addition, I would like to learn to . . .
- To accomplish these goals I need to replenish the intimacy prerequisites of . . . (Select from: sense of self-worth; trust; courage; positive regard for others; tolerance for ambiguity, conflict, and imperfection; self-disclosure; interdependence; or intimacy role models—including learning new relationship skills.)

WHERE IS INTIMACY ON YOUR LIST OF PRIORITIES?

As influential as the tug-of-war between your need for intimacy and your fears is the contest between your need for intimacy and other needs or pursuits that you have deemed equally or more important. Here are a list of some of those needs. Reorder them to reflect your priorities, inserting *establish and maintain intimate relationships* in the spot where it fits on your hierarchy.

- having and getting ahead in my career
- attaining financial security or wealth
- not changing my life-style
- avoiding pain
- not taking risks
- keeping my secrets
- proving that I do not really need a relationship in order to be happy
- having no one to answer to but myself
- parenting
- other

YOUR PRESCRIPTION FOR CHANGE

Although establishing an intimate relationship or nurturing the relationship you do have need not be your top priority, you will have to give it more priority than you have in the past if you want this area of your life to improve. To do this, you must compromise—taking *some* time, energy, or attention from one area and donating it to another. You do *not* have to give up anything completely or forever, and, contrary to what you may believe, you *can* have professional success and satisfying personal relationships at the same time, be a good parent and maintain a social life, or reconcile any other seemingly mutually exclusive needs. You can also rearrange your priorities again at any time.

To write your personal prescription for change, answer the following questions:

- What do I need to do or have more of in order to fulfill my need for genuine intimacy?
- What can I do less of in other areas of my life in order to free up some time, energy, and attention for intimacy?
- What are three compromises that I am willing to make immediately?
- What intimacy prerequisites do I need to replenish in order to achieve my goal?

WHICH COME HERE/GO AWAY DANCE STEPS DO YOU DO?

In your well-meaning, yet not always conscious, efforts to meet your need for intimacy while keeping your fears at bay, and to have close relationships without compromising in other areas of your life, you unwittingly develop belief and behavior patterns that both prevent you from getting what you want and bring about the very consequences you had hoped to avoid. Although it was never your intention, by doing the same dance over and over again, you erect barriers that stand between you and genuine intimacy.

As described in Chapter 4, you may turn intimacy paradoxes into either/or propositions and neglect or avoid personal relationships so that you can single-mindedly pursue professional success. As described in Chapter 5, you may turn intimacy paradoxes into if/then equations that predict certain disaster and then attempt to have intimate relationships while still concealing your real self from others. With little confidence in your ability to get the "real thing," you may settle for and get hooked on intimacy substitutes—either the substances and activities described in Chapter 6 or people and relationships as explained in Chapter 7, or both. You will also have difficulty finding or committing yourself to a truly intimate relationship if:

- you *have trouble making decisions or expressing personal preferences.* As a result, you may be indiscriminating and try to have a satisfying relationship with anyone who chooses you rather than doing the choosing yourself. Or you may go to the opposite extreme, keeping your options open "just in case" somebody better than your current partner comes along.

- you are *drawn to danger, intrigue, drama, or challenges.* As a result, you may find yourself attracted to individuals who may be dangerous, intriguing, or dramatic, but who are not the least bit interested in a lasting relationship. You may dedicate yourself to the ultimate challenge: involving yourself with people who are unattainable—married men and women who do not intend to leave their spouses, individuals who have made it clear that they are not interested in you, or matinee idols, rock stars, and magazine centerfolds whom you worship from afar. Or you may simply grow bored with a relationship as soon as the excitement of the chase and romantic phase has worn off.

- you *place a great deal of emphasis on the sexual aspect of any relationship.* The only time you feel close to your partner may be when you are in bed—sex being the only way you know how to express affection. You may use sex as a weapon, withholding it rather than explaining what's bothering you. Or you may use it to distract or appease your partner, seducing your lover in the middle of an argument or in response to requests for more closeness and self-disclosure. With chemistry as your only connection to another person—and no emotional intercourse to sustain that chemistry—your relationships tend to be short-lived or rife with conflict.

- you have *unrealistic expectations for your partner and your relationship.* Perhaps you bought lock, stock, and barrel the romantic myths portrayed in novels, movies, or television shows and expect the passion and intense closeness that marked the beginning of your relationship to continue at the same level indefinitely. You may sincerely believe that intimacy does not change over time; that someone who really loves you will know what you need without being told and meet your needs without being asked; that people in a good relationship rarely get angry or disagree; or any number of other "unreasonables." Your unmet expectations create resentment, frustration, and disappointment. Because you do not realize that your standards are too high for any flesh-and-blood human being to meet, you assume that you are in the wrong relationship with the wrong partner and either end it or work overtime trying to make reality live up to your perceptions.

In addition to the beliefs and habits you *do* have, the information and skills you lack also present an obstacle to intimacy. You may have little experience with relationships that include mutual trust, positive regard, and sharing. Indeed you may have only a hazy notion of what a warm, loving relationship can be like. You *need concrete information about how relationships work.* And because of your lack of knowledge and experience you may not be able to:

- detect signs that other people are interested in getting to know you
- accept nurturance, emotional support, or compliments
- respond to someone else's self-disclosure in kind, or determine what personal data to share with others, and when
- assert yourself when you are being treated unfairly
- resolve conflicts constructively, negotiate mutually satisfying compromises, or express affection

Before you can feel safe and comfortable with other people or sustain an intimate relationship, you will have to *develop the basic skills for making meaningful contact with other human beings and strengthening intimate connections once they are formed.*

YOUR PRESCRIPTION FOR CHANGE

Think about the the examples of obstacles just described. Then on a sheet of paper list the attitudes, beliefs, behavior patterns, and skills you lack that may be preventing you from finding the genuine intimacy you want and need. For instance, do you constantly bring work home from the office in the evenings and weekends? Do you clam up when people attempt to get you to talk about yourself? Are you afraid to go to new places?

Place an asterisk (*) beside the five obstacles you most want to dismantle and then order them in rank—denoting the obstacle you would like to work on first with the number 1, the one you would like to tackle next with a 2, and so on.

WHERE DID YOU LEARN TO DANCE?

I have found that one of the most useful of all diagnostic and relearning tools for individuals and couples with intimacy or relationship problems is the *genogram*, or family tree technique, developed by family therapist Murray Bowen and explained in detail in the book *Genograms: The New Tool for Exploring the Personality, Career and Love Patterns You Inherit*, by marriage and family therapist Emily Marlin. Creating your own genogram enables you to spot relationship patterns and problems that have been passed from generation to generation, identify sources of unfinished business, and make connections between your past experiences and your present-day beliefs and behavior. When you and your partner both draw and compare family trees, you are able to find explanations for many of your previously bewildering conflicts and recognize the ways in which you are reenacting scenes from the past. In fact, genograms are such eye-openers and provide such an excellent starting point for positive change that I have most of my patients create them during their initial sessions.

Using Rebecca's genogram (found on page 175) as a guide, draw your family tree, beginning with your grandparents. Use a square (□) to denote male family members and a circle (○) for females. For deceased family members, place an X inside their symbol (×) and write their age, the year, and the cause of their death beside the symbol. Write the present age of living family members inside their symbols.

Marriages are indicated by drawing a connecting line from one symbol to another, slightly below the symbols. If a marriage ended in divorce, place a double slash through the line (—/ /—). Write dates of marriages and divorces right above the line. Offspring of marriages are indicated by drawing vertical lines from the marriage line to the appropriate symbol; keep in birth order, moving from left (the oldest) to right. Draw double lines (= = =) before family members who had particularly close bonds to one another and squiggly lines (⌇⌇) between family members whose relationships were marked by conflict.

Having completed a basic family tree, you can then begin to explore specific sources of conflict and confusion. You might want to examine any or all of the following:

- addictions or compulsive behaviors (A = alcoholism; D = drug abuse; E = compulsive eating; W = workaholism; G = gambling; S = sex addiction; SP = spending; C–D = codependency; PP = people pleasing)
- abuse (indicate *victims* with PA for physical abuse; SA for sexual abuse; VA for verbal abuse. Denote *perpetrators* with the same abbreviations plus the suffix "er." Some family members may be both.)
- roles (hero, scapegoat, lost child, mascot)
- general demeanor (cold, unemotional, melodramatic, unpredictable, aggressive, violent, warm, loving, self-sacrificing, unreliable, trouble-making, depressed, nourishing, happy-go-lucky, etc.)
- treatment received from parents or others (neglected, overindulged, overprotected, criticized, pushed to be perfect, nurtured, blamed, etc.)

GENOGRAM: Rebecca, 33-year-old, computer software developer, single

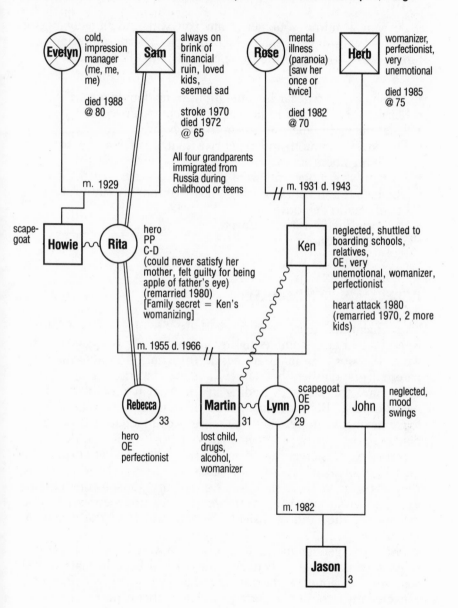

Evelyn — cold, impression manager (me, me, me) died 1988 @ 80

Sam — always on brink of financial ruin, loved kids, seemed sad

stroke 1970 died 1972 @ 65

Rose — mental illness (paranoia) [saw her once or twice] died 1982 @ 70

Herb — womanizer, perfectionist, very unemotional died 1985 @ 75

All four grandparents immigrated from Russia during childhood or teens

m. 1929

m. 1931 d. 1943

scape-goat

Howie ⌇ Rita

hero PP C-D (could never satisfy her mother, felt guilty for being apple of father's eye) (remarried 1980) [Family secret = Ken's womanizing]

Ken — neglected, shuttled to boarding schools, relatives, OE, very unemotional, womanizer, perfectionist

heart attack 1980 (remarried 1970, 2 more kids)

m. 1955 d. 1966

Rebecca 33
hero OE perfectionist

Martin ⌇ Lynn
31   29
lost child, drugs, alcohol, womanizer

scapegoat OE PP

John — neglected, mood swings

m. 1982

Jason 3

- illnesses, financial ups and downs, criminal activity and incarceration, employment history, sibling rivalries, affection or conflict in marriages, family secrets, patterns of defiance and conformity, and so on

As you examine your genogram you will undoubtedly notice patterns beginning to emerge. By completing the following sentence stems, you can bring those patterns into clearer focus.

- Problems that reoccur in generations of my family are . . .
- Marital relationships in my family are characterized by . . .
- Rules my family members seem to live by are . . .
- The most common and repetitive sources of conflict between family members are . . .
- My family's strongpoints were . . .
- The beliefs and behaviors that I learned from my family and that I continue to demonstrate are . . .
- My unfinished business seems to be . . .
- Other connections are . . .

REBECCA'S GENOGRAM

"A problem that reoccurs in generations of my family is infidelity," Rebecca said after completing her genogram. As you can see, she wrote the word "womanizer" beside the symbols representing her paternal grandfather, her father, and her brother. "All three of them have this habit of trading in the woman they're with for a newer model," Rebecca elaborated. "They're always on the lookout for someone younger, prettier, more accommodating . . ." Suddenly, Rebecca stopped speaking. Her eyes opened wide and a surprised expression appeared on her face. "That's what I expect the men I get involved with to do," she said. "I try to be who I think they want me to be so they won't go looking for someone else *the way the men in my family always have.*" Her statement is just one example of the kind of insight you can gain from the genogram technique.

From her genogram Rebecca also discovered that her perfectionism was a belief or behavior she learned from her family and that she continues to be influenced by today: "My grandfather expected my father to be perfect, and my father expected me to be. My mother was always trying to be perfect enough to hang onto my father. My brother tried to be as good in school as I was. We were all trying to be better than we really believed we were, and we were always failing to measure up."

Seeing how many times the words "cold," "distant," and "unaffectionate" appeared on her diagram, Rebecca commented, "I never realized how undemonstrative my family was, but in every generation there was a cold fish, someone who couldn't or wouldn't show his feelings and didn't want anyone else to either. No wonder I never let anyone see me cry or admit it when I'm scared or sad. It seems like the thing *our* family didn't want anyone to know was that we are human."

Like most of my patients, Rebecca's observations were primarily focused on what was wrong with her family, and yours may be as well. But I urge you to look for positive patterns also. In addition to its faults, your family had strongpoints. For instance, Rebecca recognized that a strong survival instinct had been passed down to her from grandparents who survived the pogroms in Russia and countless hardships while emigrating to America; from her mother who survived her divorce without becoming bitter and resentful; and from her father who survived a heart attack. And they all survived with very little emotional nourishment. Other strong points of Rebecca's family were the value they placed on education and hard work, as well as the tolerance of people who are different from them, which Rebecca attributed to her mother's habit of "taking in strays—troubled kids, relatives who were going through hard times, characters she made friends with somehow, all kinds of people."

YOUR PRESCRIPTION FOR CHANGE

Complete the following sentence stems.

- The strengths that I developed as a result of my family relationships which I would like to enhance are . . .
- The intergenerational patterns I would like to break are . . .
- The unfinished business I need to complete is . . .
- The intimacy prerequisites I must replenish in order to accomplish these are . . .

If you are involved in a long-term relationship, and your partner is willing to create a family tree of his or her own, you will gain additional insight by comparing and discussing each other's genograms. Not only will this help you to learn a great deal about each other, but it will also illuminate the source of many of the problematic interactions in your relationship. If your partner is not interested in using this technique, you can still increase your understanding by sketching his or her family tree based on information you already have available to you. In addition, whether you do it individually or as a couple, I recommend sharing your genogram with a supportive third party—a friend or therapist who may be able to spot connections that you miss or ask thought-provoking questions.

TAKING A RELATIONSHIP INVENTORY

Another way to identify your repetitive relationship patterns is to conduct a relationship inventory. Like the "searching and fearless moral inventory" recommended in step four of twelve-step recovery programs, a relationship inventory delineates your history of problems and strengths in intimate relationships.

Starting as far back as you can remember, write a chronology of your attempts to find intimacy. Include relationships that never quite got off the ground and short-lived ones as well as long-lasting ones and marriages. You may even want to write about "best" friendships since they are often as intimate as romances. Describe:

- what attracted you to your partner and what attracted him or her to you
- the early "courtship" stage and "honeymoon period" of your relationship
- what happened and how you felt once the "honeymoon" was over
- any distancing behaviors you noticed in yourself or your partner
- sources of conflict (what you argued about, things about your partner that drove you up a wall, and vice versa) and how you resolved those conflicts
- the amount of intimacy in the relationship and signs of it (trust, open communication, being and sharing your real selves, etc.)
- what you liked about the relationship, and what you handled well; what you regret and wish you had handled differently; and *anything from a previous relationship that repeated itself in another*

YOUR PRESCRIPTION FOR CHANGE

Once your inventory is complete, take out a sheet of paper and divide it horizontally into halves. In the top section list any recurring problems you uncovered. Underline three that you most want to prevent from occurring again.

In the bottom section list any intimate behaviors or ways of relating to your partners that worked for you. These are the strengths on which you will build as you unravel the intimacy paradoxes in your life.

FILLING YOUR PRESCRIPTION
FOR POSITIVE CHANGE

Habitual behaviors and self-defeating attitudes thrive in the darkness. When brought out into the light of day and seen for what they really are—old and unnecessary excess baggage—they make you uncomfortable, perhaps even uncomfortable enough to get rid of them. In this chapter you focused a spotlight on your old habits and have hopefully reached the point of being able to say, "No, I don't want to keep thinking and feeling and doing these things. I'm ready to try something new." That is the first step. The second is: to believe that you *can* change; to be willing to try; to patiently pursue the realistic goals you have set and take pleasure in each small success; to practice new behaviors and act in spite of your old fears and skepticisms. You will have to stop listening to the internal voices that say, "This won't work" or "There's nothing you can do." As long as you believe that, you are doomed. Instead, try reminding yourself that *anything you do differently is more effective than doing nothing or doing the same old thing over and over again.* Your negative habits are not your destiny. You *can* develop new habits—positive ones that enhance your life and relationships. The final section of this book will show you how.

In Chapter 9 you begin the process of actually removing the obstacles to intimacy and extricating yourself from your endless come here/go away dances by replenishing the three most basic intimacy prerequisites—*self-worth, trust,* and *courage.*

Replenishing the remaining intimacy prerequisites—which is the subject of Chapter 10—provides you with effective techniques for establishing and maintaining mutually satisfying intimate relationships.

You may also need to overcome individual psychological problems like depression or marital difficulties, complete unfinished business from the past, or recover from addictions, compulsive behaviors, or codependency. And you will probably need outside help to do that. Chapter 11 describes the peer support and professional services that are available to you and where you can find them.

BECOMING A CANDIDATE FOR GENUINE INTIMACY:
How to Build Self-Worth, Trust, and Courage

When a house is built on a shaky foundation of crumbling cinder blocks, no matter how many times you remodel the exterior or redecorate the interior, the walls will creak, the floors will warp, and the basement will keep on leaking. And while any building will sustain some damage from strong winds, heavy rain, or earth tremors, these natural disasters are bound to reduce an already unstable structure to a pile of rubble. So it is with relationships in which one or both parties lack vital intimacy prerequisites.

Try as you might, you cannot build a new house from the sticks of wood and scraps of siding left after your old house has been demolished. Likewise, you can neither hope to pick up the pieces of a broken relationship nor to establish and maintain close, nourishing ones by adopting the same old attitudes and behaviors.

The strategies and suggestions in the remainder of this book show you how to *go back to basics and replenish your supply of intimacy prerequisites.* To discontinue your come here/go away dance and unlock the intimacy paradoxes in your life, you need new ideas, new skills, *and* a new foundation on which to build truly intimate relationships. This chapter lays the groundwork, preparing you to experience intimacy by simultaneously replenishing the personal resources of *self-worth, trust,* and *courage.*

183

GETTING REACQUAINTED
WITH YOUR REAL SELF

When you begin to lay the groundwork for genuine intimacy, you are apt to discover that the plot of land on which you hope to build your new home is about as sturdy as a sand dune. Your self-image may be too negative, and your sense of self-worth too shaky, to sustain a close, nourishing relationship. You simply may not know yourself well enough and feel comfortable enough with who you are to be and share your real self with another person—and that is the cornerstone of any truly intimate relationship. Thus, to fortify the foundation for genuine intimacy and prepare yourself to be intimate with other people, you must become intimately acquainted with yourself.

The whole of your identity is comprised of a number of parts:

- a Helpless, almost infantile, part of you that longs to be nurtured and cared for. If you are aware of this part of yourself, you may look upon it with disdain, labeling it weak, cloying, babyish, or needy. Yet, the nourishment it craves you do in fact need and may not have received during crucial stages of your development.
- a Feeling part that registers anger, sadness, excitement, or fear and tries to draw your attention to what is going on inside you. Unfortunately, you may expend most of your energy trying to silence this part of yourself instead of listening to it.
- a Thinking part that attempts to interpret, fix, and control the circumstances you encounter. Enamored of logic and cold, hard facts, it comes in handy when problems need to be solved but can also be used to justify self-destructive behavior or explain away realities that you would prefer not to face.
- an Impulsive part that feels urges and acts on them without considering the consequences. This is the part of you that seeks immediate gratification and does not like to take no for an answer, handling frustration very poorly.
- a Visionary part that I like to think of as a "higher self." It holds your hopes for the future and the image of who you could be, as well as the values and ethics that guide you through trying times. This is the door to your spiritual self.
- an Intuitive part that supplies you with hunches, insights, and creativity. Not to be confused with the deceptions and illusions conjured up by your thinking part to deny reality, intuitive information is reliable and works to your advantage.
- an Empathic part that is sensitive to other people's feelings without wanting or needing to make things "all better." A well-

spring of compassion, this is the part of you that lets people and life touch or move you.

- a Sensual part that tunes into life physically—fully experiencing the senses and sensual pleasures. It also tips you to the fact that something is wrong via bodily symptoms such as tingling sensations, heart palpitations, ulcers, or backaches.
- a Playful part that enables you to be spontaneous and have fun and makes it possible for you to laugh at yourself and the absurdities of life.

Some of the items on this list may seem foreign to you; the very idea that they might actually be facets of your identity may be frightening. Still others may represent sides of yourself that you wish you *did* have, and you may feel sad or angry that whoever was handing out spontaneity or creativity or faith forgot to give you any.

The fact of the matter is that *every item on that list is part of you.* You have simply gotten into the habit of ignoring or stifling some of those facets of your real self.

YOUR IDENTITY PROFILE

Using the list I just provided as a frame of reference, answer the following questions:

1. Which parts of yourself did you recognize immediately?

2. What are at least three things that each of those parts "make" you do? (Does your impulsive part send you on shopping sprees or compel you to eat a whole bag of cookies? Is your empathic part the reason you end up listening to everyone's sob stories?) Try to think of positive examples as well as negative ones. (Does your sensual side make you an attentive sexual partner or help you stick to a healthy diet and exercise program? Does your helpless side prevent you from isolating yourself for too long and motivate you to call a friend or schedule a quiet evening at home with your lover?)

3. Of the parts you recognize, which do you like? Why?

4. Which do you dislike? Why?

5. Which aspect of your personality seems to be "in charge" most of the time? How does relying on this side of yourself help you? How does it hurt you? What might happen if you allowed another part to have more influence?

6. Whether or not you recognize them as facets of your identity today, which items on the list were previously dis-

couraged or prohibited by important people in your life (parents, teachers, peers, partners, others)?

7. Which seemed unwise or unsafe to express or pay attention to during your youth?

8. Which do you consciously try to keep under control today? How do you do that (anesthetize feelings with substances or activity, criticize yourself severely whenever you act impuslively, tightly schedule your time, believing you're not allowed to "goof off," etc.)?

9. Which are you least likely to let other people see? Why?

10. Which do you wish were a more active part of you? What do you think is stopping you from recognizing and unleashing this aspect of yourself?

Take a few moments to think about your answers and then complete the following sentence stems:

- I learned that I have lost touch with . . .
- I learned that I seem to be afraid of . . .
- I learned that I need to tap into the resources of . . .
- The aspect(s) of myself I would most like to get to know better is (are) . . .

Each facet of yourself has its own wisdom, something vital to teach you about being and sharing your real self with others. To obtain that wisdom and integrate the various parts of yourself into the whole of your identity, you must become friends with the many aspects of your real self.

Whenever I am treating a patient who seems to be stuck viewing a situation from only one angle and has lost touch with one or more parts of himself, I assign those parts to some empty chairs in the room. The patient then addresses questions to each lost part, moving to the corresponding chair and, *as that part of himself,* answers the question. Moving from chair to chair, the patient not only views his circumstances from new vantage points but also becomes less fearful and more accepting of his whole range of emotions and attitudes. You can obtain the same benefits from the following variation on this Gestalt therapy technique.

THE INNER DIALOGUE EXERCISE

Choose one side of yourself that you would like to know better and visualize a person who you imagine might give full rein to this side—a young child, a wise old hermit, a gypsy with a crystal ball, or any other image that makes this part of yourself seem real and alive. You may even want to give your "imaginary friend" a name.

Then take out a sheet of paper and write a dialogue between you and your new friend. Ask any questions you would like answered and respond in the voice and from the point of view of this other part of yourself. Some topics for "discussion" might be: what that part of yourself tries to tell you; how it feels and what it wants to do when you ignore or try to control it; how you think it can hurt you; how you feel about what it has made you do; why you have treated it the way you have; and so on. Do not ponder or even think too intently about what you are writing, just keep the dialogue going even when it seems irrelevant or silly.

Here is an excerpt from a dialogue between Ellen and the playful part of herself, which she visualized as a ten-year-old child named Polly:

POLLY: Hi, my name is Polly.

ELLEN: You seem familiar. Have we met before?

POLLY: Yup. But that was a long time ago.

ELLEN: Where have you been?

POLLY: Right where you left me, stuffed in your old toy box, locked up in the attic collecting dust. Thanks to you, neither of us is having fun anymore.

ELLEN: You sound angry.

POLLY: Wouldn't you be if no one paid any attention to you? You've been ignoring me for years and years. You don't even like me. You think I'm not important.

ELLEN: Well, I do have a lot on my mind, a lot of responsibilities . . .

POLLY: All work and no play makes you dull, dull, dull.

ELLEN: Maybe that's why Gary is always off somewhere looking for excitement.

POLLY: Oh please, don't start that again. I'm not here for Gary. I'm here for you. I want to make you laugh and have fun and stop worrying so much. Aren't you tired of being so serious all of the time?

ELLEN: Yes, but . . .

Ellen's dialogue with Polly went on for several more pages and included Polly telling Ellen that she was the "silly one" for thinking that if she turned her back on Gary for even an instant, he would disappear altogether. "Look, with or without Gary, you gotta get a life," Polly said at one point. "You gotta loosen up and have some fun. Nothing earthshaking. Just something that doesn't have anything to do with taking care of anyone." Neither of these ideas was new to Ellen, but somehow "hearing" them in this dialogue hit home. The conversation ended with Ellen and Polly making a list of fun things to do and Ellen promising to "take Polly out" once a week.

I encourage you to try this dialogue technique, preferably with each part of yourself, over the course of several weeks. You can continue to use the technique whenever you are not sure "where you're at" or feel stymied in any area of your life. You might even try calling a "committee meeting" and asking for input from various parts of yourself. If you conclude your dialogue by writing statements beginning with the words, "I learned . . ." or "I discovered . . . ," you can bring new insights into clearer focus. And if you negotiate a "peace treaty," as Ellen did with the playful part of herself, you can come up with ways to nurture that aspect of yourself in the future.

"REPARENTING" THE WOUNDED AND NEGLECTED PARTS OF YOURSELF

Another way to look at these parts of yourself is to view them as children whom you tend to treat the way your parents or other influential people treated you. For instance, many of you eat when the helpless part of you feels needy because your parents comforted (or rewarded) you by giving you sweets or extra helpings at mealtime (or punished you by withholding these things). Similarly, when your feeling part runs up a red flag of sorrow or anxiety, instead of paying attention to it, you might tell yourself that you are too smart to feel that way or berate yourself for being childish and weak. That was probably what your parents or teachers once told you.

Also like real children, these various parts of yourself occasionally rebel. Refusing to submit to your control, your feeling part throws a tantrum, and afterward you are racked with guilt. Or your thinking part concocts an elaborate story to cover up the latest drinking binge indulged in by the impulsive part of you, and you are a bundle of nerves as you worry about getting caught in your lie.

Whether one of your "inner children" is trying to help you fulfill a legitimate need or is running amok, you punish yourself—just as your parents punished you for misbehaving. But self-punishment does not help you get to know and accept your real self. In fact, your punitive, hypercritical treatment of yourself is one of the greatest deterrents to building and maintaining a positive sense of self-worth. More helpful by far is "reparenting" your inner children, giving them what they did not get in the past—acceptance, comfort, and a set of reasonable, consistent limits. This does *not* mean finding someone else to supply what you did not receive previously (as overattachers so desperately try to do). Nor does it mean that you should indulge your every whim. Instead, you must use your imagination, what you have learned from taking care of others, and even skills described in books on child rearing, to treat yourself lovingly and respectfully.

LEARNING TO LIKE YOURSELF

If I had to name the one preconceived notion most likely to prevent an intimate relationship from getting off the ground, it would be: *"If this person really knew me, he or she would not like me."* Convinced that this is true, you build walls that keep other people at arm's length, never having the chance to learn that you are not as horrible as you think. The problem is not that other people really would dislike and reject you if they discovered your imperfections, but that you do not like yourself and *cannot imagine anyone loving or accepting you the way you are.*

If I were to ask you to write down everything that you think is wrong with you, chances are that you would have absolutely no trouble coming up with a long, depressing list. However, if I also asked you to call a cease-fire and to stop bombarding yourself with "should have," "could have," or "a better person would have" messages long enough to view your imperfections objectively, you would discover that:

- you have probably done nothing bad enough to warrant the self-punishment you are heaping upon yourself;
- you could be a Mother Teresa—a highly evolved, chaste, and honorable person—and from time to time "mess up" in the ways that you find so unforgivable;
- even if, at some previous point in your life, you acted in ways you thought were dumb, insensitive, or inadequate, you would most likely handle a similar situation differently today. Your old label may not apply to you now;
- on the rare occasions that your theories of how other people will react to the "real" you are tested, the response you receive is mild in comparison to the one you expected;
- you are a card-carrying member of the human race, fallible, scarred and frightened—just like everyone else.

Obviously you are not perfect. No one is. There are things that you do not do as well as other people, things you have done that you are ashamed of, people in your life whom you have hurt, and people you could not stop from hurting you. The same can be said for everyone you have ever met or will ever meet. Yes, you may need to make amends to certain people. You may need to work on aspects of yourself. But none of your imperfections are fatal and the sum total of all of them are only part of who you are. You are *more* than your weaknesses and deficiencies. Everyone is. Unfortunately, you may devote so much energy to worrying about and concealing your flaws that you become completely oblivious to your accomplishments and positive attributes.

POSITION AVAILABLE: INTIMATE PARTNER

If we went about applying for jobs in the same way that we approach intimacy, most of us would be unemployed. We are so sure that we are lousy candidates for the position of intimate partner, so convinced that we have nothing to offer, that we walk into our "interviews" assuming that we will not get the job. We underestimate our abilities and make, at best, a halfhearted effort to convince others of our real qualifications (although we may try to fool them by creating false impressions).

Imperfect as you may be, you are more qualified than you think you are. In fact, if you could present your positive qualities without falsifying them, and appreciate where you are now instead of constantly focusing on how much better you wish you were or how much harder you could try, you might finally recognize that you are indeed worthy of genuine intimacy.

Superlatives and awe-inspiring facts are not required to be an intimate partner. You may not be a genius. You may have never completed college. But that does not detract from the fact that you have common sense, are practical, mechanically inclined, or a sports trivia buff. Nor do you need to be the best at something in order to count it among your accomplishments and positive attributes.

With that advice in mind, it is time to "rewrite your résumé" so that it highlights your positive attributes instead of merely concealing your flaws. Here are some guidelines to follow:

1. Describe the position you are seeking (what you are looking for in an intimate relationship).
2. Identify your physical attributes. Stand in front of a mirror and describe yourself *objectively*—as if you were helping a police

sketch artist draw a composite picture. Then go back and underline the characteristics that are appealing or attractive. If you find that too difficult, try underlining the features that are not unappealing or unattractive. Do not draw comparisons between yourself and people you know or the media image of physical perfection.

3. List *anything* that you do well and *every* positive attribute you can think of. Start small and go for quantity. For instance, are you: a good listener, organized, loyal, thoughtful, cheerful, enthusiastic, willing to try new things, determined, easygoing, flexible, well-read, quick with a joke? Do you: make people feel comfortable, understand others' ideas, appreciate their quirks and uniqueness, keep a clean house, make a good doubles partner at tennis, know how to tune up a car or pack for a ten-day trip in one suitcase?

4. List anything you enjoy doing.

5. List the many topics you could comfortably discuss without feeling *completely* out of your league.

6. List the many things you wouldn't mind encouraging others to talk about so you could learn more.

7. Describe what you have to offer to a partner in an intimate relationship.

8. Summarize the prior experiences that qualify you for the position of intimate partner. If your past experiences with intimacy have been limited or negative, you may find this difficult to do at first. It may help to refer back to the genogram and relationship inventory in Chapter 8 as well as think about ways that you adapted to trying circumstances which may have made you stronger, more sensitive to another's pain, better able to roll with the punches, and so on.

I consider this résumé-writing strategy to be not just a practice exercise that you do once and leave behind, but rather a lasting source of reassurance and encouragement. Hang onto your résumé and reread it whenever you are low on confidence or obsessing about what is wrong with you. As you would with a professional résumé, update this personal résumé from time to time. At three- to six-month intervals record any new skills, attitudes, and positive habits you developed, as well as the strengths you have rediscovered along the way. Reminding yourself that you are better than you thought you were and getting even better all the time gives a shot in the arm to any change effort.

LEARNING TO TRUST

As you come to know and more fully express your personal strong points and the various facets of yourself, your fears about revealing imperfections diminish. You expend less energy concealing your flaws or maintaining your masks and are more willing to be and share your real self with others.

However, *mistrust* may still prevent you from letting down your guard. Like a bulldozer that hits a layer of solid rock while digging the foundation for your new home, you may be stymied by your fear of making yourself vulnerable and of being hurt or abandoned. There are no shortcuts for building trust. You must chip away at that layer of bedrock a little at a time, conducting "reality checks" to determine who you can trust, whether you are confusing past experiences with present circumstances, and how your defensive reactions may be hurting instead of helping you.

REALITY CHECK ONE:
SOME PEOPLE REALLY ARE UNTRUSTWORTHY

Ultimately, intimacy requires a leap of faith. You must act in spite of the risk of failure or pain. However, you will not make much headway in learning to trust by doing a gainer off the high dive into what might prove to be a dangerously shallow pool. Before taking the plunge, you have every right to test the water to reassure yourself that you are placing your trust in someone who is in fact trustworthy.

As I've pointed out before, some people truly are not, most notably, addicts of any kind. If someone you are just getting to know seems to be a heavy drinker, drug user, gambler, or so on, you are well-advised to hold back until you can determine where you will stand in relation to his or her supply. Try casually suggesting that you spend a day or evening doing something that does not include his or her "drug" of choice. Or politely ask him or her not to engage in that activity during a date. The reaction you get should be quite telling.

Your betrayal detector may also be giving you an accurate reading and appropriately warning you to proceed with caution if you are in the presence of someone who:

- pumps you for information about yourself, but clams up or changes the subject whenever you ask about him or her
- has a hot temper and is easily provoked to lash out at you or others

- is consistently rude to secretaries, waiters, store clerks, or anyone else he feels superior to, expecting them to drop everything to attend to his needs
- repeatedly "forgets" to call you (or others) when she said she would or repeatedly changes or cancels plans at the last minute, assuming you'll all understand
- lies to cover up his or her mistakes, to impress other people—you name it
- regularly "bad-mouths" or gossips about other people, especially if the information he or she shares is preceded by comments such as, "I probably shouldn't be telling you this, but . . ." or "She made me promise not to say anything, but . . ."

These behaviors do not prove beyond a shadow of a doubt that someone cannot be trusted. However, if you witness them, you would be well-advised to move slowly, following the advice for safe self-disclosure that you will find in the next chapter.

REALITY CHECK 2:
DISTINGUISHING BETWEEN THE PAST
AND THE PRESENT

When you feel suspicious of someone but cannot really say why, you may be responding to unfinished business from your past rather than anything that is actually occurring in the present. Ask yourself one or all of the following questions:

1. Does this person look, act, sound like, or in any other way resemble someone who hurt me in the past?
2. Has something like what is happening now ever happened to me before? What was the outcome of *that* situation?
3. When have I previously felt the way I am feeling right now? What was going on then?
4. Do I think that situations, arguments, or relationships like the one I am experiencing right now *always* end up hurting, disappointing, or frustrating me?

If your answers to these questions do reveal a connection between the past and the present, ask yourself: *Is what happened then really happening again now?* Then identify all of the ways the present-day person or circumstances *differ* from your past experience and all of the ways *you* are different than you were when you had the painful experience. If there are actual similarities, think about how you handled the situation unsuccessfully then and list all of the options you have for handling things differently now. Choose one and put it into action. This enables you to deal with your immediate circumstances as well as put an old fear to rest.

REALITY CHECK 3:
KNOW YOUR SORE SPOTS AND
HOW YOU PROTECT THEM

I once had a patient who felt gravely wounded whenever her boyfriend teased her. "So how did it go in court today, Perry?" he would ask, playfully making reference to the fact that my patient, like Perry Mason, was a criminal lawyer. She assumed, however, that he was devaluing her chosen career and showing that he did not respect her or her aspirations. If she got dressed up to go out for the evening and her boyfriend wolf whistled at her and made a comment about having to fight off his competitors all night, she thought he was telling her that she was dressed too provocatively, and she changed her attire. Her relationship with this man was doomed. He teased to show affection, but each time he did this, he hit a sore spot—my patient's belief that teasing was actually criticism in disguise.

No matter how kind, sensitive, or trustworthy they may be, people inadvertently bump into each other's sore spots, causing knee-jerk defensive reactions. You misinterpret other people's motives, assume that they are intentionally trying to hurt you; you withdraw or "hit" back and then walk around with your dukes up ready to fend off new attacks. Clearly, this chain of events makes you *more* mistrusting and less likely to get close to people.

Because mistakes are made and feelings get hurt in any intimate relationship, it is in your best interest to know where your sore spots are, so: Take a sheet of paper and divide it into three columns. In the left column list all your sore spots—areas of your personality or life about which you are particularly sensitive. In the middle column indicate what inflames those sore spots—things people say and do that "hit you where you live." And finally, in the right-hand column list the ways in which you typically protect yourself from, or retaliate for, having your sore spots attacked.

Review your lists, then try some of these alternatives to reacting the way you typically do.

1. *Give people the benefit of the doubt.* Unless they have previously proven to be vindictive or untrustworthy, try to assume the best about others. Like my patient's boyfriend, your partner may not have known that his or her actions would hurt you.

2. *Don't leap to conclusions.* Whatever your vulnerabilities are, they tend to color your perception of everything that happens to you. For instance, if you are sensitive to rejection and your boyfriend sounds less than thrilled to hear from you when you call, you think, "He's annoyed with me for calling. I must be coming on too strong and he's thinking about telling me to take a hike. I'd better end this call right away and maybe cancel our weekend plans, to give him some space." Of course, rather than being poised to reject you, your partner might have a wicked headache or be on his way out the door to confront a problem employee or have just ended a disturbing telephone conversation with his depressed mother. You do not consider those possibilities. You get all worked up and even make a decision to cancel your weekend plans based on behavior that may have absolutely nothing to do with you.

3. *Take responsibility.* If something your partner says or does offends or upsets you, say so. Instead of assuming you know the reasons behind someone's actions, *check it out,* inquiring about that person's intentions. Don't be afraid to explain your feelings and ask your partner to try and be more sensitive to them in the future.

4. *Desensitize yourself.* Taking truly innocent teasing so personally was my patient's problem, not her boyfriend's. Although she had the right to ask him not to tease her, she also needed to take a cold, hard look at why she found his behavior so painful in the first place—and you need to do this too. Use "Reality Check 2" to ferret out and overcome unfinished business from the past. Then, use the "Negative Self-Talk" strategies found at the end of this chapter to revise your thinking and reduce the likelihood of overreacting.

Building trust also involves developing a more accepting attitude. You must recognize that certain people and circumstances simply are the way they are and learn to live within the parameters of those realities, instead of beating your head against a wall trying to change reality to suit you.

Trust, in yourself and others, grows naturally when planted in the soil of faith in a higher power. You can let go of many fears and stop trying to control everyone and everything by getting in touch with the visionary side of yourself and strengthening your spiritual beliefs and practices.

Finally, you learn to trust by participating in what psychologists call "corrective emotional experiences"—trying out new behaviors and taking well-thought-out risks that are designed both to deliver positive results and help you face your fears.

LEARNING TO TAKE RISKS

Intimacy offers only one guarantee—there are no guarantees. There is no way to establish and maintain intimate relationships while "playing it safe" and never taking any chances. Even making surface-level connections involves taking risks—going to new places; introducing yourself to new people; smiling at someone who catches your eye.

Getting close to someone during the romantic phase of a relationship poses new risks—sharing your true thoughts and feelings; deciding whether or not to have sex; discussing sexual histories, sexually transmitted diseases, preferences; taking time away from work or friendships so that you can be with your new partner as often as possible, and so on. As time passes there are still more risks to take—discussing the future of your relationship and other long-range plans; letting the other person see your imperfections and know about your sore spots; standing up for yourself and telling your partner about behavior that is unacceptable to you; allowing another person to give to you, and on and on. Indeed, for as long as you are involved in a relationship you will be taking chances—reaching out for probable gains even in the face of possible losses.

RISK TAKING COST/BENEFIT ANALYSIS

List twelve relationship risks that seem frightening, but which you need to take to get closer to people. Feel free to use any of the examples I just gave.

Rank order your list. Assign the number 1 to the risk that is your top priority to take. This might be the most difficult risk or the easiest; the one you have been struggling with the longest or a relatively new idea. It is up to you. Assign the number 2 to your second-highest priority, and so on until all of the risks have been assigned a different number between 1 and 12.

Write your number-one risk at the top of a sheet of paper and then divide the page below into two columns. Label the left-hand column "Benefits" and list everything you could gain by taking the risk. Label the right-hand column "Costs." List anything you stand to lose and any consequences you fear you will suffer.

For example, you might want to get to know a new neighbor, an attractive, unattached individual with whom you casually converse whenever you run into each other in the hall or at the grocery store near your apartment building. Let's say that you would like to invite that person over to your place for dinner. The potential *benefits* of taking that risk might include:

- spending a pleasant evening with that person
- getting to know him or her
- enjoying a stimulating conversation and feeling good about the things that you discover you have in common with that person
- making a new friend
- perhaps sowing the seeds for a more intimate relationship in the future
- chipping away at your anxious feeling about approaching or getting closer to other people

The potential *costs* might be:

- having your invitation turned down and feeling rejected, embarrassed, etc.
- spending a miserable evening with someone who turns out to be a crushing bore
- spending an anxiety-provoking evening tripping over your own tongue, wondering if you are making the right impression or enduring long stretches of uncomfortable silence
- hearing all about your neighbor's lover and having your hopes for an intimate relationship dashed
- drinking too much wine and acting like an idiot
- having the other person come on to you and refuse to take no for an answer
- proving once again that taking risks only leads to disappointment and failure

Your "cost" list is likely to be longer than your "benefit" list. The items on it are probably more vivid in your mind and reflect the negative consequences you typically anticipate and fear, regardless of the specific risk you are considering.

Give each cost and benefit a numerical weight between 1 and 100 based on how much you want to receive each benefit and how much you do *not* want to pay each cost. Total each column and compare.

Repeat the process for at least three more risks on your list.

After completing this cost/benefit analysis some of you may discover that the probable gains for certain risks outweigh the possible losses, and that actually taking that risk would be well worth your effort. However, most of you will simply confirm what you already believe—that the price you might pay outweighs the benefits you might obtain. If that is the case, you can either continue to talk yourself out of taking the risks that genuine intimacy requires *or* you can make risk taking safer by building your self-confidence and conquering your fears.

BUILDING CONFIDENCE IN YOUR ABILITY TO TAKE RISKS SUCCESSFULLY

Take out another sheet of paper and write down *fifty risks* that you have taken successfully—fifty things that you once could not do but can do now (tying your shoes, riding a bicycle, living someplace other than in your parents' home) or that you were once afraid of but no longer fear (the dark, shopping mall Santa Clauses, having to pump your own gas, riding on the subway) or that you thought you would fail at but succeeded at (landing a job, passing a test, getting a raise, meeting someone you liked on a blind date). In no time you will have fifty examples of risk-taking success. Contrary to what you keep telling yourself, *you have taken hundreds, even thousands, of risks during your lifetime and reaped countless benefits without suffering the horrendous consequences you feared.* You will probably forget this again the next time you feel afraid to take a risk. So keep your list handy and refer back to it for encouragement.

Now think of ten risks that you can take just for practice. They need not have anything to do with intimacy but must involve an unfamiliar or mildly anxiety-provoking activity. For instance, you might pull into a service station and ask for directions; smile at twelve strangers you pass while on your way to lunch; eat a meal at a restaurant by yourself; change your hairstyle; walk your dog down a different street than usual, and so on. Take one risk a day for the next ten days, paying attention to your thoughts and feelings before, during, and after each activity. Then add each to your list of fifty successful risks.

FIVE TIPS FOR CONQUERING FEARS

Tip 1: *Investigate your fear.* What do you really mean when you say that you are afraid of rejection or ridicule or making mistakes? Exactly what do you expect to happen? Would that really be so bad? Would it be worse than the loneliness, frustration, or inadequacy you feel because you are not in a satisfying intimate relationship? Go one step further and develop a worst-case scenario. Incorporating every gory detail, visualize yourself taking the risk and having your worst nightmare come true. You will quickly see and hopefully have a good laugh over how carried away you can get while conjuring up catastrophes. You can also ask yourself what the chances are that these horrors will really come to pass.

Tip 2: *Talk to your fears.* As you did with the various parts of your identity, write a dialogue between yourself and your fear.

Ask it to explain itself and its perspective on what might happen to you if you took certain risks. Even if you agree with it, take an opposing point of view and present a case for taking action anyway.

Tip 3: *Anticipate and prepare for fearful consequences.* Worrying about the consequences you might suffer does not magically prevent them from occurring. However, anticipating that which you fear and preparing yourself to handle whatever happens does reduce the anxiety you feel prior to taking a risk. Being as specific as you can be, identify the consequences you fear and then come up with a plan to deal with them. Shut your eyes and visualize yourself putting your plan into action. Visualize it working out. Write it down if you want to. Once you have developed your contingency plan and, through visualization, gotten the "bugs" out of it, you can stop worrying about that particular stumbling block. You know what you will do if you encounter that fearful consequence. You can even check your notes to reassure yourself that you can and will salvage something from the "disaster" if it occurs. You do not need to keep working yourself into a frenzy over it. When those particular worries come to mind, simply remind yourself that you "have it covered," and then focus your thoughts on something else.

Tip 4: *Manage your anxiety.* First, learn to relax. Find a relaxation technique that suits you by consulting any book on stress management or obtaining one of the many relaxation tapes currently on the market. Practice it until you can get yourself into a physically relaxed state and stay in it for ten to fifteen minutes.

Conjure up an image of a calm, relaxing place and practice visualizing it each time you relax.

After you are comfortable with the first two steps, relax, visualize your calm scene for a few minutes, and then begin thinking about the risk you want to take. You will immediately notice yourself getting tense and anxious. Keep thinking about that risk until you actually feel uncomfortable. Then use your relaxation technique and your calming thoughts to bring you to a relaxed state once again. Practice this until you can comfortably visualize yourself taking the risk.

This technique demonstrates that you can indeed control your anxiety. With practice, you will be able to take a few deep breaths, picture your calm scene, and feel less anxious in real-life situations—including those that present risks you have previously been unable to take.

Tip 5: *Go out and get what you fear.* Make intimacy paradoxes work to your advantage by turning something you fear and try to avoid into a goal that you must try to achieve. If you are afraid of rejection, go to a singles' group or a social function and try to get rejected by at least five people. If you are afraid of being ridiculed, at the next gathering of friends, relatives, or co-workers, tell stories that poke fun at yourself. If you are afraid that you will have nothing to say to people who try to make conversation with you, give yourself an assignment to say nothing for the first hour of a party or meeting. You will make three important discoveries. First, the consequences you feared are not as bad as you thought they would be. Second, they do not occur as easily or as often as you imagined. (The rejection assignment in particular requires hard work on your part. People simply are *not* out there waiting to reject you.) Finally, the consequences themselves become less frightening.

STOP SABOTAGING YOURSELF

As you were reading the suggestions and completing the strategies in this chapter, did thoughts like the following cross your mind?

- "This will never work. Nothing ever does."
- "I can't do that. I'm not good at these kinds of things."
- "This is hopeless. I could think for a week and I wouldn't come up with a single thing I do well."
- "Is this worth it? Maybe I should just accept the fact that I'm not cut out for intimacy."

These statements are examples of *negative self-talk*—the critical, pessimistic, and self-defeating messages you convey to yourself countless times each day and even more so in situations that challenge or frighten you. It is as if a mean-spirited overseer is observing everything you think, feel, or do and making comments about it. Most of these comments seem to be negative judgments about who you are and what you are capable of, as well as predictions of impending doom. Negative self-talk also attributes meanings to everything that goes on around you. Like a patient of mine who assumed that men who did not make passes at her on a first date found her unattractive and that men who did were only after a meaningless one-night stand, you interpret *whatever* happens nega-tively. As a result, you intensify your fears, talk yourself out of taking risks, and sabotage your efforts to find genuine intimacy.

Fortunately, you can stop sabotaging yourself by using a process called *cognitive restructuring,* a concept developed by the father of cognitive therapy, Aaron T. Beck, M.D., and described in depth in the book *Feeling Good,* by David D. Burns, M.D.

First, learn to recognize the negative self-talk you typically use. In *Feeling Good,* Dr. Burns categorizes self-defeating thoughts as follows. (Try to think of at least one example of your own for each category.)

- All-or-Nothing Thinking: Thinking, "If I can't do it as well as so and so, I won't do it at all," or eliminating potential partners because they are lacking one or two characteristics you seek.
- Overgeneralization: Seeing a single failure or negative event as part of a never-ending pattern of defeat, thinking, "I never know what to say" or "I always wind up with the losers."
- Discounting Positives: Instead of taking pride in your attributes and accomplishments, you think, "I am *only*: average looking, an accountant, okay at tennis. . . ."
- Filtering: You focus on the negatives and ignore the positives. When someone says, "You've been a pleasure to be around since you've stopped drinking," you think, "My God, what must she have thought of me when I *was* drinking?"
- Mind Reading: Believing you know what people are really think-ing despite what they tell you, you say to yourself, "Boy, does *she* think I'm an idiot" or "I know he would really rather be with that blonde over there."
- Fortune Telling: "He won't call" or "This will never work" and other predictions about how things will turn out.
- Magnification/Minimization: "The date was a complete disaster," or "It's not so bad. At least he doesn't beat me" and other distor-tions of reality.
- Shoulds: "I should be married by now" or "I should have kept my mouth shut" or "I shouldn't have been so devoted to my career" and other self-criticisms.
- Labeling: Instead of thinking, "*I did* something stupid, embarrass-ing, or unsuccessful" you believe, "*I am* stupid, foolish, or a failure."

After you have identified the negative self-talk you use, take a closer look at it and try to pinpoint its source. Most negative self-talk stems from judgments other people made about you in the past.

You internalized those messages, and even though they might not have been accurate then and probably do not describe who you are and what you can do today, you play them back to yourself on a seemingly endless tape loop.

Try to observe what happens to you whenever you convey these critical or pessimistic messages to yourself. How do you feel? What do you do or not do? Do you slouch or sigh, feel sick to your stomach, grit your teeth, or have other physical reactions?

Pay attention to the events that trigger negative self-talk. Knowing what sets off self-defeating thoughts can help cut self-sabotage off at the pass. You can use one, two, or all three of the following techniques to *circumvent negative self-talk*.

1. Turn Off the Tape: When self-defeating thoughts come to mind and undermine your resolve, you can simply stop them by visualizing a stop sign or imagining a voice inside your head shouting, "Shut Up!" If you immediately focus your attention on something else, your negative self-talk will be summarily dismissed. It helps to practice this technique by intentionally starting your negative self-talk tape, stopping it, and focusing on a task at hand until you feel confident that the technique works.

2. Rewrite the Script: Although there may be elements of truth in some of your negative self-talk, few if any of those put-downs or gloom-and-doom prophecies are accurate perceptions of you or the world around you. They are too all-encompassing; too skewed toward blaming you for circumstances that are beyond your control; more focused on events from the past than the realities of the present. It is more beneficial to think something like, "I did that and I did not like what I did. I *wish* I had handled the situation differently, and if I encounter it again I will." Your revised self-talk acknowledges your behaviors and your feelings. In addition, it offers hope and a suggestion for future use rather than making your circumstances seem unalterable and talking you out of doing anything about them.

   Similarly, you can change, "I always say the wrong thing" to "I sometimes say things that I later regret" or "He thinks I'm desperate" to "I'm feeling desperate and I'm worried that it shows. I think I'll just take a deep breath and listen to what he's saying instead of panicking." Take some time now to rewrite some of the negative self-talk you have already identified.

3. Make Substitutions: You can replace negative self-talk with positive affirmations—healthy thoughts deliberately planted in

your mind to provide encouragement and reminders of what you do have going for you.

Drawing from the strategies you have already completed, write at least a dozen positive statements about yourself beginning with the words, "I am . . . ," "I can . . . ," "I believe . . . ," or "I am proud of . . ."

Read them aloud, slowly, listening to your own words and letting them sink in. Read them again with even more conviction. Then read them at least once a day everey day and whenever you are facing someone or something that typically arouses anxiety or triggers negative thinking. This repetition is a must. It will take practice for affirmations to make a dent in the negativity that you have unwittingly been practicing for years.

I recommend increasing your list of positive statements as often as possible—until you have almost as many uplifting things to say to yourself as you once had "downers." Additional affirmations can be found in inspirational books, poems, or songs. I particularly like this adaptation of the serenity prayer: "God *has* granted me the serenity to accept the things I cannot change, the courage to change the things I can, and the wisdom to know the difference."

On this positive note, let's move on to the next phase of reconstruction—developing the skills and attitudes that will make your new home one in which intimacy will flourish. The next chapter shows you how to replenish the intimacy prerequisites of *positive regard for others* and *self-disclosure; tolerance for conflict* and *interdependence;* and *intimacy role models.*

HOW TO BUILD A CLOSE, NOURISHING RELATIONSHIP:
Replenishing the Remaining Intimacy Prerequisites

This chapter adds interpersonal skills to the foundation of personal resources you developed in the last chapter. It shows you how to build and "weatherproof" a close, nourishing relationship by replenishing the intimacy prerequisites of *positive regard, self-disclosure, tolerance,* and *interdependence.*

Just as building a house without a blueprint to follow is an invitation to disaster, so is trying to establish or improve a relationship without knowing what you really want. To get the most from the advice and exercises you will find in this chapter, take some time now to create a vision of the end result you hope to obtain.

DESIGNING AN INTIMATE RELATIONSHIP

Taking into consideration the goals you set for yourself in Chapter 8 and what you learned about yourself in Chapter 9, draw a mental picture of the relationship you would like to have or how you would like your present relationship to be *one year from today.*

First, make a detailed wish list. Grandiosity is permissible. Specificity is essential. If you are not involved with anyone now and would like to be one year from now, it is not enough to say that you want to meet a "nice" guy or a "good" woman. You need to identify the actual qualities that appeal to you. If you want your spouse to show that he or she cares about you, describe *how* you want him or her to do that. Elaborate on catchphrases like "committed relationship" or "spending time together."

After you complete your "pie in the sky" list, bring your expectations down to a reasonable and attainable level. Establish a "bottom line" standard for each lofty expectation—defining the least you would settle for in each area—and then pick a middle ground as your actual aspiration.

Finally, organize your mental picture by completing the following sentences: In the relationship I am hoping to build:

- I would . . .
- My partner would . . .
- Together we would . . .

As anyone who has ever built a home knows, even with a detailed plan you encounter unforeseen problems and design flaws that do not become apparent until construction is under way. As a result, the finished product rarely if ever meets *every* specification or turns out exactly the way you pictured it in your mind. Neither will your relationship. Try not to think of your newly drawn blueprint for intimacy as a standard for measuring success or failure, but simply as a guide, a frame of reference for building a new relationship or rebuilding the one you already have.

POSITIVE REGARD—LEARNING TO LIKE THE ONE YOU LOVE

Although working on yourself and building self-confidence, trust, or courage helps you conquer some of your *fears* about intimacy, you cannot meet your *need* for intimacy on your own. It takes two people to make a relationship, and not just any two people. It takes you and someone whom you like and respect—someone you believe is lovable and capable of loving you back. This may seem too obvious to be worth mentioning. Yet, many of you do not pick partners who fit that description or feel such positive regard for the partner you now have. While looking for an intimate partner or establishing your present relationship, you may unwittingly have fallen into one of the following traps:

- Shortsightedness. You were attracted by qualities that mattered only in the short run—sexual confidence, physical appearance, someone's potential to enhance your image, or the exciting nature of someone who "lives on the edge."
- Hero Worship. You placed people on pedestals and kept them there by never acknowledging your negative thoughts about them. Seeing attributes that were not there, you magnified good points and minimized flaws, constantly telling yourself how perfect you and your partner were for each other—though there was little evidence to support your contention.
- Finding Fatal Flaws. In your distorted view, either anyone who was not perfect was not good enough for you, or there was something wrong with anyone who thought you were good enough for him.
- Rescue Missions. You believed in and respected the person your partner *could* be but had little patience or positive regard for the person he or she really was.
- Competitions. This trap led you to dismiss and devalue potential partners because they seemed to pale in comparison to someone who was unavailable to you—often a former spouse or lover. Still holding out for the miracle that would allow you to be with the person you really wanted (but could not have), you found everyone else a waste of time.
- Waiting to Be Chosen. You got involved with anyone who seemed willing to be with you. You may have told yourself that you could learn to love him or her. You may have reminded yourself that you were not getting any younger and that you might not get another chance to be in an intimate relationship. But you never asked yourself, "Is this person attractive and acceptable to me?"

To escape those traps and enter into truly intimate relationships, you must stop doing what you have been doing and start developing a new way of looking at people and assessing their potential to be intimate with you. This does not mean that you should take a "suitable mate" checklist with you on every date or give your current partner some arbitrary rating and end your relationship if he or she does not score big. It does mean consciously setting out to discover who someone *really* is and then asking yourself if you can appreciate, willingly give to and comfortably share yourself with that person *as he or she is.*

HOW TO SEE A WHOLE PERSON

For a New Partner
You develop positive regard for a new partner in the same way that you enhance your own sense of self-worth—by creating an intimate partner résumé. Turn back to page 190 and, replacing the pronoun *you* with *he* or *she* or your new partner's name, answer the questions you find there.

You will be able to obtain some information from your conversations with a new partner and other data by observing his or her behavior toward you and other people. Pay particular attention to how he or she:

- reacts to stressful or unexpected circumstances
- interacts with family members
- expresses affection, anger, and other emotions
- responds when you express your feelings

Genuine positive regard involves accepting and being able to get along with a whole person and not just the admirable parts of his or her personality. After you have defined the other person's positive attributes, use the résumé questions as a guide and identify the qualities that you are looking for in an intimate partner which your new partner *lacks*. List the unappealing traits or irritating habits you have noticed. If you have been hurt or angered by certain behaviors but kept your mouth shut in order to maintain the glow of new romance, be sure to list those behaviors. Glossing over them now can lead to resentment in the future. Anything that you think you or your love will "fix" and any problems you think will disappear once you and your partner have settled into your relationship must go on the list. Those expectations set you up for future disappointment.

For Long-standing Partners
If you are currently dissatisfied with your relationship, you are already familiar with your partner's shortcomings. In fact, your existing perception of your spouse or lover may be quite discouraging.

As you did while enhancing your own self-image, you must develop a more charitable attitude toward your partner's imperfections. This does not mean that you should pretend his or her flaws do not exist or do not bother you. But you must try to stop blowing them out of proportion or focusing on them to the point where you blind yourself to his or her positive attributes.

You rediscover the plus side by compiling an intimate partner résumé for your spouse or lover. Then regularly review and update it to remind yourself that your partner is *more* than his or her faults.

Whether you are getting to know a new partner or trying to see an old partner in a new light, once you have a composite picture of who that person really is, ask yourself these questions:

- Am I capable of loving, trusting, and sharing myself with this individual?
- Can I accept this person as he is now, without trying to change him or expecting him to change himself?
- Am I willing to tolerate her imperfections and respect her thoughts and feelings even when they are different from my own?
- Can I give to or be in a relationship with this person without going against my own values or sacrificing my own needs?

You will have enough positive regard to sustain an intimate relationship when you can answer yes to all of those questions. Sometimes you will not be able to do that. As much as you wish a new partner will be right for you, he or she may prove not to be. Or you may not want to stay with a spouse or longtime lover who is addicted or abusive or who is not motivated to improve your relationship. Some relationships really should expire, but please do not be too hasty to draw such a conclusion about yours.

Continue to replenish your own supply of trust and self-worth. Positive regard is a natural outgrowth of both. It also flourishes as you become more adept at the necessary techniques for intimacy, especially those that help you and your partner communicate your true thoughts and feelings to each other.

SELF-DISCLOSURE: THE MEDIUM OF EXCHANGE IN INTIMATE RELATIONSHIPS

Self-disclosure means revealing your innermost thoughts and feelings to another person. But it is not just sharing deep, dark secrets. You are self-disclosing whenever you talk about your hopes and dreams, your fears, your beliefs, or significant events from your childhood. When your words or actions let people know that you notice or appreciate them, you are self-disclosing—revealing both what pleases you and that you care. Every preference you express is a self-disclosure. It conveys some aspect of your personality. There are high-risk self-disclosures, such as leveling with someone about where you want your relationship to go. And there are self-disclosures you make to encourage others to be open also—for instance, sharing how you would have felt in a certain situation and then asking if that was how your partner would have felt as well. You can even self-disclose without uttering a single word—with nonsexual touches like resting your hand gently on someone's elbow or greeting someone with a great big bear hug.

An intimate relationship cannot exist without self-disclosure, and self-disclosure cannot occur if you have developed one or more of the following negative habits:

- Accommodating. In order to win someone's love or maintain it, you present your best, most agreeable side at all times, rarely if ever revealing what is really on your mind. When someone requests your preference or opinion, you say, "I don't care" or "Whatever you'd like" or "It makes no difference to me." You aim to please and see yourself as easygoing or undemanding. Unfortunately, other people see you barring the door on which they have just knocked. If you continue to turn down their invitations to share yourself with them, they will eventually stop inviting you to get close.
- Being Preoccupied with What You Will Say or the Impression You Are Making. Prevalent among shy people and perfectionists, this habit keeps you so preoccupied with how others are perceiving you as they speak, that you often pick up only a few key words or phrases before having to respond. You are so busy listening to your negative self-talk or composing clever comebacks that you cannot hear other people's self-disclosures or pull off your own.
- Taking Center Stage. Believing that you must entertain people in order for them to like you, or that they couldn't possibly have anything as interesting to say, you are likely to grab the microphone and begin performing at the merest invitation to self-disclose. As entertaining as your monologues may be, they rarely give others a chance to get a word in edgewise and thus prevent you from getting close.
- Gutspilling. You reveal intimate details about yourself to anyone who will listen, dumping more personal data on people than they are prepared to hear from someone they do not know well and rarely returning the favor when they need a sympathetic ear.
- Pushing for Self-Disclosure. The flipside of gutspilling is pushing people to tell you more than they are ready or willing to share. You try to squeeze self-disclosures out of them, complaining that they never tell you how they feel, putting them on the spot with probing questions, or accusing them of not really loving or trusting you.

If you have any of these habits, chances are that for most of your life you had a limited supply of self-worth, trust, and courage. Afraid that you would be betrayed or rejected for revealing your true thoughts and feelings, up to this point you have avoided self-disclosure like the plague. Now you must replace your old habits by learning self-disclosing skills and practicing them—communicating your innermost thoughts and feelings gradually and seeing how they are received before proceeding further.

For easier reading, the advice in the remainder of this section is addressed to readers who are not in ongoing relationships now and hope to connect with and get close to new people. However, all of the skills I describe will also work for those of you who are already in relationships and want to connect with, and get closer to, your spouses or lovers.

SELF-DISCLOSURE SKILLS FOR MAKING CONNECTIONS

To make connections, you must first "send out signals" that you are open to making them. Those signals include catching someone's eye, smiling, laughing, maintaining eye contact for a little longer, and so on. Most of us have observed these rituals. If you have not, begin looking for them. As you watch other people make contact with each other, you will quickly be able to separate the confident from the insecure, and you will notice that the insecure give up too quickly. If someone catches their eye, they look away instead of smiling. If someone they try to connect with does not respond immediately, they assume he is not interested when he simply may not have seen their smile or may be as insecure as they are. Try not to fall into those traps.

Of course, everyone you signal may not signal back, but if they do, it is time to show more interest. This generally involves *saying something.* You do not need a brilliant opening line. Not only will you lose your momentum or your nerve while you try to think of one, but it will not help you in any significant way. A simple "Hello" or "Where are you from?" or "How are you enjoying the party?" will do.

Once that person responds, continue to "move toward" him or her by asking questions, maintaining eye contact, and nodding occasionally as he or she speaks.

Then begin to *make occasional references to yourself.* For instance, "I know what you mean. I was almost late myself thanks to that temperamental car of mine" or "Oh, that's a great town. I drive through it on my way to work." These references invite the other person to get acquainted with you. If your invitation is accepted, he or she will respond, usually by asking a question such as, "What kind of car do you drive?" or "Where do you work?" Now the speaker is moving toward *you* and will be the listener for a while. Eventually, as you did, he or she will signal a readiness to disclose more by making passing references to his or her own life. If you hear these references and invite him or her to say more, the focus shifts again. You are now on a two-way street and with each direction change, the conversation—and your connection—becomes more satisfying and intimate.

Naturally, this process will not always proceed as smoothly as I just described. The first glitch you are apt to encounter occurs when the other person does not accept your invitation to get acquainted. If you are nervous about self-disclosure in the first place, you will immediately assume that the other person is not interested in knowing you. Before you give up, come up with at least two other explanations. Then try again. If you do not receive any encouraging responses after several tries, you can throw in the towel and move on. If you want to make yourself miserable, call your experience a rejection or a failure. If you do not, call it a decision—*your* choice not to waste your time trying to connect with someone who has chosen not to connect with you.

Sometimes your conversation will be flowing nicely only to abruptly grind to a halt. You will feel panic rising as you contend with the dreaded awkward silence. Go back several steps and ask an easy question. "Have you been to the buffet?" or "Do you know so and so?" will suffice. Or you can just count slowly to ten, twenty, or thirty and see what happens. Every moment spent with someone need not be filled with talk.

EMPATHIC LISTENING

- "I can't believe you think that."
- "You shouldn't feel that way."
- "What you need is . . ."
- "You don't really mean that."
- "What a strange (silly, dumb, rotten) thing to say."

These are just a few examples of *conversation stoppers*. They effectively interrupt the flow of self-disclosures because, regardless of the actual words spoken, the message received is: *"You had better back off because it is no longer safe to share your true thoughts and feelings."* The person who receives that message reacts to it by clamming up, becoming defensive, or changing the subject.

Most of us stop conversations without realizing it. In fact, we are frequently surprised or baffled by the reactions we get to what we believe are intimate overtures. We may even be convinced that other people are incapable of or unwilling to share themselves with us when in reality, we have discouraged them from self-disclosing. Whether you want to get closer to someone you just met or someone whom you have been involved with for years, you must break the conversation-stopping habit and replace it with a new skill—*empathic listening.*

You listen empathically by:

1. *Giving your full attention to the speaker's words and actions.* Instead of worrying about what to say next, listen to what is said to you and absorb the nonverbal messages transmitted by facial expressions, tone of voice, and body language.
2. *Focusing on feelings.* Try to understand the emotions behind the other person's words and actions rather than merely reacting to what appears on the surface.
3. *Reflecting back what you heard* in a sympathetic, nonjudgmental way. Rephrase or restate the speaker's message as you understood it without ridiculing, criticizing, or suggesting that the other person should think differently. I find it beneficial to begin reflections with "It sounds like you . . ." or "I think I hear you saying . . ." rather than "You think . . ." or "You feel . . ."
4. *Giving the speaker an opportunity to verify your perception or clear up any misunderstanding.* End your reflection with a clarifying question such as, "Is that what you meant?" or "Am I on the right track?"

After you have listened empathically, you might try asking additional questions, explaining how you feel about what you have heard, sharing a similar experience you have had or offering some self-disclosures of your own.

Although it is not necessary to go through the entire empathic listening process for every interchange during every conversation, this skill is essential for emotionally charged discussions and useful when you want to understand another person's point of view and encourage him to tell you more. Empathic listening is a skill that you will have to practice in order to feel comfortable with it. But remember, communication is a two-way street. If you go overboard and *only* reflect back what you hear, you prevent the other person from getting to know *you.*

MAKING HIGH-RISK SELF-DISCLOSURES

Share. Check. Share. That is how to self-disclose *safely*. If sharing your real self with others is new to you, or if you are revealing personal information to someone new, blindly rushing forward and blurting out intimate details about yourself is a great way to get burned. The way to get close is to express your real feelings in small doses and gauge other people's reactions. If they do not judge or invalidate what you have told them or betray your confidence, then you can share more. Be sure not to let your fears or unfinished business distort your perceptions. Use the reality check strategies from the last chapter to help you decide when and if it is safe to disclose more.

As you use self-disclosures to get closer to new people or to your longtime lover or spouse, you will feel as if a cloud that was hanging over you or your relationship has drifted away. However, that cloud may return from time to time, when you want to share information that might jeopardize your relationship, such as an embarrassing confession or expressions of anger. These are all high-risk self-disclosures with real potential to hurt you, your partner, or your relationship. Before making them:

1. *Examine your motives.* If they primarily involve relieving a guilty conscience or getting back at your partner for something he or she said or did to hurt you, think twice about disclosing the information.
2. *Evaluate the immediate and long-term costs and benefits* of your self-disclosure (see the risk taking cost/benefit analysis strategy on page 196.
3. If you decide to proceed, *give careful consideration to how you will share the information.* You may want to write out a script and rehearse in front of a mirror or with a friend. Or you can tape-record your disclosure and play it back to hear how it sounds, modifying your approach as needed.

Never blurt out a high-risk self-disclosure. Let the other person know that an important revelation is forthcoming, reducing the element of surprise by saying something like, "I need to talk to you about something important" or "There is something you should know" or "I have been meaning to tell you . . ." Most of us recognize these signals and prepare ourselves to hear emotionally charged material.

After you make a high-risk disclosure, be willing to discuss it—at length and more than once. Your partner will undoubtedly have thoughts and feelings to share with you on the matter. Remember to use your empathic listening skills (even if your partner "forgets" to use them with you).

FROM CONNECTION TO CLOSENESS TO COMMITMENT

Once you have found and nourished resources within yourself and made a connection based on positive regard and self-disclosure, you are well on your way to finding the truly intimate relationship you have been looking for. But you are not there yet. You have to go one step further and decide to be in that relationship, to commit yourself to it. The sort of commitment I am referring to does not necessarily include proposing marriage or agreeing to live with someone. It is not necessarily about "till death do us part." It *is* about loving, honoring, and cherishing each other and your relationship.

You cross the fine and crucial line between being close to someone and being in an intimate relationship with that person when you acknowledge the presence of a third party in your life— the relationship itself. You value that relationship. You make room for it on your list of priorities. You anticipate the effect your personal and professional choices will have on it. Although you do not abandon your individual needs, interests, and goals, you consider your relationship before you run off to pursue them. When you have committed yourself to your relationship in this way, genuine intimacy is finally within your grasp.

Of course, acknowledging that your relationship matters to you is a far cry from actually getting it to work. To do that and sustain intimacy once you have found it, you must learn and practice techniques for resolving conflicts as well as adopt a more accepting attitude toward ambiguity and imperfection.

TOLERANCE: LEARNING HOW TO "FIGHT" FAIRLY AND WHEN TO LET GO

A conflict occurs each time getting something you want or need prevents your partner from getting what he or she wants or needs and vice versa. You want to make love but your partner wants to complete the work she brought home from the office. You expect your husband to read your children the riot act when you report their misbehavior to him, but he needs them to view him as "Mr.

Nice Guy" and does not discipline them. You expect your lover to call at an agreed-upon time or be there when you call, but your lover wants to stop for a few drinks on the way home from work or is determined not to be "bossed around" by you. These are just a few of the infinite number of needs, wants, or expectations whose collision can lead to emotionally charged arguments or endless power struggles.

If you cannot tolerate conflict, you avoid it by manipulating, accommodating, or doing nothing. If you do fight, but communicate poorly, or try to "win" rather than reach a mutually satisfying settlement, your battles do not clear the air or solve your problems. Your unresolved conflicts reoccur and escalate, creating resentment and mistrust. Fortunately, there are skills you can learn that will prevent this from happening.

LEARNING TO HANDLE ANGER

Anger is an emotion that is most often aroused by other emotions such as feeling injured, interfered with, rejected, humiliated, unfairly criticized, taken advantage of, ignored, or manipulated. These are precisely the feelings stirred up by any conflict, and the resulting anger can make it impossible to resolve those conflicts constructively. Consequently, you must:

- *recognize when you are angry.* Some clues to look for are tension, knots in your stomach, an inexplicable urge to scream or cry, complaining, feeling exhausted for no apparent reason, making sarcastic comments, or losing your sense of humor.
- *identify the real source of your anger.* Feelings are not facts. You overreact and conflicts escalate when unfinished business distorts your perception, when you take out work-related frustration on your partner, or when you see hidden meaning in other people's actions.
- *remember that you have the right to express your feelings but also the responsibility not to express them destructively.* You do not promote intimacy when you arbitrarily vent your anger, throw tantrums, or give your partner the silent treatment. You may feel like inflicting pain or giving your partner a dose of his or her own medicine, but acting on that impulse does not produce positive results and almost always creates new problems—so do not do it.
- *learn to discharge anger* by going for a brisk walk, pounding pillows with your fists, shutting yourself in the bathroom and screaming, or using other physical outlets to let off steam.
- *learn to fight fairly.*

HOW TO FIGHT FAIRLY

If you want to resolve conflicts, negotiate mutually satisfying compromises, and strengthen your ongoing relationships, there are a number of negative habits that you must get rid of immediately. They are:

- *becoming violent.* Physical violence—assaults on another person's body as well as smashing furniture, throwing objects, or breaking things—is unacceptable. Period. Verbal abuse—from coercive or inflammatory language to name calling—only fans the flames of conflict and should be avoided as well.
- *generalizing.* ("You always . . ." or "You never . . ."), *crucializing* ("If you really loved me, you would . . ." or "If this relationship mattered to you, you would . . ."), and *kitchen-sinking*—bringing up unrelated problems, old injustices, and "everything but the kitchen sink" during arguments.
- *hitting below the belt*—rubbing in your partner's weaknesses or making fun of him or her; indirect jabbing; using setups, such as asking questions that your partner cannot answer without "incriminating" himself or comparing your partner to someone you know she cannot stand.
- *poor timing*—opening fire when your partner is on her way out the door or trying to concentrate on something else; starting a discussion five minutes before company is due to arrive or in the car on the way to a party.
- *threatening.* From time to time, you *will* want to attach consequences to certain behaviors ("If you do not pick up the dry cleaning, I am not going to do it for you and you will run out of clean suits" or "Going out and getting drunk is your prerogative, but I will not call your boss for you if you can't get up tomorrow morning.") If the consequence is reasonable and you follow through, behavior change may occur. However, threatening consequences that you cannot or will not implement or ones that are just plain ridiculous ("If you don't move that trunk, I'll never speak to you again") wastes your time and prevents you from being taken seriously.
- *thinking you are right and being determined to prove it.* Stop trying to "win" at your partner's expense. You may call what you are doing "reasoning" with your unreasonable partner, but it still boils down to convincing him to see or do things your way—whether he likes it or not. The price of being right is more often than not being miserable and alone.

Many of you developed these negative habits by observing unfair fighting in your childhood homes. Some of you have been involved in relationships with unfair fighters and fought back unfairly in self-defense. Most of you simply do not know how to operate in any other way—a stumbling block that the following step-by-step procedure for resolving conflicts will help you overcome.

CONFLICT RESOLUTION EXERCISE

For the purpose of learning the procedure I am about to describe, pick a relatively minor problem to discuss. It should be meaningful but not an emotional minefield. If you do not have an intimate partner or the partner you do have seems uninterested in "just practicing," try it with a friend, relative, or co-worker.

Arrange a time to hold your discussion. A minimum of fifteen minutes of uninterrupted time is needed.

Review the following ground rules for fair fighting:

1. Agree to disagree. It is okay not to see eye to eye on this subject, and your goal is not to get the other person to adopt your point of view.
2. Agree not to use any of the unfair fighting tactics described earlier.
3. Be specific. Clearly define the problem. Rather than handing down a general indictment ("You don't pay attention to me"), talk about actual behaviors and specific incidents ("Yesterday morning, I tried to tell you that I'd be late getting home tonight, but you never looked up from the newspaper. Then you were surprised when you got home and I wasn't here."). Ask clarifying questions to bring general impressions into clearer focus. ("Do you mean that you just don't like it or that you did not like it at that particular moment?" "What was it that I said that got you going?")
4. Stick to the problem you have agreed to discuss.
5. Use "I" statements. ("I wish we would make love more often" rather than "You don't make love to me enough.") Convey your own and try to understand the other person's feelings as much as possible.
6. Be polite and reassuring whenever possible. Make it clear that even though you are unhappy with the other person's *behavior*, you still have positive regard for him or her as a person.
7. If things start to heat up, take time out to cool off or break the tension with a bit of humor, a gentle touch, silence, or a

positive affirmation like, "This is really difficult but I know we can get through it."

8. Stick to your bottom line, but leave everything else open for negotiation. Be firm, consistent, and clear about the behavior you absolutely will not tolerate. Yet be willing to make concessions as well. Your objective is not to get all of what you want or give the other person everything he wants, but rather to find a way for both of you to get some of what you want.

Once you have read and agreed to follow the ground rules, decide who will speak first. (I will be referring to that person as One and the person who listens first as Two.)

Step 1: One speaks and Two listens.

Step 2: When One has finished, Two reflects back what she has heard, paraphrasing what was said and asking if that was what One meant.

Step 3: One confirms or clarifies his position (repeat steps 2 and 3 until both of you are satisfied that One's message has been understood).

Step 4: Repeat steps 1, 2, and 3 with Two speaking and One listening. In addition to conveying her position on the matter at hand, at this time, Two can explain her feelings about what One said.

Step 5: Continue your exchange, alternately listening empathically and speaking, until you have:

- identified the here and now problem as well as any underlying concerns
- expressed your true thoughts and feelings about the matter and are reasonably certain that you heard and understood the other person's feelings
- each owned up to your respective contributions to the problem and what you might be willing to do differently in the future
- each identified a reasonable and specific change in the other person's behavior that would satisfy you

Step 6: Negotiate. Restate the problem. Review the solutions each of you proposed and brainstorm additional alternatives. Analyze the costs and benefits of each alternative. Reach an agreement on what each of you will actually do. Set a date to discuss how your solution is working and renegotiate if necessary. Be sure to leave enough time for your solution to work but not so much time that an unworkable solution stirs up new trouble.

By now you may be thinking that conflict resolution demands an enormous amount of hard work. Sometimes it does. On the other hand, many conflicts can be ironed out without going through the entire procedure I just described, especially if you and your partner routinely treat each other with positive regard and share your thoughts and feelings. Dealing with small problems and differences of opinion as soon as they arise also prevents major conflicts from occurring. What's more, you and your partner might butt heads less often and less intensely by learning to tolerate more of the little day-to-day irritants that come in your intimate relationships.

LEARNING TO LET GO

The first step of the recovery program suggested by AA begins, "We admitted that we were powerless over . . ." And just reading those words, you may immediately understand why it is so often said that the first step is the most difficult one to take. None of us wants to admit our own powerlessness. We want to believe that by the sheer force of our own wills, we can control anything, and compel other people to behave as we wish they would. No matter how many times it is proven to us that this just is not true, we go right on trying to control the uncontrollable (and grow more and more upset with both ourselves and the uncontrollable forces in our lives).

You would truly be more at peace with yourself and secure in your relationship if you could:

- stop getting worked up over behaviors that are irritating but do not really hurt you
- expend less energy worrying about the awful things that *might* happen tomorrow and mourning the awful things that happened in the past
- learn to detach—no longer blaming others for making you feel the way you do or blaming yourself for the way other people feel
- accept the fact that long-term relationships do not feel good all of the time, that people who love you will sometimes hurt or disappoint you and that you will sometimes hurt, disappoint, or disagree with people you love
- give up your efforts to steer everyone and everything in the direction *you* want them to go

How do you accomplish these goals? By recognizing that you do not have all of the answers. By admitting that you are powerless over other people, many external circumstances, and even certain internal forces—most notably your obsessions, compulsions, and fears. And ultimately, by coming to believe in and trust a power greater than yourself.

Acceptance—the ability to acknowledge reality without needing to change it—cannot be achieved without faith, without some inkling that your will alone is not enough to move mountains (or overcome the barriers to intimacy that you have encountered). You become whole—and thus capable of genuine intimacy—by strengthening body, mind, *and* spirit. I encourage you to explore your spiritual beliefs and develop your faith in God as you understand him. By doing so, you will finally be able to let go and let intimacy into your life.

INTERDEPENDENCE: HOW TO GIVE, HOW TO RECEIVE, AND HOW TO SHARE

Interdependence is the glue that holds relationships together. It is the delicate balance that enables two people to fulfill their needs, combine their resources, and adapt to each other's temperaments while maintaining their individual identities. Interdependence is achieved through a gradual process of integrating your values and habits while at the same time celebrating your differences. Although you cannot force interdependence to happen, every step you have taken thus far has made it easier for you to let it happen. However, you may still have to extract yourself from one of the following traps:

- Self-centeredness. This trap involves habitually seeking personal gain rather than mutually beneficial outcomes. It is your way or the hard way and unless you find a martyr who will sacrifice all of his or her needs to meet yours, you will end up alone.
- Keeping a Give/Get Tally Sheet. Born of mistrust, this trap involves comparing what your partner does to show he cares or meet your needs to what you do for him. It is quite exhausting, makes spontaneity impossible, and leads to countless conflicts.
- Equating Closeness with Sameness. If you are caught in this trap you expect yourself and your partner to be identical twins, to feel the same feelings, think the same thoughts, need the same things, and want your needs met in the same ways. Since your expectation is entirely unrealistic, your relationship is apt to deliver one rude awakening after another.
- Believing That One Person Can Meet All of Your Needs.

Whether you want a shoulder to cry on, a playmate, a confidant, or a swift kick in the pants to get your life back on track, you expect your patner to provide it. Having no other support system in your life, you drain your partner dry. Or you expect your partner to turn to you and only you to meet all of his needs, becoming jealous of the time he spends with family or friends.

Although interdependence is not a skill and you grow into rather than learn it, there are several measures you can employ to escape from these traps and replenish this intimacy prerequisite.

THE CARING DAYS EXERCISE

As you've seen, an interdependent relationship is based on reciprocity, a mutual exchange of affection, emotional support, and encouragement that takes place when you find a comfortable balance between giving and receiving. Many a come here/go away dance begins with the inability to find that balance. You get stymied by your fear that more will be asked of you than you are willing to give or by your assumptions about what someone is supposed to do to show that he or she cares. This exercise, adapted from Richard B. Stuart's *Helping Couples Change: A Social Learning Approach to Marital Therapy*, can begin to remedy those problems.

1. Separately and without consulting each other, you and your partner should each list twelve caring behaviors. List acts that your partner could perform to show that he or she cares; your partner should list the things that you could do.
2. Make sure caring behaviors are *described in positive terms* ("Ask me how I spent my day" rather than "Don't ignore me so much"), are *specific and understandable* ("Clear the table and do the dinner dishes" rather than "Help around the house"), are *small* things that could be done on a daily basis in short periods of time, and are things that have *not been the subject of recent conflicts*. Here are a few examples: Give me a hug when you get home from work; call during the day; bring me flowers or a little gift; leave me a little note saying something positive; fold the laundry; make a dinner or dessert I really like; ask me what restaurant or movie I want to go to; bring me a cup of coffee while I get ready for work; play with the kids when I get a phone call or one of my friends drops by; etc.
3. When each of you has completed your lists:
   a. Share them.
   b. Negotiate. Each of you has a right to refuse to do something that makes you uncomfortable or that you think requires too

much of you. *However*, you and your partner must come up with an alternative so that there are twelve doable items on each of your lists.

c. Post your lists on the refrigerator door or the bathroom wall or any place else where they can easily be seen.

4. Then do four items from each other's list *every day*. You can do more than four caring behaviors if you want to, but *not* to "one up" your partner. This is not a contest to see who cares more. Nor is it another way to keep a give/get tally sheet. Do these things whether or not your partner makes similar gestures and do them without expecting your partner to thank you for or even acknowledge your caring behavior. Finally, do them even if you do not *feel* caring. When developing a new habit—in this case giving and receiving caring gestures—your behavior often changes before your attitudes or emotions do. Acting *as if* you care is not dishonest but simply a way to practice a new skill.

As time passes, you may want to expand your lists or discuss the impact giving and receiving care has had on you and your relationship. You may need to confront any problems that have cropped up. For instance, if you have an underlying fear of being overwhelmed by demands, you may repeatedly "forget" to show you care. If you find it difficult to be on the receiving end, you may brush off your partner's caring gestures or unwittingly distance yourself after them (suddenly getting very busy around the house, leaving the room, or picking that moment to criticize your partner about something else). In addition to reassuring you that your partner does care and increasing closeness, this exercise also brings these hidden barriers to intimacy out into the open, making it possible finally to dismantle them.

To promote interdependence you need a life of your own. If you have been living through and for your partner, you must begin to develop independent interests. Get involved in group activities at work, at church, or in your community. Seek and accept support from friends, relatives, a therapist, or a self-help group as well as from your partner. Derive a sense of accomplishment from hobbies or projects of your own. Although you may be reluctant to believe it, these *separate* pursuits actually enhance your relationship and make togetherness a pleasure rather than a chore.

Of course, if your own and your partner's lives are *too* separate, you need to be together more often and to collaborate rather than constantly trying to handle responsibilities and problems independently.

You also promote interdependence by recognizing that both you and your partner need your own "space"—a certain amount of privacy, the freedom not to share your thoughts and feelings until you are ready to do so, possessions or activities that are yours and yours alone. Discuss these boundaries and agree to respect them, recognizing that they will move from time to time. Also realize that your relationship does not exist in a vacuum. Try to be sensitive to outside pressures that affect the way you and your partner relate to each other. For instance, when your spouse is under the gun to meet a work deadline, you may need to back off and be willing to receive less attention from him or her for a while. Conversely, if your lover is worried about a seriously ill parent, you may need to move closer and provide extra emotional support.

Finally, you promote interdependence (and intimacy in general) by playing together—joking around, acting out fantasies or being silly, childlike, even a bit bizarre in each other's company. There is no way to get around the fact that it takes hard work to maintain an intimate relationship, but not all work and no play. Pet names, little rituals, reminiscing about funny things that happened to you earlier in your relationship (even if they did not seem funny at the time), and mock fights are all ways to be playful with and enjoy each other. Having fun *together* most definitely brings you and your partner closer together and is one of the joys that make intimate relationships so desirable and well worth the effort you pour into them.

Having explored the personal and interpersonal ingredients for establishing and maintaining truly intimate relationships, there is just one more place to look for the key that can unlock the intimacy paradoxes in your life. You will find it in the next and final chapter of this book.

11

GETTING HELP

Self-help strategies like those found in the last two chapters can unlock the intimacy paradoxes in your life and pave the way for close, nourishing relationships. However, to actually discontinue your come here/go away dance and relate to people in new ways, many of you may need more information and assistance than you can find in this book. Unfinished business, addictions, compulsions, codependency, and most of the other problems I have described simply cannot be resolved overnight or single-handedly. You will need help. Breaking negative habits and dismantling barriers to genuine intimacy is an ongoing process. You will need support, encouragement, and guidance every step of the way. This chapter explains what resources are available to you as well as how to find and get the most from them.

INTIMACY ROLE MODELS

As you no doubt discovered while completing the genogram exercise in Chapter 8, by far your most influential role models for intimacy were your parents and other family members. Their beliefs and behavior had such a powerful impact on you that their habits may have become your own and, regrettably, some of those habits have prevented you from finding the relationship you want or feeling satisfied with the relationship you have.

Naturally, you cannot turn back time and learn different lessons from your old intimacy role models. Nor can you reasonably expect parents, siblings, high-school sweethearts, or ex-spouses to supply in the present whatever they were unable to offer you in the past. But even though observing and imitating the actions of intimacy role models saddled you with many of your negative habits, it is still one of the most effective ways to develop new, more positive ones.

Recognizing that everything they do will not necessarily work for you and that you will not necessarily want *everything* they have, begin looking for people who are walking the emotional and spiritual path you want to follow and observe their behavior. Keep in mind that your goal is *not* to become exactly like them or constantly to compare yourself to your new role models and criticize yourself for not being as smart or self-confident as they appear to be. Instead, try to remain true to yourself but open to the skills other people may have to teach, adopting only those actions and attitudes that help you obtain the results *you* desire. Here is one way to do that:

1. Identify a situation that is difficult for you and that you would like to learn to handle differently than you have in the past (saying "no" to inappropriate requests, accepting a compliment, conversing with someone you just met).
2. Find someone who handles that situation effectively. This might be your boss, your spouse, a neighbor, or even a stranger whom you happen to notice having a good time at a singles' bar.
3. Study that person's behavior. If you want to, you can ask her to tell you what she would do in the situation you identified as a problem for you. But your best bet is to watch your role model in action, paying attention to every detail from the way that person stands or positions her body to what she says and how she says it.
4. Make a step-by-step list of what you observed and try to imagine yourself actually doing each item on the list. If certain steps seem like too great a .stretch, modify them to suit you. For instance, if you notice that while making small talk, your role model often brings up the topic of fishing—which he is knowledgeable about but you are not—substitute a topic that you feel more comfortable discussing.
5. Visualize yourself going through the entire process, using relaxation techniques to lower your anxiety level. Then do what you have visualized.
6. Evaluate the results, recognizing that—like a new pair of shoes—the behavior you are "trying on" may feel uncomfortable

at first. In fact, your immediate inclination may be to say, "I don't know, this just isn't me" or, "I feel like I'm putting on an act." The truth is that at this point you are. However, you are not evaluating how well a new behavior fits, but whether or not it got the job done.

If the behavior you have chosen to emulate nets you the results you desire or simply works a bit better than what you have done in the past, keep practicing it. Through repetition the new behavior becomes more comfortable and you can incorporate it into your growing repertoire of interpersonal skills.

If someone else's approach does not work for you, there is no reason to keep using it. Rather than trying harder to make your new role model's behavior fit you, accept that in this particular area the person you admire does not have anything useful to offer you. Remain open to other things you might be able to learn from him or her and look for other potential models to emulate in that particular area.

TWELVE-STEP RECOVERY PROGRAMS

If you have become dependent on intimacy substitutes, your addictive or compulsive behavior is unquestionably creating an insurmountable obstacle to genuine intimacy. You simply cannot form or maintain satisfying relationships until you have extracted yourself from the vicious circle of dishonesty, guilt, shame, and self-centeredness that is part and parcel of any addictive disease. The *first* item on your blueprint for change must be to embark upon the road to recovery.

If you are or have been involved with an addicted, compulsive, or otherwise dysfunctional person, your obsession with another person's unmanageable behavior and your compulsion to control your partner and your relationships are also self-destructive and counterproductive. Before you can find intimacy and derive pleasure from a relationship, you too must take action to recover from the progressive disease of codependency. Involvement in a twelve-step program based on the principles and practices of AA is the route to recovery I emphatically recommend.

In an atmosphere of safety and acceptance, fellowships like Alcoholics Anonymous, Narcotics Anonymous, Overeaters Anonymous, Gamblers Anonymous, and Sex Addicts or Sexaholics Anonymous, as well as groups for codependents and family members affected by another person's addiction or compulsive behavior

(Al-Anon, Alateen, Nar-anon, etc.) offer support, understanding, and a proven program for overcoming addictions and compulsions of all kinds. Charging no dues or fees and having no membership requirements other than the desire to discontinue your addictive, compulsive, or codependent behavior, "Anonymous" fellowships offer you a new way of life based on honesty, self-respect, compassion for others, acceptance, and faith in a higher power. They promote physical health, emotional well-being, and spiritual growth by encouraging people with a common problem to share their experience, strength, and hope with each other.

On any day of the week, in communities throughout the United States, men and women who share similar concerns and life experiences meet to talk about their struggles and their triumphs—without being judged. They hear about the steps they can take to treat their addictive disease—without being coddled or coerced. They learn, perhaps for the first time in their lives, that they are not alone, that other people have been where they are *and* have moved on.

Your involvement in the fellowship and anything that you say at a meeting is kept completely confidential, freeing you to finally be honest with yourself and others. Sponsors—fellowship members who have walked down the road before you—introduce you to the recovery process and guide you through it. They offer support and encouragement on a daily basis, both listening to your concerns and sharing what they have learned along the way. A twenty-four-hour "lifeline" is also available. By jotting down telephone numbers from a list that is circulated at every meeting, you can have someone to call whenever you need a sounding board, a shoulder to cry on, or help resisting the temptation to return to your old habits. Yet another "tool" for recovery—program literature—provides additional advice and inspiration.

To find a group dealing with your particular problem, check your local telephone book or contact one of the national resource centers listed in Appendix B.

USING THE TWELVE STEPS TO UNLOCK INTIMACY PARADOXES

The balanced way of life taught by "Anonymous" fellowships is available to anyone. You need not have an identifiable addiction, compulsion, or codependency to take advantage of the principles and practices on which recovery programs are based, and if you are recovering from an addictive disease, your program need not be restricted to that one specific problem. The twelve steps can help you work through any conflict or confusion in your life—including your intimacy and relationship problems. In fact, I use them as a framework for treating all of my patients.

For those of you who are not familiar with the twelve steps or who have never considered using them on anything other than a specific addictive or compulsive behavior, let me run through them now and briefly describe how they apply to intimacy and relationship problems.

1. We admitted we were powerless over alcohol—that our lives had become unmanageable.
2. Came to believe that a power greater than ourselves could restore us to sanity.
3. Made a decision to turn our will and our lives over to the care of God as we understood him [her, or it]. (I've added the material in the brackets.)

Replace the word *alcohol* with *relationships, intimacy paradoxes, people pleasing,* or any other problem, and you have taken the first step toward overcoming it.

You have acknowledged that an intimacy problem exists and that nothing you have done thus far has solved it. You have punched a hole in your wall of denial, admitting that everything is not okay, that something is, in fact, beyond your control and destroying your peace of mind. As terrifying as it may be and as reluctant as you may be to do it, admitting your own powerlessness is the only way to let go of your old attitudes and behavior patterns and make room for new ones.

Step 2 asks you to consider an alternative—getting help. Naturally, you must first believe that help is available, that someone or something can do what you alone could not. And this belief does not develop overnight. It is the result of a spiritual pilgrimage, a gradual process of loosening your grip on the reins of control and allowing faith in a higher power to slowly work its way into your life. The higher power you recognize can be a support group or a professional therapist. Or as I do, you can place your faith in a loving God.

Step 3 takes you to a turning point—the point where you choose to conduct yourself differently than you have in the past. It is the point at which you decide to let go and let a higher power help you. You have reached it when you can say, "Because I cannot control my partner (or my anxiety about meeting people or my fear of abandonment or my inability to let other people nurture me), I will leave it in the hands of my higher power, trusting that although I may not get what I think I want, I will get what I need." This is not a one-time decision. Indeed, you may have to "turn things over" to your higher power countless times a day—every time your fears about intimacy surface, tempting you to return to your self-defeating habits of manipulating, controlling, or avoiding anxiety-provoking situations.

4. Made a searching and fearless inventory of ourselves.
5. Admitted to God, to ourselves and to another human being the exact nature of our wrongs.
6. Were entirely ready to have God remove all these defects of character.
7. Humbly asked him [her, or it] to remove our shortcomings. (Again, brackets mine)

These steps may conjure up distasteful images of going to confession and being assigned acts of contrition or being sent to the principal's office and having to write, "I will not do thus and such" one hundred times. Yet, when you take them, you do not receive absolution or punishment. Instead you discover a way out of the vicious circle of guilt, shame, and deceit that has been damaging your self-esteem and undermining your relationships.

The Step 4 inventory is not unlike the strategies you completed in Chapter Eight or the intimate partner résumé you created in Chapter Nine. It is a way to identify your strengths as well as your deficiencies, and it provides you with a detailed picture of what your relationships have been like in the past and what they are like now so that you can determine how to improve them in the future.

Step 5 lightens the burden of guilt and shame by sharing it with others. It also proves that you will not descend into a black hole of depression or be struck by lightning if you reveal the flaws you have for years been working overtime to conceal. In fact, there are few things more healing than getting your secrets out into the open.

Step 6 paves the way for letting go of your old demons and getting on with your life, and Step 7 finds you asking for the direction and guidance you need to develop new, more productive habits. Asking a higher power to remove your shortcomings enables you to stop beating yourself up over the mistakes you have made in the past. But it does not let you off the hook when it comes to the present and future. Faith alone does not lead to genuine intimacy. You must act on your own behalf, exercising the power you do have over your own attitudes and behavior.

8. Made a list of all persons we had harmed, and became willing to make amends to them all.
9. Made direct amends to such people whever possible, except when to do so would injure them or others.

Although you may have become "intimacy disabled" as a result of being hurt or disappointed by people who were supposed to care about you, don't forget you have hurt and disappointed others because of it. Addictive, compulsive, or codependent behavior does the most visible damage to the people in your life and your relationships with them. Yet any barrier to intimacy is "other-destructive" as well as self-destructive. By pouring all of your energy into a single-minded quest for success, you may have neglected the people you love, taken your work-related frustration out on them, or even sabotaged their progress because you could not bear the thought of them being more successful than you. Welded to your perfect-person mask, you may have demanded perfection from others, damaging their self-esteem with your constant nit-picking and criticism. Whatever part you have played in your intimacy and relationship problems, Steps 8 and 9 ask you to take responsibility for it—to identify the mistakes you have made and to do something to repair the damage.

How do you make amends? By talking with people you have harmed or writing to them, acknowledging the damage you have done and letting them know what you will try not to do in the future. By giving them the opportunity to tell you how your behavior affected them and the freedom not to forgive you if they feel that they cannot. If it is mutually agreeable, you may be able to reestablish your relationships with people you once harmed.

Of course, there will also be people you choose not to contact directly at all. You may not know where to find them or you may realize that you would disrupt their lives by walking back into them now. Your only recourse is to forgive yourself and make a commitment to treat people more kindly and respectfully in the future—which is also how each of us makes amends to ourselves for the pain our old attitudes and actions caused us.

10. Continued to take personal inventory and when we were wrong promptly admitted it.
11. Sought through prayer and meditation to improve our conscious contact with God as we understood him [her, or it], praying only for knowledge of his will for us and the power to carry that out. (Again, brackets mine)
12. Having had a spiritual awakening as the result of these steps,

we tried to carry this message to alcoholics, and to practice these principles in all our affairs.

Like recovery from addictions, compulsions, or codependency, the creation and maintenance of truly intimate relationships is a lifelong process. The last three steps keep you on track by promoting conscious living—awareness of what is happening while it is happening rather than acting out of habit and regretting it afterward. Step 10 prevents guilt over specific *human* errors from mushrooming into the self-destructive shame that can drive you back into your old behavior patterns. It makes it possible to resolve conflicts as they occur rather than allowing them to fester and form a wall of resentment that separates you from the people you love. Step 11 continues the process of accepting and letting go of circumstances that are beyond your control. Keeping the need to control or avoid that which you fear at bay, your growing trust in and comfort with your higher power prevents you from turning off the new path you have chosen to follow. And by living according to the principles you have learned, you are able to share that path with other people, to be yourself with them and finally have the close, nourishing relationships you desire.

This brief synopsis can only touch on the balanced way of life that following a path defined by the "Twelve Steps" can provide. For those of you who want to learn more and incorporate those steps into your life and relationships, I recommend the following resources (most of which are also listed in Appendix A):

1. Carnes, Patrick, *A Gentle Path Through the Twelve Steps*, Comp-Care Publications, 1985.
2. Halverson, Ronald and Deilgat, Valerie, *The Twelve Steps: A Spiritual Journey*, Recovery Publications, 1988.
3. Halverson, Ronald, and Deilgat, Valerie, *The Twelve Steps: A Way Out*, Recovery Publications, 1982.
4. Larsen, Earnie, *Stage II Relationships: Love Beyond Addiction*, Harper and Row, 1987.

OTHER SELF-HELP AND SUPPORT GROUPS

Whether or not they are based on the twelve steps of AA, self-help and peer support groups are excellent resources for removing obstacles to intimacy and putting your new ideas into practice. Involvement with people who are "in the same boat" as you relieves your sense of isolation, broadens your perspective on your problems, helps you develop trust in other people, and gives you an opportunity to improve your social skills. The process of helping yourself while helping other people has proven so effective that peer support groups for victims of abuse, victimizers, widows and widowers, divorcé(e)s, adult children of alcoholics, families of the mentally ill, and almost any other population imaginable exist in most communities. To locate groups in your area contact:

THE NATIONAL SELF-HELP CLEARINGHOUSE
33 West 42 Street
New York, NY 10036
(212) 840-1259

Singles' organizations (such as Parents Without Partners) can also be valuable resources for you. You may have a tendency to sell them short, but they do allow you to meet new people and in addition to holding social events, many of them also run support groups.

PROFESSIONAL THERAPY RESOURCES

Sometimes barriers to intimacy have been in place for so long that you require the advice and guidance of a well-trained professional therapist to remove them. Sometimes your unfinished business, negative self-talk, depression, or marital strife are more effectively and expeditiously unraveled with the insights you obtain from someone who has extensive knowledge about the human psyche and experience in the field of psychology or family therapy. Sometimes you simply feel more comfortable sharing your troubles with someone whose job it is to listen and be supportive. Regardless of your specific reason for seeking professional help, here is some information that can improve your chances of actually getting the help *you* want and need.

A therapeutic relationship is like an intimate one. It requires trust and the ability to share your innermost thoughts and feelings with another human being. Just as you cannot be intimate with everyone you meet, you cannot necessarily be helped by every therapist who happens to hang out a shingle. All therapists are not alike. They have different styles, different areas of expertise, and different theoretical perspectives that affect their approaches to treating patients. Consequently, the first professional you consult may not be able to supply the kind of help you need. Recognizing that your own anxiety about seeking help may be getting in your way, try to give the therapeutic relationship time to work. If, after several therapy sessions, you still feel that you are not being helped, discuss your concerns with your therapist, clearly stating what is bothering you and what you would like to be different. A reputable therapist will hear you out, try to meet your needs if that is possible, or refer you to another therapist if it is not. You have the right—and a responsibility to yourself—to part company with a therapist who is not helping you or who does not respond to your feedback.

In general, effective treatment for intimacy and relationship problems begins with an extensive intake evaluation that examines all of the possible factors that may be contributing to your present-day distress. This evaluation may include a complete medical workup to identify or eliminate physical causes of problems like depression or sexual dysfunctions. And it always involves gathering a detailed personal and family history. In my practice, I use the genogram as a diagnostic tool. I also use questionnaires and/or standardized psychological tests. Regardless of the methods, anyone who is going to be able to help you work through conflict or confusion about intimacy will find out about your family background and previous relationships. Intake sessions also provide you with an opportunity to find out about your therapist. If you have a sense of the specific barriers you would like to dismantle, it is your responsibility to determine whether or not the therapist is equipped to help you in that area. Ask about his or her expertise and experience with addictions, codependency, stress management, or any other specific concern.

I believe that the best approach to treating individuals, couples, and families is an *integrative* one that addresses your physical, emotional, interpersonal, and spiritual needs. I also recommend looking for therapists who provide *comprehensive* services and offer all or most of the different treatment options I am about to describe.

Group Therapy is an especially effective treatment option for people with intimacy and relationship problems. Like self-help groups, it offers you a safe place to practice honest communication and develop trust. However, with a therapist present to facilitate interactions, you are encouraged to take more risks than you might in a peer support group. Although the most useful, eye-opening insights frequently come from other group members, group leaders offer suggestions and provide guidance for using assertiveness and communication skills, revising negative self-talk, giving feedback, and responding appropriately to other people's self-disclosures. Groups give you the opportunity to test out your theories about

your effect on other people, discuss and rehearse upcoming interactions, and receive feedback that can help you fine-tune your approach to anxiety-provoking situations. Groups comprised of both
men and women can be particularly beneficial for patients of either
gender who want to obtain a better understanding of the opposite
sex's point of view.

Individual Therapy offers you more one-on-one attention and
may be more comfortable for those of you who have trouble trusting
people. Particularly beneficial for resolving unfinished business and
uncovering long-buried emotions, individual therapy gives you an
opportunity to concentrate on specific intimacy prerequisites and
conduct an in-depth examination of one or more areas of conflict
and confusion. By getting to the bottom of your negative behavior
patterns, you improve your chances of breaking old habits and
replacing them.

Couples Therapy helps identify the attitudes and behaviors that
may be blocking intimacy in your current relationship. If a couple
enters treatment complaining of sexual problems, specific sex
therapy techniques may be employed. But regardless of the problem, enhancing *emotional intercourse* and improving interactions
outside the bedroom as well as in it is the ultimate goal. It is
important to recognize that couples therapy is *not* designed to keep
two people together at any cost. Indeed, during the course of
treatment, you and your partner may decide that you do not want
to repair your relationship or that no matter how much either of you
changes, the relationship will still not meet your needs. By coming
to this conclusion in therapy rather than without it, you will be
able to walk away with more peace of mind and be less likely to
repeat your unproductive behavior in your next relationship.

Family Therapy involves treating the family unit as the patient so
that all members can work together to improve relationships and
communication within the family. This approach prevents unhealthy habits from being passed on to the next generation and
stops family members from unwittingly supporting one another's
dysfunctional behavior. By involving parents and children in
therapy, a "bad" child who is holding the family together by
providing parents with a subject on which they can agree or a
young "hero" who serves as one parent's confidant(e) and prevents
parents from communicating about their problems can be identified, and the entire system can change for the better.

In addition, because your attitudes and behaviors were "inher-
ited" from your family, Family-of-Origin Therapy may offer you a
vital key for unlocking intimacy paradoxes. Whenever possible I try
to conduct at least one session with my patients' parents, siblings,

and other close relatives. Not only does this give me new information about my patients, but it also gives my patients an opportunity to begin communicating with their family in new ways as well as let go of old grudges and resentments. This may pave the way for improved relationships within the family or simply help my patients realize that the fears they have been harboring since childhood are not so monstrous after all—and that they can conquer them.

MORE HELP FOR HELPING YOURSELF

GET IN SHAPE

Your physical health affects your state of mind, and your state of mind affects both your willingness and your ability to actively participate in an intimate relationship. If you are too tired to get off the couch and go out to meet people, if you are too stressed out to concentrate on what other people are saying to you, if you are too down in the dumps to socialize or care about anything, there are actions you can take to eliminate the physical causes of these maladies. You can consult a nutritionist, or read articles about nutrition, and change your diet to one that gives you more energy. You can exercise regularly to release tension as well as tone your body and improve your appearance. You can make a fifteen-minute relaxation technique part of your daily routine. By doing these things, you will discover that your outlook on life has improved dramatically.

GET INVOLVED

An antidote for self-centeredness and self-pity, involvement in community or church/synagogue activities is an excellent way to connect with people, improve your social skills, and feel less isolated while at the same time serving others. There are countless volunteer organizations that desperately need your help. Although you will want to make sure not to go overboard, working with those organizations enables you to put your old caretaking habits to good use instead of employing them to coerce or control a partner to whom you are overattached. Participation in church/synagogue-related activities offers the extra added bonus of exploring your newly activated spirituality and strengthening your faith in a higher power.

GET SMART

The more interpersonal skills you develop and the more you learn about yourself, other people, and relationships, the better equipped you will be to handle whatever your own relationships throw at you. Seminars, weekend workshops, and semester-long courses that teach communication skills, assertiveness, stress reduction, time management, or visualization techniques help replenish intimacy prerequisites. Bible study classes, meditation courses, and conferences sponsored by "Anonymous" fellowships enhance spirituality and promote recovery from addictions, compulsions, and codependency. Marriage encounter weekends and couples communication courses strengthen your existing relationship. And if you are not in a relationship, these educational experiences can also double as social opportunities, enabling you to meet new people *and* have something to discuss with them (the course). To find out about workshops and courses in your area, contact and ask to be put on the mailing list of the churches, synagogues, community colleges, adult education programs, singles' organizations, mental health clinics, and men's, women's, or couples' resource centers that frequently sponsor such programs.

Also helpful is "bibliotherapy"—reading books or listening to tapes that can provide additional insight into the sources of conflict and confusion in your life. There are many, many excellent resource materials available in the addictions, self-help/psychology, and inspirational sections of any bookstore. The recommended reading list found in Appendix A contains the books I most often suggest to my patients and which I believe you will find beneficial as well.

A FEW PARTING WORDS

Whether you gain it from this book, a twelve-step program, psychotherapy, or any other resource, insight is the foundation for change. However, insight alone will not change you. You must take action. You cannot just think differently than you have in the past or be more aware of what you are doing. You must *do things differently*. In this book I have offered what I believe are sound suggestions for steering your life and relationships in a new direction. What you do with those suggestions is entirely up to you. If you choose to follow a new path, however, go gently along it. Slowly and conscientiously find a middle ground where you can be aware of your actions without becoming a perennial navel gazer, where you can share your real self with someone without clinging to or smothering that person, and where you can maintain your independent identity without isolating yourself from others. When you strive for this sort of balance, neither fulfilling your needs nor protecting yourself from your fears can control your life or undermine your relationships. And that is the ultimate key to the intimacy paradox.

APPENDIX A:
Recommended Reading

Beattie, Melody. *Codependent No More*. Center City, Minnesota: Hazelden, 1987.

Bowen, Murray. *Family Therapy in Clinical Practice*. New York: Jason Aronson, 1978.

Burns, David D. *Feeling Good: The New Mood Therapy*. New York: William Morrow, 1980.

Carnes, Patrick. *A Gentle Path Through the Twelve Steps: A Guidebook for All People in the Process of Recovery*. Minneapolis, Minnesota: CompCare Publications, 1989.

———. *Out of the Shadows: Understanding Sexual Addiction*. Minneapolis, Minnesota: CompCare Publications, 1985.

Colgrove, Melba, H. H. Bloomfield, and P. McWilliams. *How to Survive the Loss of a a Love: 58 Things to Do When Nothing Can Be Done*. New York: Bantam Books, 1977.

Dobson, James. *Love Must Be Tough*. Waco, Texas: Word Books, 1986.

Earle, Ralph, and Gregory Crow. *Lonely All the Time: Recognizing, Understanding, and Overcoming Sex Addiction, for Addicts and Co-Dependents*. New York: Pocket Books, 1989.

Forward, Susan. *Men Who Hate Women and Women Who Love Them*. New York: Bantam Books, 1987.

Gravitz, Herbert and J. D. Bowden. *Recovery: A Guide for Adult Children of Alcoholics*. New York: Simon and Schuster, 1987.

Halverson, Ronald S. and V. H. Deilgat. *Twelve Steps—A Way Out: A Working Guide for Adult Children from Addictive and Other Dysfunctional Families*. San Diego: Recovery Publications, 1982.

243

Halverson, Ronald S. and V. H. Deilgat. *Twelve Steps—A Spiritual Journey: A Working Guide Based on Biblical Teachings.* San Diego: Recovery Publications, 1982.

Kiersey, David and M. Bates. *Please Understand Me: Character and Temperament Types.* Buffalo: Prometheus Press, 1988.

Larsen, Earnie. *Stage II Relationships: Love Beyond Addiction.* New York: Harper and Row, 1987.

Marlin, Emily. *Genograms: The New Tool for Exploring the Personality, Career, and Love Patterns You Inherit.* Chicago: Contemporary Books, 1989.

Marlin, Emily. *Hope: New Choices and Recovery Strategies for Adult Children of Alcoholics.* New York: Harper and Row, 1987.

Milam, James Robert and K. Ketcham. *Under the Influence: A Guide to the Myths and Realities of Alcoholism.* Seattle: Madronna, 1981.

Miller, Joy and M. Ripper. *Following the Yellow Brick Road: The Adult Child's Personal Journey Through Oz.* Pompano Beach, Florida: Health Communications, 1987.

Miller, Sherod, Elam Nunnally, and Daniel Wackman. *Talking Together.* Littleton, CO: Interpersonal Communication Programs, 1979.

Missildine, W. Hugh. *Your Inner Child of the Past.* New York: Simon and Schuster (Pocket Books), 1963.

Norwood, Robin. *Women Who Love Too Much.* New York: Simon and Schuster (Pocket Books), 1986.

Peck, M. Scott. *The Road Less Traveled.* New York: Simon and Schuster (Touchstone Books), 1978.

Powell, John Joseph. *Why Am I Afraid to Tell You Who I Am: Insights on Self-awareness, Personal Growth and Interpersonal Communication.* Allen, Texas: Argus Communications, 1969.

Scarf, Maggie. *Intimate Partners: Patterns in Love and Marriage.* New York: Random House, 1987.

Schaef, Anne W. *Escape from Intimacy.* New York: Harper and Row, 1989.

Schaeffer, Brenda. *Is It Love or Is It Addiction?* Center City, Minnesota: Hazelden, 1989.

Schneider, Jennifer. *Back from Betrayal: Surviving His Affairs.* New York: Harper and Row, 1988.

Seamands, David. *Healing for Damaged Emotions.* New York: Walker and Company, 1987.

Smith, Ann W. *Grandchildren of Alcoholics: Another Generation of Codependency.* Pompano Beach, Florida: Health Communications, 1988.

Stuart, Richard B. *Helping Couples Change: A Social Learning Approach to Marital Therapy.* New York: The Guilford Press, 1980.

Wegscheider-Cruse, Sharon. *Another Chance: Hope and Health for the Alcoholic Family.* Palo Alto, California: Science and Behavior Books, 1981.

————. *Choicemaking.* Pompano Beach, Florida: Health Communications, 1985.

Woititz, Janet G. *Adult Children of Alcoholics.* Pompano Beach, Florida: Health Communications, 1985.

————. *Struggle for . . . Intimacy.* Pompano Beach, Florida: Health Communications, 1985.

APPENDIX B:
Resource Organizations

ALCOHOLISM AND THE FAMILY

Alcoholics Anonymous World Services (AA)
P.O. Box 459, Grand Central Station
New York, New York 10163
(212) 686-1100

Alcoholics Anonymous—General Services Office (AA)
468 Park Avenue South
New York, New York 10016
(212) 686-1100

Al-Anon Family Group Headquarters
1372 Broadway (at 38th Street)
7th Floor
New York, New York 10018
(800) 245-4656
(212) 302-7240 (in New York area)

Alateen
Call Al-Anon (cited above).

National Association of Children of Alcoholics (NACOA)
31706 Coast Highway
South Laguna, California 92677
(714) 499-3889

Children of Alcoholics Foundation
200 Park Avenue
31st Floor
New York, New York 10166
(212) 949-1404

DRUG ADDICTION

American Atheist Addiction Recovery Groups (AAARG)
2344 South Broadway
Denver, Colorado 80210
(303) 722-1525

Cocaine Anonymous—National Office
P.O. Box 1367
Culver City, California 90232
(213) 559-5833

Drugs Anonymous
Look for groups in your area.

Narcotics Anonymous—World Services Office (NA)
P.O. Box 9999
Van Nuys, California 91409
(818) 780-3951

Nar-Anon
Check local listings.

National Cocaine Abuse Hotline
(800) COCAINE (800-262-2463)

National Institute of Drug Abuse (NIDA)
Parklawn Building, 5600 Fishers Lane
Rockville, Maryland 20852
Information Office: 301-443-6245
For Help: (800) 662-HELP (800-662-4357)
For Employers: (800) 843-4971
For Literature: National Clearinghouse for Information
        P.O. Box 416
        Kensington, Maryland 20895

EATING DISORDERS

American Anorexia/Bulimia Association, Inc.
133 Cedar Lane
Teaneck, New Jersey 07666
(201) 836-1800

Overeaters Anonymous—National Office
4025 Spencer Street, Suite 203
Torrance, California 90504
(213) 542-8363

O-Anon
Check local listings.

SEX ADDICTION AND THE FAMILY

Sex Addicts Anonymous (SAA)
P.O. Box 3038
Minneapolis, Minnesota 55403
(612) 871-1520

Codependents of Sexual Addicts (COSA)
P.O. Box 14537
Minneapolis, Minnesota 55414

Sexaholics Anonymous (SA)
P.O. Box 300
Simi Valley, California 93062
(818) 704-9854

S-Anon
P.O. Box 5117
Sherman Oaks, California 91413
(818) 990-6910

Sex and Love Addicts Anonymous (SLAA)
Augustine Fellowship
P.O. Box 119
New Town Branch
Boston, Massachusetts 02258

National Association on Sex Addiction Problems
(800) 622-9494

COMPULSIVE GAMBLING

Gamblers Anonymous
National Council on Compulsive Gambling
444 West 56th Street, Room 3207S
New York, New York 10019
(212) 765-3833

Gam-Anon
Check local listings.

COMPULSIVE SPENDING

Debtors Anonymous
Check local area for groups, or for Shopaholic groups.

Spender Menders
Check local listings.

CHILD ABUSE (PHYSICAL AND SEXUAL)

Adults Molested as Children United (AMACU)
P.O. Box 952
San Jose, California 95108
(408) 280-5055

Incest Survivors Anonymous
P.O. Box 5613
Long Beach, California 90805
(213) 422-1632

Incest Survivors Resource Network, International, Inc.
P.O. Box 911
Hicksville, New York 11802
(516) 935-3031

National Child Abuse Hotline
Childhelp USA
P.O. Box 630
Hollywood, California 90028
(800) 4-A-CHILD (800-422-4453)

Parents Anonymous—National Office
6733 South Sepulveda Boulevard, Suite 270
Los Angeles, California 90045
(800) 421-0353

Victims Anonymous (VA)
9514-9 Roseda Boulevard, #607
Northridge, California 91324
(818) 993-1139

Victims of Incest Can Emerge Survivors (VOICES) in Action
P.O. Box 14809
Chicago, Illinois 60614
(312) 327-1500

IF YOU CAN'T FIND IT LISTED HERE

National Self-Help Clearinghouse
33 West 42 Street
New York, New York 10036
(212) 840-1259

INDEX